LONELY NO MORE

OTHER BOOKS BY KAREN MAINS

Friends and Strangers: Divine Encounters in Lonely Places
Karen, Karen
Key to a Loving Heart
Making Sunday Special
Open Heart, Open Home
The Fragile Curtain
The God Hunt: A Discovery Book for Children
With My Whole Heart
You Are What You Say

CO-AUTHORED BOOKS

Child Sexual Abuse: A Hope for Healing
Living, Loving, Leading
Parenting Us: How God Does It
Tales of the Kingdom
Tales of the Resistance
The God Hunt: A Discovery Book for Men and Women

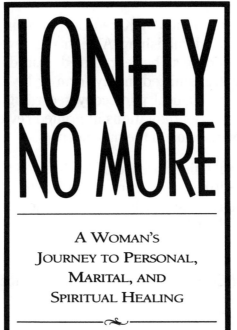

LONELY
NO MORE

A WOMAN'S
JOURNEY TO PERSONAL,
MARITAL, AND
SPIRITUAL HEALING

KAREN
BURTON MAINS

WORD PUBLISHING
Dallas·London·Vancouver·Melbourne

Scripture quotations are from The Revised Standard Version of the Bible (RSV), copyrighted 1946, 1952, © 1971, 1973 by the Division of Christian Education of the National Council of the Churches of Christ in the U.S.A., and are used by permission.

Library of Congress Cataloging-in-Publication Data

Mains, Karen Burton.
    Lonely No More/Karen Mains.
       p.   cm.
    ISBN 0–8499–0880–9 :
    1. Mains, Karen Burton.   2. Christian biography—
United States.   3. Identification (Religion)
4. Marriage—Religious aspects—Christianity.
I. Mains, David. II. Title
BR1725.M3162A3   1993
209'.2—dc20
[B]   93–16548
                                          CIP

3 4 5 6 7 8 9 LBM 7 6 5 4 3 2 1

Printed in the United States of America

To Eddie Bishop,
self of my self,
and to the persistence
with which he wooed me to
love him.

My deep gratitude to the God-given gifts of Harold Fickett;
writing master, mentor to my wounded creative soul,
patient adviser, gentle counselor, friend, editor.
This book is truly a collaboration between his insights
and my tellings—all without destroying the sighs and
rhythms of my odd but very personal writer's voice.
Only I know what he has done for me.
May every struggling artist one day be so fortunate.

Contents

Introduction

$\mathcal{I}$ count on the quiet in the old stone chapel. Here the business of the congregants is prayer and worship. A smile perhaps. A nodding head. The rustle of the pages of a prayer book. The creaking of the pew kneelers. Noise—chatting, laughter, greetings—these are sloughed off like muddy gardening boots. A plaque on the outside door declares: This church is open daily for prayer and meditation. The worshipers of St. Mark's parish expect the quiet.

The five outside steps, worn in the middle like old steps should be, lead to tall double doors lathered with layers of weathered red paint, a wooden cloisonné. The doors groan slightly as they open. The round iron handle softly drops. I hear all of this as I pray on weekdays, gladdened in the chapel by my aloneness. Someone enters behind me. Privacy, not to be caught and held, scurries away. I draw my soul tight to my side, covering the bare thing that has been dancing before the altar, that has been weeping or stretching in prayer before God. Others, too, find solace in the quiet, or a place to rest from shopping, or they come to admire the architecture of the nave and sanctuary.

The building itself is constructed of faded river stone, crumbling patiently with time, seemingly soft to the eyes, a mellow blonde. The cornerstone was laid in 1868 with joy and praise to God. It is an unobtrusive marker in the community, a memorial in this river town (to any who care to note) to the holy. Above all is a handsome three-tiered tower topped by the belfry that shelters one bell, cast long ago in England. Above the Victorian homes, above the tree line, above the Fox River which (mostly well-behaved) bisects Geneva, Illinois, this bell has tolled its solitary tone for decades.

On Sunday mornings an usher greets worshipers in the tiny vestibule. He or she stands to the right, by the radiator painted brown that hunches beneath the clear-glass arched window. A bell rope dangles from the steeple tower, behind the usher's head, often tickling the back of his ear. A smile. The proverbial lapel carnation, white or red. A worship bulletin thrust into my hand. I move on through the black, inside double doors. Into the quiet, into the softly lit, somber silence.

Phrases of the Lord's Prayer are needlepointed in painstaking stitches (approximately 2.5 million in all) on each kneeler on one side of the church, eight rows, front to back. On the other side of the center aisle, the Ten Commandments have been stitched. Long ago parishioners also adorned their needlework project with stylized replicas of native Illinois wildflowers. On this rich heritage, on this labor of love, I now kneel. The church is gathering. We bend to pray, backs curved, shoulders hunched, foreheads hidden in folded hands here in the quiet of St. Mark's parish church on Sunday morning. The paint is worn in regular intervals on the plank floors beneath our feet. Hundreds before me have stood for the entrance processionals, sat for the readings, stood for the creed, knelt for the general confession, moved toward the altar for communion, stood for the blessing. Week after week, the pew kneelers have sung their worship song as they've swung down and up. Light filters through the leaded glass windows. I lift my head and read. The painted grisaille is a place mark; here my eyes begin, here I pause, here I stop reading the design.

Someone pulls the rope that dangles from the steeple. The lone bell duly tells the sleepy town that worship in this small place is joining hands with worship the world over. The acolytes now brandish their brass candle lighters. The smaller ones stretch their arms and fumble for the fat candles. A wee drama. Will the wicks take the light? The flame flares. We, watching, sigh relief. The bell peals the morning air. The processional is forming. Our rector, vested in cream and white and Pentecost green, stands at the ready. The choir, bunched together in the cramped nether spaces, holds hymnbooks, their white surplices brushing black undercassocks. The bell tolls again. A tall acolyte elevates the cross. The red book of the gospel is lifted high. The entrance hymn unfolds down the aisle as the singers pass in twin rows. The sopranos, a variety of vocal textures. The mostly mellow bass (except for one who distinctly rumbles). The edged vibrato of the tenors. Quiet defers to liturgy, the Sunday work of the people. It bows to plainsong, to responsorials. It submits to melodic Taize songs, to the limbering organ.

I am part of the work of this people, of the others before me I have never known, and of those who will follow when I am dead and perhaps forgotten. This is a safe place to do this work of worship, the work of the people—the communal adoration of God. I have attended this church for almost a year. I am not much known and little is required of me. I am not interrupted; my mind is not cluttered with organizational details. I am not scanning the congregation thinking of whom I must catch and whom I must ask to work on church committees. Consequently, I am left to pay attention (in quiet moments, for an hour here, an hour there) to my own soul.

Many of us, if not all, at some time or another need havens along our human pilgrimages. We need safe places, safe people. Something has savaged us. We flee to sanctuaries where we can hide and mend, bide our time until we

11

are willing to venture again along the risky way. Without realizing I was in danger, I chanced upon the quiet of a safe place, the nave of St. Mark's Episcopal Church. One Sunday morning I saw a clear and startling picture of myself as a refugee.

Starving, pitiful, her limbs ravaged by malnutrition, her body bowed by hunger, she raised a clawlike hand in supplication. I close my eyes to see her clearer. Her hair falls loose, thinning and lusterless on her shoulders; it brushes against her unwashed garments, all faded a dusty dun. Her eyes implore, rimmed luminous with pain, wide in her narrowed face. She is barefoot, and I know that this starving woman is a self of myself.

White mildew flakes of malnutrition crack her flesh, scale her arms, her face; the corners of her mouth split. "Please, please," she seems to plead. "Don't send me away. Hide me, shelter me. Please don't harm me."

I was forty-one when this picture of my own refugee status came to mind. My father had died when I was thirty-seven, my mother on my thirty-ninth birthday. Often lonely for the nurture and kindliness of an older generation, was I suddenly displaced because I had no parental homeland? Was I more of an orphan than I knew? Some part of me was a starving refugee, as real as the women I had once seen lifting to me their fevered babies in the refugee camps in Somalia. I hold up a weakened wrist, a rusted tin cup for food, empty in my hand. "Bread, bread," this part of myself whimpers. "Feed me. Give me water."

What strangers we are to ourselves, even those of us who have been careful to tend to inner journeys. We think we know the truth about our own personalities. But we are wanderers, dispossessed persons searching for homelands, lacking passports and guides to lead us to safety. Some part of my psychology or my emotional life or my spiritual being has been savaged and needs sanctuary. But what part? Why? What should I do?

12

I set myself on a pilgrimage, a sojourn, a wilderness wandering. This journey through my inner exile, plodding and pain-filled, unknown on this Sunday morning, is to take eight years. Perhaps even then it is not fully accomplished.

Discovery

$\mathcal{I}$ have holed up for breakfast at Baker's Square Restaurant in St. Charles. The solemn autumnal morning nods to me outside the window beside which I sit. Going-to-work cars still shine their headlights. Last night's rain left scattered puddles on the highways. The sound of splashing tires is a comforting accompaniment to my reveries. The world is a serious orange and gold, not bright or glowing as under the sunlight, but in some places actually a paper-bag brown. Straggling storm clouds are westering. Patches of pewter sky peek and hide. The world feels intimate, leaning close like the two women at a nearby booth who bend their heads to listen intently to each other's conversation.

My table is spread with a prayer notebook, a day organizer, and a Bible. I have been concentrating on pencil-editing two chapters from a recent writing project. Breakfast away from home with desk work is a way to clip the filaments that mentally connect me to laundry room and kitchen, to telephone, to vacuum cleaner, to broadcast studio, to people who need me. I take the back roads and two-lane highways past empty fields and farms to the surrounding towns. There, close to home but not at home, I find a mostly empty eating spot. It is an act of transition, like going to an office. Since ordinarily I wake between four and four-thirty, eight o'clock is nearly my lunch time. I have already worked for hours, and suddenly I begin to long for a skillet brunch—sliced potatoes and ham, chopped onions and green peppers, two poached eggs, melted cheese. I grab paper paraphernalia and go to where I will not have to cook, to clear, or to clean up after myself. "Coffee?" This word spoken by a waitress is one of the kindest greetings I know.

I brainstorm with myself on the draft sheets. Sloppy notations, descriptive phrases, and sentence fragments are scribbled all over the columns and headers of my printouts. Grandparents with their little grandson are shown to the table across from mine. I watch the body language of the child's mother as she abdicates her parenting responsibilities. She gratefully scootches into the seat while the older couple coax the child. For this restaurant moment, they eagerly assume what she has temporarily set aside.

Lifting my eyes to continue thinking, I stare at the far end of the large room, and it is then I notice the man waiting at the cashier's counter. What a handsome man! Like a heroine in a popular romance novel, I actually catch my breath. Tall, well formed, the man is about my husband's age, perhaps a decade older than me. His head and broad shoulders are perfectly proportioned to the rest of his body. I like the full wavy hair, dark but graying. I have, with my own passage into the forties, noted a certain tender susceptibility to men with gray hair. There is something vulnerable about them, something in this pigmenting that tells of life passing. The man has the kind of face, particularly in profile, that I find attractive; a rugged irregularity, not too perfect, not too fine-lined; something square and strong in the jaw. The manager is slow. The waiting by the cash register continues while I watch a little longer.

What makes a man like this attractive to me? There's a sort of nobility about his body. He exudes a physical confidence that is natural, unstudied, and appealing. However, I realize what has really caught my eye: the man is wearing tan riding breeches and fitted knee-high black boots, polished and smart. A black turtleneck stretches over his broad chest and tucks trimly into the beltline inside his loose, open jacket. He either has spent the last hours on the bridle paths or will spend the next few hours there.

I am suddenly filled with an irresistible longing. What a perfect morning to ride! The smell of stables comes rushing at me. I hear leather creaking, a horse neighing. I feel the pull of the stirrup during mounting, the balanced thrust of the English saddle in motion, the pound of hoofs on a solid trail, yellowed by fallen maple leaves and sodden from the night's rain. I remember how I love the gentleness between beast and rider, the nuzzle of a velvet nose in my hand or the press of haunches against my side and ribs. I remember the puffs of frosty breath when the animal sighs.

This man has not looked at me. He has not for an instant noticed me. Our eyes have not met in any way. Yet I consider walking over to him, flashing my brightest and best smile, and asking, "Oh, are you riding today? May I come along?" I go so far as to check my attire: jeans, ankle-high boots, two pullover sweaters. I could do it. With effort I restrain myself from this most uncharacteristic and unseemly behavior. Somehow, this is more than just fantasy. I detect desire, insistent desire pushing at me. But desire for what? I know what I would do if the man glanced my way, read my mind, and grinned, "Oh, you like to ride! Well, let's go." Without a thought or look behind me, I would abandon the last hour of well-formed plans, all my papers and projects. I would ditch them in favor of this excellent make-sure-you-wear-wool day and take off with him!

But I am a virtuous Christian wife, faithful to my husband in both thought and action. I sit tight. The man strides out the door. I am first amazed, then troubled by the pull of a total stranger upon me. What does this mean? I know what some of my acquaintances would diagnose: lust. I breathe a prayer to be spared foolish middle-age sexuality. "Oh God, save me from all that. Let me use my creative energy more productively." Then the interesting thought pushes to the surface: Would I have been so attracted if the man had been wearing a business suit? I decide probably not. I might have looked up admiringly and approved of this extremely nice-looking, middle-aged man. But I would soon have returned to my work, to all the list making and list checking that convinces me I am accomplishing much.

The riding breeches represent something to me . . . what? A work morning given to personal pleasure represents . . . what? Does it stand for a moneyed world of leisure I have never experienced and will never know? Is that it? If a woman had been standing there in riding jodhpurs, would I have been so taken? No. I would have noticed her and thought with some envy, "Lucky gal," and forgotten her. What does a handsome man in riding breeches represent to me? What is this sudden desire for? Is it for him or for something he symbolizes?

In celebration of the season, I buy pumpkins on the way home and melon-colored chrysanthemums and, for good measure, a basket of ornamental gourds. Then I take a long, unscheduled walk down the prairie path and watch the geese fly in the wet, gray sky, follow the deer track into a clump of thickets, and sit on a stump listening to the peculiar contrast of birdsong against the quiet. I come home, my lungs saturated with the healthy smell of earth mold and damp air. I warm cider on the stove and fill a mug. I turn the classical music station on high so that sound thrums through the whole house. I try to work, but I think again about the man in riding breeches waiting at the cash register. On a weekday morning. This afternoon the thought of him still disturbs me.

I stand barefoot on our front porch and lift my eyes to the young May morning. Our brown house is nestled in a wooded plot; brambles tangle with wild chokecherry trees across the driveway in front. (My mother-in-law kindly calls this "the natural look.") The old English sheepdog roams, sniffing rabbit tracks. His fur, silky and long, gathers twigs and pods and leftover dried fall leaves. It is almost time for his annual summer shearing. A chickadee cries from its perch. The two purple plum trees against the garage bear delicate cream and pink blossoms.

Ordinarily I am ecstatic in May, wired the whole month by exultation, but—nibble, nibble—something is laying across my innards and chewing, bite by bite, at my joy.

I press my fingers against the freshly painted front doors. They are a shade richer than the leaves of the plum trees. Mixed and re-mixed by the hardware salesman, he demonstrated amazing patience as I searched for the exact tone of maroon/wine/plum that appears randomly in the brickwork of the house and here and there when the sun shines on the old paving bricks I salvaged from a city alley, just steps ahead of a neighborhood demolition project and the Chicago police. I place my palm on the door to feel the texture of the paint. If blinded, I might just sense this color through my fingers.

"Joshua," I call. The dog has roamed out of sight. The weekend ahead is full. Jeremy, our youngest, in junior high, and I are leaving at seven this Saturday morning for a trip downstate to Western Illinois University in Bloomingdale. He and a friend, Rob Barrett, much to their amazement, have won first place in the local young author's competition and are to gather with hundreds of other schoolchildren to receive recognition for their achievement. Jeremy is at that stage of adolescence where his nose has grown faster than his face. His sandy hair is browning (but I, his mother, still see him as a towhead). He can be annoyingly adamant about principles that are dear only to him.

I pause in this one quiet moment to wash out what is troubling me. A weight lies within, like when the cat impudently curls up on my stomach during my nap. In slumber I know that something has plopped on me, but I cannot come up from sleep enough to push the half-heavy thing away. The morning is cool, lush, and green, but exultation does not bubble up out of me.

The dog has already disappeared inside, through the slightly ajar door. He is my boon companion when the house is empty, sleeping at my feet in the study where I work for hours alone. I bend my head and press the still-warm coffee mug to the place on my forehead between my eyes, the very place where my mother at my age wore a distinct frown scar—from migraines perhaps, her particular defense against discontent. Later, hopefully, I can tend to the unknown weight that presses within me. For now, still in my house robe, I lift my mug to the morning, a salute at least to this luscious beginning, a new day.

All the children will be home this weekend. Their calling cards are the piles of abandoned shoes on the remnant of bedroom carpet in the front hall. Because we have three sons, the mound mostly consists of jogging shoes with some deck shoes, and because we have one daughter (home from college), usually a pair of women's size six-and-a-half flats. Shoelaces limply intertwine. I can't remember ever asking the children to discard their shoes when they entered the house, but it is a habit, despite the messy welcome, that I am not about to discourage.

How else do I know when the children come home? I play this mental game as I do a few quick morning chores. I fluff couch cushions, straighten magazines, stow discarded belongings on the up and down staircases—one step for each offspring's things. When the boys practice dance steps in front of the floor-length mirror in Joel's room, the blue-and-white delft chandelier downstairs in the kitchen bobs on its chain. Random flame-shaped bulbs, loosened from their sockets, go dim. Coats and jackets never make it to the front hall closet. The detritus of education—notebooks and school theme papers, notices of fees or social events, lists of phone numbers, piles of textbooks, pens and pencils and fine-line markers—proliferate on every surface. The kitchen counters tell a tale: powder from the cheese packet of an instant macaroni dinner, drying blobs of pancake mix, crumbs. Empty, used glasses multiply. The laundry room door jams against a mountain of jeans. The children are home.

The house will stretch out like a concertina in the hands of some street musician. It will expand with the rhythm of their lives; steps pounding on the stairs, the showers on full-blast, the dog barking and chasing at their heels as they hurry through the rooms.

David Barrett, head of the nearby hospital's pathology department, and his wife have volunteered to drive us to Bloomingdale in their van. They will be here shortly. Before our departure I wake Melissa, our second child, home from Miami University before summer session. "Melissa, please let your dog out." She is to meet Grandpa and Grandma Mains for an eight o'clock breakfast and is perfectly capable of letting out her own dog without my prodding. This mothering dies hard. I carefully guard against my habitual tendency to coach, but good habits that have outgrown their usefulness are as hard to break as bad ones.

Her English setter, an angling adolescent pup, with brown markings on a field of cream fur, has scrambled into the three-quarter-size Victorian walnut bed. He scrunches his back on the bedspread and rolls; his four feet paw the air. Melissa turns sleepily from her face-down position, her long blonde hair dragging across the pillow. Ten pounds slimmer than her winter weight, she has already acquired a fashionable, golden tan. I pass along necessary information. "Jeremy and I will be home sometime this afternoon. Dad flies out to Toledo this morning." She informs me of her theater plans for an evening in the city.

I walk on down the hall to my own bedroom. David, my husband and father of this brood, is packing. Diligently, methodically, he checks the list at hand. I have learned never to offer help; he has a suitcase system that

I unintentionally offend. Once in a while, pressed by time constraints, he will allow me to fold his shirts. I watch my husband of almost twenty-five years. Nearly fifty, he is handsomely graying at the temples. I lean against a corner of the bureau, tucking myself out of his way. We chat about last-minute information—the airport pickup time, a quick rundown of general family activities, my own weekend plans. David always asks in these private spousal moments, trusting my assessments, "Is everyone OK?"

I like the way this room has come together. The raspberry wallpaper like smooth yogurt. The lean oak-grained wardrobe, acquired from a friend in one of her sporadic household rearrangements, standing tall against the wall. My lace and satin wedding dress hanging on an antiqued brass hook. The collection of Canada geese (they mate for life, we're told): first-edition prints, signed and framed—the china geese, a mother with goslings—the water pitcher with its long gooseneck—the hand-carved wooden goose and gander. The draped Laura Ashley-patterned curtains, the matching dust ruffle. An Amish log cabin quilt David bought in St. Mary's, Ontario, for our wedding anniversary covers the bed. Its variegated patchwork of rose, wine, mauve, and maroon are all hues that in some way surfeit me emotionally, suffuses my eye.

This is my hideaway at the far end of the house; a place where I can nap and read and pray and close the door against the pulsing forces roaming lively outside these walls. My study adjoins it across the hall. The children find me here, and they are welcome. I am an interruptible writer (or pray-er, or napper). They congregate and chat. The boys take flying leaps from the hallway and bounce belly up on the bed beside me where I sit propped by pillows and bolsters, reading and making notes and organizing the external material events of my life. The sheepdog finds me and plops on the carpet by the bed

24

where my hand can pull his curling coat and scratch behind his ears.

A van honks outside. I quickly kiss David good-bye. Travel separations are one of the hallmarks of our marriage. One of us is always going or coming. I no longer cry the way I did when, as a young mother, for the very first time I had to stay home with a baby and wave my husband on his way. I decided early that I would be in perpetual pain if I did not learn to manage separations.

The Bloomingdale campus is teeming with hundreds of budding young authors. We listen to a lecture by a "real" author, find a place for adult chats and coffee while Jeremy and Rob are involved in workshops. David drives home while his wife Anne dozes in the front passenger side. I talk to him from the second seat. Our conversational eye contact is mediated through the rearview mirror. A Catholic by confession, he expresses a longing to live the kind of personal and professional life significant enough to be worth dying for. He discusses voluntary missionary medical service.

The sheepdog, a floppy, lovable clown, greets us when we pull into the driveway at home. Within seconds, our high school sophomore, Joel, graced with undeniable charm and enviable good looks, comes striding out of the house. He conjures a charming, crooked grin (what the rest of the family, not to be impressed, dubs his "*Gentleman's Quarterly* Pose"). His sweater dangles casually from hooked fingers over one shoulder. A car filled with a brace of older classmates screeches in behind the van. Joel is fifteen and chafes at his driving dependency. He is politic enough to ensure his continual popularity with these upperclassmen since they are strategic to his mobility. All have parts in tonight's high school musical, the innocuous *No, No, Nannette.*

Jeremy settles into early evening activities. He is an absorbed cartoonist who requires hours alone in his bedroom in the basement. Sometimes we lose him for days down there, but I understand his need for creative solitude (and indeed, his tolerance of artistic chaos). I change my clothes, then head off (without David, of course) to our small group, which includes four other couples, meeting this evening at the home of Harold and Luci Shaw, a mile and a half away. Much of the evening is spent playing an aggressive game of "Dictionary." Most of us are word people, but I detect that in some this competition has evoked the instincts of sharks. Midway in the evening, I feel myself detaching, swishing emotionally away from the hilarity. A gulf seems to fix itself between me, the room, and the people in it. Fatigue probably. Too many people in one day.

I return home around 9:30 that evening just as our eldest son, Randall, pulls his gray Honda into the driveway. "Hi, Mom!" Returning for the weekend from Northern Illinois University, he has a week left before finishing his junior year. Travel preparations are under way for a summer on a soccer team as part of an evangelistic outreach in the barrios around Mexico City. Randall is the family business man, having inherited some of his Grandpa Mains's interests. He is financing his collegiate board and room and his incidental living expenses through a small enterprise he has appropriately named BODYWORKS, a t-shirt imprint and supply company that fills orders for dorm floors, campus groups, and Christian clubs. The buses in DeKalb, Illinois, bear advertisements designed and painted by Jeremy: "BODYWORKS" the full-length placards shout. This is almost a family cooperative. In addition to tuition payments, I have contributed $1,000 to the new business and am amazed that my son is an economics major and shows financial acumen. The BODYWORKS catalog is ready to go to the printers. Jeremy has just completed the artwork (admittedly under some brotherly deadline duress).

Soon, Melissa and her date arrive from their evening in the city. A theater major, my daughter is full of evaluations regarding the deficiencies of the musical. None of the Mains children have ever been accused of hesitancy in the offering of opinions. Joel hits the house, exuberant with closing-performance and cast-party highs. We sit on the church pews in the living room debating dramatic curves and the lack of narrative line in most popular musicals. Jeremy, drawn by the discussion and having satisfied his need for solitude, moseys up from his basement hideaway, and suddenly, except for David, we are a family complete.

All my children are performance hams. Melissa's date and Jeremy have trained the dog to dog-yodel to a country gospel favorite, "God's Love Is Like a Cannonball." This record is put on the player and the young men (all four of them) whip cushions off the couch. With these soft, neuter dance partners in hand, they execute fancy step work as they mime the words to the song, further accompanied by canine howls. As is frequently the case when my children gather, I laugh so hard my stomach muscles begin to spasm. Excusing myself to retreat to the quiet of the raspberry bedroom, I literally cannot stand to laugh more. Always an early riser, I now feel the lateness of the hour.

As I pause on the bottom step, we coordinate Sunday plans. I enjoy the subdued quiet of the early eight o'clock service. My children all opt for sleep and the later 10:15 service. Melissa's friend will hurry to O'Hare after church to fly out for a job interview in Pittsburgh. My daughter (and her puppy Sebastian) will drive back to Oxford, Ohio. Joel needs to spend Sunday afternoon striking the set in the high school auditorium. Randall promises to help me plant some grapevines. Hopefully, my accordion house will contract again. By late Sunday afternoon, perhaps, things will settle. Maybe I will read, take a walk, have time for meditation and for straightening the rooms before I meet David at the airport.

I crawl under the covers, weary. My children are still laughing in the living room. Like smoke, the conviviality seeps through the floor and the baseboards. I pull the quilt up to my ears and sink into the sheets. I love all this activity, this great wheezing as the house bellows in and out, the amazing physical and intellectual beauty of this clan—but it always wearies me. I am often teased about being the only mother on the block whose young children put her to bed first so they could enjoy "their personal moments."

I reflect on the activities of each day before I fall asleep. It is part of my quieting ritual. I find that the unknown weight, despite all the activity, despite the energy and the socialization of this day, is pressing on me still. Surprised, I give it a name, this heaviness: It is loneliness. I am lonely! How can I be lonely today, with all this life? David is gone, yes, but I have been surrounded by children, neighbors, friends, acquaintances. How can I possibly be lonely?

This is a blight that seems to be creeping across my middle years. More and more frequently I say to David, "I just feel alone, so alone." For some reason, I am not making significant connections with other humans in a way that satisfies me, that nurtures. Friends there are, people there are, family and work colleagues, but tonight I feel an all-too-familiar disconnection, a disassociation, an unhealthy separateness. It feels as though I am there for others, but there is no one there for me. I cannot absorb their love.

Am I loved? That is the nagging thing that has been a dead weight on me all day. The cat that has been sleeping within wakens, stretches, and sharpens her claws.

I pull the satin edge of the blanket diagonally across my face, like when I was a child needing comfort. I feel the slight brush of silk across one eye, across the bridge of my nose, my lips. Loneliness curls again within, settles down, but it is waiting. I can feel its dormant presence. It always presses just on the lower surface of my abdomen, and it will not go away. Tonight, although I give myself a psychological shake (You are a woman who has every reason *not* to be lonely!), I cannot think of one person who is there for me.

"I had this dream last night," says Joel. Barefoot, wearing a mismatched t-shirt over wildly patterned surfer shorts, my son curls languidly around the kitchen corner. I have been having a happy cooking morning, one of my too-infrequent rituals on the weekends when I am not traveling. Today I'm putting together dishes for Sunday dinner and for the busy days of next week. Groggy still, mussed and musky from late sleep, Joel rummages in the cereal cupboard and drags out the Bisquick baking mix, the Aunt Jemima's lite syrup jug, and sets my grandmother's cast-iron skillet on the stove. He is hungry for pancakes.

On the Saturdays when I'm absorbed in a cooking marathon, sooner or later each member of the family passes through, chatting and ruminating over toast or leftover pizza. Cereal bowls, empty mugs, orange juice containers, and a dwindling coffeecake intermingle with mixing bowls, measuring spoons and cups, dishes, pots, and a plethora of chopped ingredients. While I stir, pour, sauté, and wash, various family members stand beside me and talk. "Here," I thrust a dishtowel into their hands. While they dry the dishes, last night's social events are discussed, as are weekend plans, the irritants and joys of friendships, the personalities of teachers, and (in our house), inevitably, theology.

"Well, tell me your dream," I say to my son. Whenever I say this to my family, I hear Tevye's wife from the musical *Fiddler on the Roof:* "Tell me what you dreamt and I'll tell you what it meant." Joel's dreams are unusual, to say the least. He has the ability to pause the unrolling sequences if he is unhappy with his dream's themes and begin again. His dreams these last months have been filled with lurid coloration, with danger, with warnings. He stops and re-starts them several times, often reporting, "I didn't sleep much last night." I wonder if this is vivid, creative imagination or if his adolescent anxieties are all cloaked in frightening symbol and hidden import. The meaning in most of them is unintelligible to me.

Five years ago, when Joel was a sixth grader, David and I rushed him to the emergency room. Purple rods mottled his flesh, telltale marks of a galloping meningitis racing toward death. Vomiting, semiconscious, he slipped farther and farther from us, finally into the clinical, professional hands of the emergency room doctors. A call for prayer went out over the Moody Bible Institute radio station. I knew the exact moment in that hospital room when he began to heal. His flesh pinkened and the purple rods faded. Quick recognition flashed in his eyes; the indomitable humor returned (though spoken drowsily with a thick tongue). Unutterably relieved, I watched my son face away from death and look back onto me toward life. He has a memory, evoked at certain terrifying moments, of a black, hooded creature staring from a corner of his hospital room, standing behind the nurse as she administered the I.V. I am convinced my son has seen Death and, by the mercy of God, has lived.

Though I observe all my children with a practiced kind of benign neglect, I have particularly watched Joel. I have watched, the way all mothers do, these children of ours who have stared at Death and survived. My shrewd maternal eyes marked the slow progress through the rest of sixth, seventh, and eighth grade: a certain mental fatigue, more-than-normal exhaustion at the end of day, an internal body thermostat unable to adjust quickly enough to Midwestern cold. He layers stockings when most teens consider snow gear to be gym shoes. He avoids the ski-and-sledding parties given by friends.

Joel plops the stirring ladle into the blue-and-white-striped bowl of batter. "I dreamed that the house was burning. There was smoke and fire all over the place. I came running to the family, to Jeremy, to you and Dad. I was shouting, 'The house is on fire! The house is on fire! We've got to get out!' But no one paid any attention. You all kept doing whatever it was you were doing. I ran outside, but no one followed me. So I had to run back inside, shouting. But still, no one paid attention."

I stop my food preparation. "Have you had this dream before?" Generally, when a dream replays itself, the subjective mind is working to grab our attention. Joel admits that he has dreamed this dream before. Five or six times.

David wanders into the kitchen for a coffee refill. Joel repeats his dream for his father. "What does this dream mean to you?" I ask.

Joel tells us another dream he has with a similar theme: "There are robbers in the house. They've locked the family in the basement as they burglarize the upstairs. I say to everyone, 'Let's get out of here. We've seen their faces. They'll come and murder us!' Dad answers, 'Joel, they're not going to bother us down here. Let them have the stuff. It doesn't mean anything to us.' Mom says, 'We can't get out of here.' I'm practically screaming, 'Let's escape through the basement windows! We can break them and climb out!' But I can't make anyone listen to me. No one pays any attention."

There is silence in my Saturday morning kitchen. Then David asks again, "What does this dream mean to you, Joel?" Our son hunches his shoulders. He doesn't know . . . or he isn't telling what he knows.

I try another approach. "What kind of feelings do these dreams evoke in you?" Dream feelings are safer; they are a degree removed from frightening, everyday emotions.

31

Joel runs through a list. He feels anger, terror, rage at our lack of attention to the danger, intense frustration at not being heard.

I press on. "Do these feelings remind you of any feelings you have in your everyday life? Do you ever feel that Dad and I don't hear you, aren't paying attention to your danger, just go on with our work?"

A dam of pent-up frustration overflows. Rage follows hard on the waves of anger. Everything comes first before him: Dad is always gone, or working on a broadcast. Past pain rushes up, tumbling through the sluice gates of opened emotion—an unsettled, damaging item from when he was a little boy. To silence his eager garrulousness, I used to say, "Edit, Joel. Edit." Sharp recognition pierces me at his accusation. I had been oversensitive to imposed-upon adult listeners. I had embarrassed my child. The little boy, not the words, had been edited, deleted, publicly cut out of our conversations.

Now, his eyes fill with tears. Our fifteen-year-old son—whom I vow burst from the womb endowed with grace, handsome at every age, instinctively cavalier and charming, who has rarely encountered a socially awkward moment in his entire life—this child weeps. He weeps. The wounds are deep and gushing. We take him into our arms; we listen to his litany of grievances. This is not the time to defend ourselves. We honor his pain. I no longer edit. We ask forgiveness. But I am appalled.

I arrange for two consultations with friends who are psychological professionals. For months, for most of last year, Joel has had no safe place. An older classmate has been encroaching upon his personal boundaries. Joel has been shadowed in school hallways. He has registered for classes only to discover that the other boy has registered after him. He is stared at in choir. We have not understood his plight or the seriousness of the psychological encroachment.

I have been watching my son with a sharp mother's eye, but not watching well enough, not watching wisely enough. I have not known, for some reason, about personal boundaries. I have not seen the violent invasion of ego territory, the parasitical sucking that has attached itself to my enchanting son's soul.

Compassionate toward the social maladjustment of the adolescent who sought our son's attention, we had actually invited the awkward teen to family events, into our church circle. Yet the Scripture declares, "If any one does not provide for his relatives, and especially for his own family, he has disowned the faith and is worse than an unbeliever" (1 Tim. 5:8). Provision includes safety, certainly, and emotional shelter. Following psychological counsel, we take stern measures to protect Joel, to disable the encroachment. We forbid contact. We return gifts. We intercept phone calls. We give permission to sever contact.

On Mother's Day I head to my bedroom, close the door, crawl into bed, pull the covers to my chin, and spend the afternoon in tears. After church I visited my grandmother, who is enduring the slow decline into death we call old age. I stopped past my sister's on the way home, and her husband was rototilling a garden plot as her Mother's Day gift, and her young sons were planting it. My daughter Melissa has wired flowers from Ohio. None of my three sons, not to mention their father, has remembered me with so much as a card.

Tears on Mother's Day are not a tradition for me. Generally, I figure that two out of four offspring remembering any special occasion is a decent batting average. Of course, children don't remember their parents. Sometimes this is callous disregard, but sometimes this is part of the necessary process of healthy separation. Moreover, I have always

maintained that Mother's Day makes more women unhappy than happy. On this Mother's Day afternoon, I am
one of the unhappy ladies.

This is David's fault! I think to myself, wiping my tears
on the bed sheet. *A father is supposed to coach his sons on
honoring their mother. I coach my sons on honoring their father.* I recall that my daughter, after taking an introductory
psychology course in college, had identified some martyr
tendencies in certain female members of our family. "You
know, Mother," she remarked, "you and I suffer from mar-
tyrs' complexes." (How tactfully these children teach their
parents! "You and I," they say. "We," they say. But I know
that she knows from whom she learned this pattern. I also
know that she is correct: I have developed a tendency to
sacrifice myself and then to suffer silently.)

Melissa is right. It is time, in a mature and rational
way, to break this pattern of silent suffering. I'll take responsibility for my own self. I dry my eyes, compose my
face, comb my hair, and walk downstairs. David is sitting at
the dining room table, preparing a broadcast for the morning. Absorbed, he doesn't pay any attention to me as I stand
beside him.

"David," I say, hesitant about interrupting, knowing
the relentlessness of his broadcast schedules, understanding from my own writing struggles how hard it is to gather
one's thoughts once they fall from the page, roll off the
edge of the table, and splatter across the carpet, "I am having a rough Mother's Day."

"Hmmm," he replies, not looking up from his notes.

First mistake. I look too composed. I should have
messed my hair, not combed it. I should have crawled
down the stairs on all fours. (But with his power of concentration, would he have even noticed this?) Perhaps a fall
down the three bottom stairs, a measured slip? (Definitely
an overcompensation, dangerous to life and limb.) A piercing scream? Moaning? Groaning? (Am I actually capable of

manufactured hysterics? I have spent a good deal of energy learning to appropriately manage and express my emotional passions.) Am I willing to trade my dignity for attention? No, I am not.

I have never learned the shady art of manipulation. I do not know how to articulate my own wounds and needs so that I can be heard. And I feel the unfairness of having to coach people in how to care for me when I am in pain, particularly when I so often extend myself intuitively and sensitively to the wounded.

I start again. "Well, the boys haven't done anything. I think it's a father's responsibility to teach his sons to honor their mother. They won't know what to do unless you remind them. You know, 'Hey guys, Mother's Day is coming. How about a little card, a surprise sweet roll in bed for your ole' mom. A little bunch of daisies? Not much, you know. She doesn't need anything fancy or costly. Just a remembrance—to show her how much we appreciate her.'"

David's head bobs up. He looks at me briefly. The message I read is: "Oh, I can't believe this is coming up now when I'm pushing so hard to get this broadcast done." His eyes actually shift back to the paper. He jots a quick note. I have one fleeting impression of how many married conversations have been conducted without eye contact. He isn't really listening to me. His thoughts are still on his work. Swallowing my pride, I announce, "For all three of my sons to overlook me today indicates basic male neglect in this family."

Maybe it's the word *neglect.* Maybe emotion is making my tone strident. Eye contact! Still, I notice that the pen is not put away. David does not leave his work and draw me to sit beside him on the couch. He doesn't say, "I hear you. Give me five minutes to finish this thought, then let's go take a walk together." Instead, there's a disclaimer. "Melissa sent you flowers. And you said you were going to Gram's . . ."

My determination to be heard is not to be diverted by his matter-of-fact surprise. "Melissa did send flowers, and that was lovely and thoughtful. And I did go to Gram's, and that's hard on me because she's so frail. And I'm missing my own mother today," I reply. "But it is the boys I'm talking about. It's the boys who haven't done anything. Furthermore, you haven't done anything."

Sometimes, in a flash of moderate hostility, during a moment of self-centeredness, I find myself saying words that bring me to discoveries I hide when I am being nice.

"But Karen," my husband replies, finally looking at me. I gaze into those beautiful brown eyes with their sweeping black lashes. "But Karen, you're not my mother." This logical explanation should wipe away any emotional dissatisfaction.

Instantly my assertiveness is deflected. He's right, I think. I feel badly that I have interrupted his writing. What is wrong with me? I'm being immature. Childish. How can I expect my husband to help me when I don't really know myself what's wrong? I'm the emotional expert in this family, the spouse in charge of interpreting psychological linguistics.

I climb the stairs again, close the bedroom door, and try to nap. "Well, of course," I think. "How foolish of me. I am not David's mother." Despite my capitulation, indignation begins to assert itself. "Hey lady. You have not received a fair hearing. What does he mean, 'You're not his mother?'" Tears and fury rise with a clear-eyed rationality. A new thought: I am the mother of his children. I make sure his children honor him on Father's Day, and he's not my father.

The complications of these overwhelming emotions demand that I attempt to attack the central issue. Why have my emotions grabbed this particular day to make their painful point?

Obviously, I am grieving my loss. My mother is dead. Mother's Day is going to remind me that I have no mother to love and no mother to love me. It will remind me that my grandmother is too frail with age and her own grief to comfort me with her usual flowery card, *To My Granddaughter on Mother's Day.* All her letters to me were invariably scrawled, "To Sweet Sue (my middle name) from Your Old Gram." And I miss them. No longer having a mother to care for on Mother's Day, I am suddenly overwhelmed by my own needs.

But there is something more here, something about that whole area of male neglect. If one, just one of my sons had left a card on my bedside table this morning, would I now be wallowing in tears? What does it mean to me that none of the men in my family have thought of me today?

Why has my subconscious grabbed hold of this symbol, Mother's Day, and stamped its feet in a temper tantrum of hurt and anger? I follow the downward spirals of questions and descend into the cellar of my own self. I feel like a child left alone in the basement with the lights out.

"Neglect, neglect," the child howls, kicking the scrub buckets, banging a broom on the laundry room door, pounding on the hot water pipes. "I'm down here in this dark place where I have been relegated, making an outrageous racket because it will be a whole year until Mother's Day comes again!"

Sometimes the only way to calm an outrageous child is to ask, "Tell me what has happened? If you can tell me who has hurt you, if you can tell me what is wrong, I will try to understand and make it right."

So I open the cellar door and listen carefully to what this neglected self seems to be screaming. This is not childish behavior on my part, I decide. I have no past pattern of self-centeredness on Mother's Day. No, this is true emotional pain with some undisclosed cause. Grief is overloaded with outrage, but for what am I grieving? Am I grieving the loss of my mother? Or am I grieving the loss of some part of myself that has been crowded by my mother's life? Again, why has this very legitimate pain all been set off by lack of male attention? What is the outrage about?

Mary Patterson, aged two and a half, bumps downstairs, her pajama-clad bottom pounding on each rung. Being in this pastor's home in California on Sunday morning evokes echoes of the years David and I spent in an inner-city pastorate in Chicago. I remember my children as toddlers, their delicious, warm bodies, still fuzzy from sleep. I remember them all reaching for hugs and cuddling my nose into their fragrant necks. I hear again the noise as our children grew. The walls of the house on Grove Street like a sound chamber, reverberating with calls and cries and bawls and hollers. Laughter whoops as my children chase each other. Feet in quadruplicate on the bare hallway floors. Doors slam. In the kitchen, I hear little boys jumping upstairs from their bunk beds, shaking the hardwood floors.

I am at the age when my rich past informs my present, but I am not so old that I prefer to live in my memories. They just catch me as I hurry by, trip me in my forward momentum, surprise me with their power. For a brief instant, little Mary Patterson scootches down the stairs, and I hear and feel and see what has been but is now gone.

Lauretta, Ben Patterson's wife and mother to this brood of children, three boys and one girl, is attending a retreat in the mountains along with other women from Irvine Presbyterian Church. All are due to return late this afternoon. Dad is in charge of this Sunday morning scenario. I admire his patience, tolerance, and good humor in the face of David's and my Laurel-and-Hardy travelogue (so typical of our life together).

We reached the Pattersons' after midnight last night, seven hours behind schedule. After delivering plenary addresses for a Sunday school convention in Peoria, we caught our flight to California at O'Hare. Our scheduled forty-five-minute layover in Utah stretched to several hours, by which time John Wayne Airport, our destination, was closed. We were rerouted to LAX in Los Angeles and took an airport van to John Wayne, where we called a limousine that rendezvoused with Ben at the entrance to the appointed housing development. It was only after we unloaded our suitcases in the Patterson driveway that David realized he had overlooked his all-important briefcase in the darkened limousine trunk. A panicked moment. A call to the limo service. A ride back to the rendezvous point. To bed finally, with relief, then up early for two worship services.

I often think of our life as a silent, black-and-white comedy movie with the episodes and scenes accelerating to double-time. Perhaps I fear that at triple-speed the sixteen-millimeter film will split and flap around the old camera reel, the way film broke when I was a child in school.

Our late arrival is the reason this afternoon that David is asleep upstairs and Ben and I are cleaning up from the Sunday dinner that Lauretta prepared ahead of time. Dan and Joel and Andy, the three boys, run outside to play. The littlest one, adorable Mary with her fat cheeks and blonde hair, now drowsy, is tucked away for her nap. The kitchen is tidied. Ben and I are good housewives. We take mugs and fill them with fresh coffee as a reward for our work, and we begin to chat. We chat as sunlight slants gently across the floor. We chat as the mellow leisure of a Sunday afternoon lulls us. We chat while children's happy voices, eagerly calling out play schemes to each other, sound through the patio doors. We are waiting for Lauretta to come home and for David to wake, and we talk more as these events delay. We are in a sanctuary, safe in the seclusion of this afternoon kitchen.

Ben traces for me his ragged sortie into Christianity. He recounts (with laughter) his hasty courtship of Lauretta and their adjustments during early married life. Mentioning his male buddies of those years (they called themselves "The Brotherhood"), he describes their bond as sort of a "Christian motorcycle gang." Ben and I consider the male pact, an intense covenant that often exists in men's friendships. We investigate how this differs from friendships between women. We examine the nuances, the delights and dangers, of cross-gender relationships, and we chew on the question: Can Christian men and women be friends? We are leisurely enough to discover and reveal personal pains. We share our amazement at the fact that our closest friends often seem the most oblivious to our hurts. We decide that this neglect is not limited to either sex. I am tender toward Ben's amazing vulnerability; his eyes tear when he talks, and he is not embarrassed by his feelings.

Ben is also an avid reader and an agile thinker. We trade titles, significant books published over the last year that have trimmed our mentalities. Paul Johnson's *Modern Times* (which I haven't read but which I make a note to purchase) is highly recommended. Both of us are in the throes of recalcitrant projects, and we talk about writing and the agony of it and the need for good Christian writers to support each other and the lack of decent critical review systems in evangelicalism.

The whole time this is happening, I realize I am waiting for Ben to excuse himself. He must have some important work to do, some reading that needs to be finished, some last-minute preparations for Sunday evening, for whatever crucial business meeting is coming up next week. (He's not leaving! Oh, my—well, what about this other idea? We explore the influence of our mothers on our separate lives.) I feel as though I have eased unintentionally into some ensconced moment with no beginnings to fear or endings to intrude, just a middle going gently on and on and on.

Of course, real time returns—happily. Lauretta sweeps breathlessly into her kitchen. Arms wide in greeting, overflowing with enthusiasm to report the good work of God in the lives of church women who have gone on retreat together, eager to embrace her children and to plan a supper and to be a hostess to her guests, she joins us at the counter. The boys clamor, gathering with news to report to their mother. The toddler stirs in her crib. David rouses from sleep, comes downstairs, and laughingly recounts the tale of our bump-along journey and the frantic recovery of the abandoned briefcase. He embellishes, of course, drawing out the absurdities and enlarging the incongruities. The circle of the kitchen island, which has been a safe place for two, now enlarges itself with laughter and becomes a place for many, for those who really belong here and for David and me, welcome guests.

David and I have another four days ahead of us in California, leading workshops at the regional Congress on Biblical Exposition in Anaheim, and I think frequently about this talk with Ben. It has unaccountably warmed me. In a way, the effect on me is out of proportion to the event. A two-hour chat on a sunny Sunday afternoon is simply a two-hour chat, nice and over and forgotten. But I do not forget. I am honored that Ben would think me intelligent and interesting enough to spend conversational time with me. This has been one of those unusual, unplanned meetings that always intrigues me, where strangers touch lives for brief moments, unexpected gifts are exchanged, and both are enriched because of the time together.

What was the meaning of the fact that a slight acquaintance met me in the midst of a Mack Sennett comedy caper that is too frequently my life, stopped the unrolling double-time sequences, and gave me the gift of his unhurried attention? What is the emotion I am feeling?

It is like the morning I walked on the beach in Oregon alone, where invading crowds had not yet gathered and where I was startled by the flashing opals of early sunlight, where thousands of sun shards struck against the flapping wings of sandpipers and forced me to stop. An inward cry rose in me, "Oh, look! The loveliness of it! The great, God-blessed loveliness of it all!" The tide wet my feet, and I felt the moment too huge to be hugged to my soul alone. I, small and frail, was breaking apart under the weight of this transcendency. Suddenly, a stranger passed beside me, going in the opposite direction. He smiled, somehow knowing, and called out, "It's almost too beautiful to bear, isn't it?"

As I examine the sweetness of my two-hour conversation, I realize I have few people who can help me bear the burden of the wonder of a thousand bombarding transcendencies. There are almost no moments in my life where I can give a whole afternoon to unplanned conversation. I vow again (as I do frequently) not to lose the spontaneity that is the core of my nature, not to become so busy that I don't have time for impromptu encounters with their unexpected, rich surprises. The unscheduled afternoons of my girlhood (in which I would begin to read a whole stack of books) have shrunk through the years to a crunched hour grabbed here and there. My adult life is turning into an unending serial, where the comic hero balances forever on a tilting ladder, scrambling back and forth from grasping policemen's hands. The script narrative calls for things to go wrong which somehow, remarkably, turn right before the fade-out. But meanwhile, how do we bear the humorous catastrophe of this transit between beginnings and endings?

I also realize that there are no adult men in my life with the gift of spontaneous time to give to me. There are none I can think of who will throw away two hours on a Sunday afternoon and laugh and let the soft part of their souls show and explore ideas and listen and respond. If there are no men in my life who can take leisurely walks without an appointment to hurry toward, without endless lists and plans and deadlines crowding the moments, what does this mean?

Flying homeward, I think again about my talk with Ben. Sitting next to David, who has the enviable capacity of being able to work anywhere, I suddenly come to the conclusion that I am a vulnerable woman. Any man who would spontaneously give me the gift of his time might be attractive to me. He could be physically misshapen, bald, short, or bandy-legged. He could be egg-shaped. He could be unstylish in his dress. But if he took a sincere intellectual delight in me, if he took my thoughts and spiritual discoveries seriously, if he gave me his full attention, if he had the capacity to ditch an afternoon of appointments and say, "Hey, let's grab the moment. Let's just spend time talking!" If he could play intellectual volleyball—spike, dive, set, block, pass—I would be susceptible.

I inform David of this susceptibility. I mention what a lovely afternoon I had spent conversing with Ben, how complimented I felt by his gift of time, how rare this event seemed to be in my experience with Christian men. David agrees with me about Ben Patterson's rare qualities. I announce my discovery—I am a vulnerable woman. My husband looks at me, gives me a husbandly squeeze, a tolerant smile; he is used to my out-of-the-blue pronouncements. I know he hears me because he puts his work away and tucks his briefcase under the airplane seat.

I also suspect he hasn't really believed me.

On Saturday morning of Memorial Day weekend, I wake from what is undoubtedly the worst nightmare of my life. Shock, disbelief, rage, and holy indignation overwhelm me. I remember fragments and lie in bed stunned. I had dreamed that David was having an affair with a woman named Lynn. My husband was leaving me and our children for this dumpy, unattractive woman.

Strange. In the dream I felt so beautiful, so desirable, so attractive. How could he not love me? How could he choose any other woman? The scene in my dream suddenly shifted: I dreamed I was in bed beside David. Instantly, in the dream state, I felt overwhelming, tender compassion for my husband. Turning on my side to watch him sleep, I actually chose to love him anyway in the face of his ruinous decision to destroy everything we cherished, held dear, and had suffered to keep.

Then I really woke, swimming up into consciousness. I really turned on my side to see David sleeping beside me. I pressed my hand against the firm substance of the familiar body beside me. It was warm and lively.

No woman has ever been so glad to wake from sleep. It is not true, I think to myself, relieved. David has not had an affair. Yet my body is as exhausted as if it has been tortured.

I take some deep breaths. I will my fluttering heart to become calm. This is not a literal message from my subconscious self, certainly, but a symbolic one. I quickly realize that my subconscious has used the one symbol, a husband's sexual infidelity, that it is sure I will not ignore.

At one time I had said to David, "You don't have a mistress, you have a briefcase." The attaché case goes with him everywhere—to work, on vacations, on family outings, on trips cross-country. If I am upstairs writing or reading in my study and David returns home in the evening, the briefcase banging down on the dining room table alerts me to his arrival. I think a convincing argument could be made that David spends more time with his briefcase, gives it more attention, delights in it more than he does in me. I mentioned this once. He protested. So I said that his briefcase was his mistress, half in jest, half in seriousness, the way we do, barbing truth in humor when it is still half-truth, or perhaps only pretruth.

44

I begin to understand, lying in my marital bed in my raspberry-papered bedroom, that I must come to terms intellectually with the fact that workaholism stunts whole parts of our marriage union. I have accepted the truth rationally that a problem exists between David and me that is not minor and that will not fade away. But I have never, until this moment, begun to consider the enormous emotional suffering it has brought me. My nighttime dream is disgorging a daytime reality: I have hidden intense pain from myself in the deepest part of myself.

Stunned by this revelation, I must nevertheless spend this Saturday organizing for a celebration. In the extended families of the five couples who make up our small group, all now attending St. Mark's Episcopal Church, three high schoolers are graduating, one grandchild has been born, and one marriage-to-be has been announced. I had decided to throw a celebratory party that would include adults, children, grandchildren, and grandparents. We would share a meal and give gifts and verbal blessings to all the congratulatees. We would practice community by celebrating communally. The day set for the event is tomorrow after worship.

I have planned an outdoor spring party. The Japanese irises in the herb garden are blooming. The buds on the old-fashioned roses, my Betty Prior border, are pinking, bursting. I have purchased eight more garden chairs. Blue-and-white striped cushions are tied jauntily to all sixteen now. The weather report, however, forecasts a weekend of rain. The clouds above are ominous, dark, and heavy. The day is gray. I strip my upstairs study, store the computer, and turn my library table into a mini dining room. I spread an India bedspread over the rectangular worktable. The two round downstairs tables are set; flowers are arranged for centerpieces. I set up another table for six in David's tiny study. There are sit-down eating places for twenty-six.

We are having a Middle Eastern menu: marinated shish kebabs, an Israeli vegetable salad, curried cold brown rice, pita bread with a blended cucumber and yogurt dip. I prepare a sliced fruit tray for dessert, arrange it on a big, round basket, garnish the slices of oranges and pears and the bunches of grapes with dried figs. For adorning platter presentations, I harvest fresh spring herbs: the mints and sages, the creeping thymes, their leaves wet with rain. The small irises dance in the downpour. I clip their heads with my garden shears. They will be perfect floating in the water glasses. I do last-minute grocery shopping and prepare the remaining recipes. By five o'clock I am exhausted but finally have a moment to begin working out the meaning of last night's dream which has haunted my busy day.

Sitting in my study, with the table now crowding the room, I realize that the effects of David's workaholism are as debilitating to my inward sense of self, to my concept of myself as his wife, as the effects on a woman who has discovered that her husband was involved in a sexual liaison. This was the very clear and uncomplicated message of my dream. I sense that since there has been no outward moral breach, my pain has all been internalized. If I am going to be responsible for myself, I must determine the extent of my hurt. I must come to terms with the fact that my soul is attempting to dissolve the clots that have formed in me; I must assist somehow by coughing up this blood.

I consider again my marriage. I think of David's delight in me, his pride in my accomplishments, his creating space for my growth. I remind myself of the sacrifices we have given to each other for the sake of each other. But I begin to sense that I am deeply damaged, to what extent I do not as yet know, by a thousand small, unmarked ways over the thousands of days of our married life together. The results of David's addiction are a benign neglect that has convinced my inner self—the most central core of who I am—that I am not truly worthy of my husband's love and attention. Something terrible has happened to me at the hands of the person who in all the world loves me the most and—most terrifyingly—I have let it happen.

I refuse to be a whining wife. In a way, my emotional wounds seem trivial to me, and the seeming pettiness of them has made me mute. For some reason, over the years (apart from occasional moments of frustration) I have allowed myself to become dumb, blind, and senseless to the wounds. But this dream is shattering my perceptions. It is insisting, with the most graphic language, that I pay attention. It is shouting that the effects of this neglect in my life are not negligible.

At the same time, I am riding a carnival whirligig of celebration that I cannot abandon. I have one more dessert to make and name cards to print. This is an intergenerational gathering, with children and high schoolers sitting at all the tables with adults; I am providing some questions for conversation starters. I write these out and slip them into envelopes. I need still to set up a makeshift serving buffet in my study for the upstairs eaters, to cube and marinate the meat for skewering, to make sure the outside barbecue is scrubbed, to move some of the yard chairs into the basement where rain will force us to gather after eating, and to wash my hair and figure out some clothes for tomorrow that will do both for church and for hostessing.

I make a prayer appeal, an intercession that is becoming age-old for me.

Dear Lord, I need you to be my Organized Householder. I need you to help me pull all these loose ends together in time for tomorrow. I am just so weary. I know that you are a Husband who never leaves me, who is never too busy to give me attention or to lend me a hand. Thank you. I know that to most women I would be considered blessed beyond measure. And I am blessed. But I am coming to understand that you want me to be a truthful woman. And there are truths about myself I do not see.

Collapsing into bed, I finally have time to touch my own deep pain. The intellectualizing is over. Like a medieval physician, in the middle of the night, I incise an artery in my emotions. I bleed spurting unwholesome black humors into a basin. Tears roll down my cheeks and onto the pillow, and I turn, hunched with hurting. David is still working; this is not the hour nor the place for confrontation. Nor do I as yet have the words. Exhausted by my emotional bloodletting, I fall asleep around 2:00 A.M.

The next morning I gratefully worship in the early service. The austere quiet of the eucharistic service, a liturgy without music, soothes me. The chapel is somber, but accents of red—here and there in the carpet down the center aisle, in the now-and-then covers of the Book of Common Prayer in the hymn racks, in the diamonds of glass in the leaded windows—these all wink at me, wiggle their fingers in greeting and smile. The homily is about Christ being our Vine, about how we need to live our lives rooted in Him. I rest my physically weary and emotionally battered self in that truth.

The celebration is a wonderful success. All are fed, all are welcomed, all are blessed. Gifts are given to the newborn, the graduates, and the recently engaged to be married. The vine life curls about us; it binds us together. We are friends. We are children. We are common celebrators. After all the guests leave, my pitch-in, clean-up crew begins to work their magic, and I am sent to bed. I hear my sons, strong and manly, down in the kitchen, drying dishes, flipping rolled towels against each other's rear end. They hoot and shout. The house feels happy as though it had its own personality and humanity. The phone rings. Melissa reports that her car is fixed and she will be coming home after all. Jeremy, who has transformed himself into a paragon of assistance this weekend, comes into my bedroom. He has a question.

"It was great, Mom. But what do you get out of it?" He kisses me and leaves me to consider his inquiry.

What do I get out of these grand events, these heroic gestures? I think wearily, "There must be something besides three days of hard work, a financial hole in my household budget, and right now, a lot of physical pain." I grab my journal and list ten ways in which I have received benefit. Most are simple things, sweet and simple things. The newborn's smile when I finally had time to hold him in my arms, his beautiful cooing breath, his trusting slumber, the warm, damp heaviness of him on my shoulder. A rare kiss from my mother-in-law. A child, a namesake actually, little Karen, slipped her hand into mine and held it. One of the teens, Kristin Shaw, hugged me and said, "I love you." What did I get out of it? A principle that my subjective self forcibly underlined by injecting my terrible dream into my plans for celebration.

The principle is this: I must never forget it. If you are going to stare at truth, if you don't want the birthing of agony to tear you apart, give it a hard look only when you are in the middle of celebrating life. Let the pain come, because it must come. Let it rend your soul asunder, but only when you are surrounded by newborns and the conversations of friends. Cry in the night because crying is party to this human estate and because you have no choice, but also rejoice. Celebrate life passages no matter the distress, no matter death or terror or loss. How do I rejoice today? By picking out the bugs that crawled from the irises into the water glasses and laughing. By being grateful for all the hands that helped. By finding a corner out of the commotion to let down my hair with my longtime buddy Marlene, "to gossip and be wicked" with each other and to howl with healing laughter.

I realize I am more wounded than I know. The work of this great affair has collided head-on with my emotional calamity, and my body is the casualty. I stay the most of the next day, Memorial Day Monday, in bed. I nap. I read. I sleep. I drag myself downstairs for leftovers, everything good and cold from the refrigerator, eaten with my fingers. I suspect that I have a barefoot journey over broken glass to travel in the days ahead. I begin the hard work of sorting things out.

A friend calls to thank me for the grand celebration. He and I have known each other for more than twenty years. I share my dream and the emotional reality it is imposing on me. "You certainly picked a good weekend to begin this journey," he comments with irony. But I haven't picked this timing. This juxtaposition was none of my doing. May, gray-green, is outside my windows. Mist rises like billowing spring steam, gently. Lamplight warms the empty rooms. It is quiet. Frederich Buechner says it all so well in one line from his book *Godric:* "What's lost is nothing to what's found, and all the death that ever was, set next to life, would scarcely fill a cup."

The vine life is curling all around me. It is rooting deep despite my pain, and I must not ever forget. I must not ever forget it, despite the sound of my husband's briefcase that I can hear banging downstairs, being opened for a long evening full of work.

"That's not your self-destructive habit, Dad," says Melissa.

Today all our children are home, two high schoolers and two college students. We are gathered in the living room. They sprawl on either side of the fireplace on the two church pews. Their feet are crossed at the ankles; heels are propped on the old oak kitchen table. My retired handyman had sawed the thick, turned legs to proper coffee table height for me. ("You sure you want me to do this, lady? Can't put 'em back on once I saw 'em off.") Melissa, knees crossed and the top one bouncing, dangles her shoe off the tip of her toe.

David has announced the plans for next year's Fifty-Day Spiritual Adventure, a program for accelerated spiritual growth we offer through "The Chapel of the Air" during the traditional Lenten season for individuals, families, small groups, and churches. The topic this year is "Fifty Days to Welcome Christ to Our Home." One of the disciplines is a centerfold titled "Overcoming Self-Destructive Habits," in which the participants chart a chosen debilitating personal pattern in an attempt to understand its cycles and then to overcome it.

David confesses to his grown children the self-destructive pattern he has identified. He has a weight problem and requests their prayers as he attempts to begin to overcome this.

There is silence. My four children observe their father with uncanny fixed stares. "That's not your problem, Dad," Melissa says again, no longer the shy little thing who could scarcely converse with strangers.

"No, that's not your problem," says Randall, the eldest, always straightforward with any of his opinions to the sacrifice of social niceties.

David is taken aback. He had been so open, so vulnerable about his extra twenty pounds. "No?" he says, leading with his chin. I've tried to help him to be a little more politic. "No?" he inquires of his children, who exude self-confidence and ease, knowing somehow that they have surrounded their father's forceful personality and that they have him outnumbered. Then my husband sticks out his jaw: "What do you think my self-destructive pattern is?"

"Your problem is workaholism," they respond instantly, as though prompted. As though they had practiced this question-and-answer scenario in some secret sibling society. "You're a workaholic," presses Melissa. "That's right," insists Joel. They laugh together at his obvious incredulity.

Taken in ambush, David squirms. He protests. He just has too much work to do. He flails in self-defensiveness. He denies. The chorus of truth rises to one single note spoken firmly, surely, in unison. They cite patterns. They give evidence of years of incidents. They report observations from yesterday, today, this morning. They corner him, and all four move closer for the final apprehension.

My husband looks each child in the eye, then proceeds to "head count," the old divide-and-conquer parenting tactic. "Randall, do you think I'm a workaholic?" "Melissa, do you think I'm a workaholic?" "Joel, do you think I'm a workaholic?" "Jeremy, do you think I'm a workaholic?"

Not one of them wavers. Not one equivocates. Without being brutal in their truth-dealing, they are nevertheless obdurate. "You're a workaholic, Dad. Face it. No doubt about it."

Amazing. We are at what sociologists call "critical mass," a consensus large enough to effect significant change.

"Karen," implores my husband, appealing by his look for me to lend him wifely backup support, "Do you think I'm a workaholic?"

How can I be less forthright than the four children sitting before me? How can I not match their amazing adamancy? I choose to speak the truth as well, to side with my children against their father. "I think you are a workaholic. And I think you are compulsive about your work patterns and cannot stop yourself from overworking."

Although I have been saying this in one form or another for the last five years, I have not been heard. But today, critical mass has been reached; one, two, three, four, five against one. David finally hears this determined, spoken consensus. Submitting, he writes "Workaholism" down in the fifty-day spiritual adventure, in the place marked "Overcoming a Self-Destructive Habit." He begins to chart his own disability because his family has spoken truth to him in joined chorus.

Once, at a social dinner, I sat beside a psychologist who worked with executives addicted to their job responsibilities. For obvious reasons I was particularly interested in how he helped their wives come to terms with the influence of this addiction on them and on their families. "You know," he said to me confidentially, leaning over the chicken cashew casserole, "I've come to the conclusion these guys are never going to change."

And I thought, *Then you don't know David Mains.* One of the qualities I love about this man I married is that as stubborn as he can be, as singly focused with no room for the leisure and recreations others enjoy, once he is convinced about truth, once he understands that it is the Holy Spirit that is convicting him, he sets his mind to the undertaking like he does everything else in his life. With unshakable determination.

David works through the disciplines of the adventure five separate times. He fills his chart over and over and fails. He begins to own the truth his children have spoken. He can see for himself that he is driven by a compulsion over which he has little control. He attempts to modify his behavior. He starts outward and works inward. He confesses over national radio that he has a problem with workaholism. A listener writes to commend him for his courage in admitting that he is an alcoholic. David responds and kindly notifies her of the mistake, but he also tells her that he is beginning to understand that changing the patterns of workaholism may be as difficult to accomplish as changing the patterns of alcoholism.

"How's David?" people ask me, friends who love him (but for whom he doesn't have much time, so much work to do). "How's David?" listeners across the nation inquire, many of whom admire the creativity, the practicality, and the significance of his spiritual direction in their lives (but don't understand that the very nature of the broadcast—the deadlines, the thin budget of time and finances—contribute to his compulsion to work all the harder). "How's your husband?" my friends politely question.

"David's fine," I reply. "He's working hard at not being a workaholic."

Lazy, slothful, still with sleep, I lie on my side in the carved mahogany fourposter. I arch my toe to tag the bed board. Luxuriant bouffants of mosquito netting poof around me. Morning peeps indolently above the veranda balustrades, their intricate fretwork more distinct as light steals softly into the master bedroom. All Antigua, all 108 square miles of her, calls to me. The fragrant bougainvillea in the overgrown garden outside presses the air sensuously. A lackadaisical island breeze stirs the drapery on the bed. The room is windowed on two sides, unlocked, uncovered, all wide. We are guests in this once-upon-a-time sugar plantation, Parham Hill.

I slip from the bed, from my husband curled still in slumber, his back toward me, through a French door to the outside veranda. Still nightgowned, I perch on a tipsy three-legged stool, knees tucked beneath me, my chin a triangle on the backs of my hands resting on the paint-peeled railing. I am an audience to mornings. I love to watch the curtain rise on each day, to applaud these premier performances. I lean close in my box seat and wait, eager for the overture.

A rooster crows, his alarm a gargled stage call. Below me, a garden amphitheater crescents. I can just see the scarlet in the jasmine vines, thickly twining, macerating with interminable tendrils the pillars and foundations. Crumbling outbuildings, all props and sets for deterioration, stand forlorn. They loom frowning in the shadows cast by the dim wattage of the new sun's bulb. Squinting in the twilight, I trace the faint outline of an old stone terrace descending toward what looks like an abandoned swimming pool. Hills in the far distance roll and loop gently onward toward the sea. A spotted goat trots across the lawn directly beneath me.

Day bursts suddenly above the horizon. The outdoor theater sky blazes in a chorus line of gaudy flashing veils— red, gold, rose, purple, yellow, cerise. They bleed, blend, then blur at last away. Awed by this shocking striptease, this lurid uncovering of the hidden skin beneath the blue dressed sky, I rise on my knees and balance on my tipping pedestal. I raise my hands in ovation. Suddenly, around a nearby clump of trees, a man appears, a worker following the goat trail. I duck behind the balustrade until he has passed. The sunrise drama is over.

Chilled, I crawl back through the netting, beneath the stiff, line-dried cotton sheets, tucking my cold toes and my body close to the warmth of my sleeping husband. The morning light, julienned by the louvers of the open wooden shutters, now lies lambent in the room. I press my nose into the nape of David's neck, embrace his form with my arms, fold my knees behind his legs. He catches my hand, hides it within his own palm, pulls it tight against his chest, all without waking. It is so good to share an exotic locale with him.

Eagerly I begin to plan the day. It is then I notice his briefcase, waiting closed on the bedroom desk. I fear that wretched disappointment lurks ahead.

Our friends, Shirlene and Tom Dunkerton, had invited us to share this trip to the Caribbean sugar plantation inherited by a work associate of Tom's. So I had schemed and pushed this short February trip onto our already crowded calendars and even scraped together the money from royalties and honoraria to pay for our share. Marital negotiations had been conducted also. "I'll have to bring work with me," my husband warned.

Tempted as I was to barter, the years have taught me that my wifely protests against work are useless. I bow to the adamancy of David's schedules. I am compassionate about his heavy responsibilities. But this looming disappointment reveals that I have been secretly investing hope in the lure of sun and good friends and a decaying mansion to contrive against the hours of work that dominate not only our everyday lives, but all of our vacations.

Today, lying curled close to his slumbering warmth in this locale filled with seductive promise, I am suddenly, overwhelmingly lonely.

Strange. Two nights ago, alone in this huge unfamiliar manor house, I was ecstatic with my solitary state! Our well-laid plans had gone awry. Shirlene and Tom were to join me in Antigua, with David arriving a day later from meetings in New York. But Tom and Shirlene's airplane had been delayed in Puerto Rico due to mechanical difficulties. Naomi, the housekeeper, met me at the darkened plantation door with the news of the Dunkertons' delay.

What I saw of the house as I passed from the front door through the entrance hall and up the winding stairs reminded me of a dowager grande dame, penniless now. Her fine, yellowed lace collar, cameo brooch pinned against her tucked bodice (a black moiré), and ivory-headed walking cane whisper deliciously of old wealth—ill-gotten, extravagantly enjoyed, and misspent.

I darkened the bedroom and changed clothes in the shadows with the windows still open. I listened to Naomi close the big house, heard her moving about downstairs, turning out lights, then felt silence descend. I was the only one behind all those locked doors. Delectable greed filled me: *It's mine, for this unspoiled moment, all mine!* I stepped out onto the sagging second-floor veranda. Moonlight painted the overgrown garden with silver, with hoary shades of artemisia. Beneath me, footsteps plodded away down a night-hugged path. Soft voices trailed off into the whispering foliage. I loved the adventurous gift of it, the aloneness of it, the space that for one evening needed not to be shared.

But now, with David sleeping beside me, with my mind leaping toward wondrous experience, I am suddenly lonely. "Now Karen," I chide, pushing away the despoiler, the disappointment. "You agreed. If David can't go shopping this morning, just take off with Tom and Shirlene. Accept what time he is able to give and don't expect his full participation. Cancel beach plans that include him; he's not crazy about water anyway. Maybe a morning of work, lunch all together, then an early afternoon visit to the historic British fortress. David can spend the late afternoon working. Dinner here at Parham Hill together, then he can work later in the evening. Remember, it's just wonderful to be here with each other. If you don't expect him to participate in everything, you won't be disappointed when he doesn't—swim, shop, explore, whatever."

Suddenly in the middle of this mental rummaging, I realize what I am doing. It is the first time I consciously catch myself protecting myself from David's work orientation. I am building barricades of some kind. What, indeed, is this defense marshalling doing to me? How can I be so delighted by aloneness one night and the very next day, with my husband sleeping beside me, be mounting a struggle to prevent aching loneliness? How often am I lonely in his presence? How long have I been this way?

Middle-age marriage is a territory little explored by mapmakers. Nor do I have a passport for this journey.

A surprise awaits me on Antigua. David joins Tom, Shirlene, and me for breakfast, served by Naomi on the first-floor veranda. As Shirlene and I plan our absolutely perfect vacation day, no mention is made of work; none of the need-to's, the must-do's intrude on our women's chatty conversation. The spotted goat plods across the porch, seeking entrance to the living room. He is shooed away.

We watch birds tumbling in the roller-coaster airways. Naomi instructs us about the markets.

The agenda includes shopping in St. John's. We drive purposely on the left-hand side into the capital city, as though this is our island home and we are not outsiders. We park on the crowded streets and vie in little shops with swarms of tourists from the cruise ships. Here David buys me a new summer frock with a matching broad-brimmed straw hat. We enjoy a rare—and therefore infinitely cherished—long, leisurely lunch in a garden cafe. A stop at a native bakery yields twisted sweet cakes, crullers to munch as we stroll through the afternoon. We climb, slanting forward, up the crooked hill to the old cathedral where we meander across broken paving stones and read the brass memorial plaques to the dead. We motor to Half Moon Bay, where waves brush our bare feet and our toes clutch the sand. We pause and talk with strangers. We watch the sun lumbering across the clouded sky. There is time; time enough to be fully alive in this sweet, gifted day.

A gentle evening shelters the plantation dining room. It grows darker as we sit at dinner. Night leans close, eavesdropping on our confidences that are all so interesting. We stay long at the table. After dessert, Naomi closes the floor-to-ceiling louvered shutters. The candles glow, flickering against the deep green walls, burning low and casting slit shadows. Coffee is poured again and again from the engraved silver service. Finally, we go to bed beneath the masses of netting. I hear a night bird call outside in the garden. The briefcase is still closed on the bedroom desk.

The next morning Tom informs us that the water pressure is down. We can use the toilet, but we are not to flush it. There will be no showers until the pressure is restored. We laugh over breakfast at the contingencies this imposes upon us. "Do you see," says Shirlene, "why I said you were one of the few couples we could invite here with us?"

On our last evening, we dine at a restaurant on a tucked hillside terrace, overlooking an ocean cove that is a favorite of Shirlene's. Sitting at an outside table, we listen to the soughing breeze whisper an irregular island reggae. We watch the remnant selvage of another sunset unravel slowly over the harbor. I wear the new dress David bought me in St. John's. It is full in the skirt and sleeves. The wind catches at it, teases. It feels soft. Everything feels soft. Inside, I feel soft.

Suddenly, raindrops fall on the table, the napkins, the stone patio. "Oh, no," I cry spontaneously. I lift my hands and implore the heavens, "Please, Lord, don't let it rain on our perfect evening!" As suddenly as the rain started, it stops. Amazed, we laugh, then laugh outrageously as we notice the quizzical glances shot our way by other diners.

The next day David and I return home. I have enjoyed luscious moments with my husband, who has given me the gift of time and is now feeling the pressure resulting from this abandon. We are molded back into conforming calendars, unrelenting lists, broadcast schedules, and the demands of phones and appointments.

But I do not forget my Antigua morning. Looking through the billowing mosquito netting, I am pulling aside a deceit in our marriage, that we are a perfect team, perfectly happy in our spousal collaboration.

I realize that I want more than a co-worker. I want a concelebrator to join with me in recognizing the glory of this living. There is no fellow aficionado. Thornton Wilder tells of the Greek myth in which the hero returns to earth for a day and realizes "that the living too are dead and that we can only be said to be alive in those moments when our hearts are conscious of our treasure; for our hearts are not strong enough to love every moment." I know that we cannot live fully and exult in the dramatic exquisiteness of every second in time, but I want a husband, my husband David, to share in a few of the moments of a few of my days. I want him alive beside me, startled to intense consciousness at some of our treasure. I want another devotee to share in my private standing ovations.

David is in town this Good Friday, and we have made plans to go to the service together. More and more frequently, his responsibilities intrude into our celebrations, and I sit alone through many special church services. Gladly, I think of him with me on this evening of commemorative sorrow. ("With me"—a little phrase, but oh, how significant!)

The children all have their own activities tonight, so I fix a special dinner for just two; something fittingly simple for this day—homemade soup and dark bread. I spread the old wood surface of the salvaged Hoosier counter with blue-and-brown plaid placemats and checked cloth napkins. We will eat in the kitchen. A salt-glazed pottery pitcher accompanies the homely setting, and a spattered blue soup tureen acts as centerpiece.

This is a gift for David, this meal. It is a way of marking our life together. I honor the moments of living by regarding them fully, by creating minor ceremonies, by forming one fleeting arrangement of beauty that satisfies my eye and then, in thankful remembering, I taste them over again.

I do not want this day to be just another day, but I want it to initiate us into the cycle of holy time. I want to stop and mark it, to participate in this memorial to redemption called the triduum, three sacred days: Maundy Thursday to Good Friday, Good Friday to Holy Saturday, Holy Saturday to Easter Sunday. At St. Mark's the choir and clergy, all garbed in somber black cassocks, enter in processional solemnity. The altar has been stripped of its lace cloths and linens. A deacon lifts a hand-hewn, man-sized cross and carries it up the center aisle. One by one, the congregation approaches in silence (barefoot if so desired), gazes upon the rough wood, stands or kneels or stretches prone, and considers the crucifixion. Many return to their seats in tears.

So, I gladly await my husband.

I neglect to protect myself, however, from disappointment. The instant David comes in the kitchen door, he goes immediately to the phone and talks for thirty minutes. I make urgent signs to attract his attention. I mouth, "The soup will cool, the bread is right out of the oven." But he is concentrated, ever adept at avoiding interruptions which, at this moment, are my importunities. The soup cools. The bread grows cold. We eat hastily. The sacrament of being, of experiencing God's gift in this present moment is marred—no, ruined.

At another time, this phone call business would have been an innocuous husbandly act. Or once, like the bruise on my thigh from rushing around the kitchen and bashing into a protruding corner, I might have noticed it days later and thought, *Wonder where that came from?* But this night, this night which is part of God's religious cycle of birth and suffering and death and resurrection, the wound I have so adroitly buried over this past decade lurks close to the surface. I am no longer distancing myself from my pain.

Silent in the car, silent on the way to the nave, silent in the church pew, I am susceptible to Good Friday. My human pain meets cosmic grief, the two somehow uniting. I am so overwhelmed with mourning that I am forced to leave midway in the service.

I mourn through Holy Saturday, and I feel two Calvaries. A midget cross-making of my own replicates the divine order of wounded time. I go down to the grave. But by afternoon, facing Easter, I look toward tomorrow, and I see resurrection. I can at last say to my husband, "A funny thing happened to me as we were preparing to share Good Friday dinner."

I am coming to terms with truth, with truth telling. How I am learning to love it—preferring truth to lies any day, even with all the pain in it. I am being continually wounded by my own loving husband! I am being wounded daily by simple neglect. I am in collusion in the pain giving. David can't change if I can't tell him what is wrong. I have not paid enough attention to my own need. How can he pay attention to it? If I do not communicate to David when neglect happens, how can he cease to neglect me? The basic pattern of my past has been to withdraw, to engage in a self-delusion that I was not hurting; then, when I surprisingly discovered pain, I nursed my own suffering.

So, on Holy Saturday, I take responsibility for my wounded, displaced self. I say to my husband, "I need you to join with me in living in the sacrament of the present moment. This being present in God's gift of life is as central to my identity in Christ as any other part of my nature. All of life is holy to me—waking is a gift, loving is a sacred act, joining in any way (the union of friend or companion or stranger) is a picture on earth of God's triune nature. When you neglect my joys, when you overlook my marvelings, when you are inattentive to the wonders I am so eager to share, I am disregarded in a part of my essential humanity. I need to feel you are utterly with me during a few moments of our common life, other than in its work orientation. I need you to be alive with me for small but continual rejoicings at the God-given gifts of our being."

One of the myths we put away in our middle years is that reality is simple and comprehensible in some formulaic fashion. Reality, rather, is a matter of complementary contradictions. David's great regard for me has granted me the autonomy and affirmation I have needed to struggle awkwardly into the continual becoming that is essential to my nature. The same husband, in his deep love for me, has wounded me nevertheless. A man gives his life to do the work of the Kingdom; the same man is driven by compulsions and becomes addicted to his work for the Kingdom.

Isn't this an essential part of the process of spiritual conversion, this living within paradoxes, this accepting joyfully the complications? Dying and rebirth is the central paradox of Christian faith. Don't I act out that mystery of Christ's redemptive work in daily, symbolic ways? Don't these symbolic acts become infused with surprising consequential meanings? I must face the darkness to see the light. I must face death (the death of the idea that I deserve a happy, perfect, untroubled existence) in order to live.

In Larry McMurtry's Pulitzer Prize-winning novel, *Lonesome Dove,* the canny, old cowboy, Gus, lies dying. One leg has been amputated and, with a cocked pistol, he holds off the doctor from amputating the other. "Since you refuse company," says Dr. Mobley, "You'll have to drink alone. I have to go deliver a child into this unhappy world." Gus replies, "It's a fine world, though rich in hardship at times." Certainly, this is a most fine world, and the troublesome complexities make it exceedingly rich in hardships.

Through my hardships I discover there's a small part of myself that hasn't grown whole along with the rest of me. It's been maimed by neglect during years of married life. I call it my "idiot-self." I'm discovering that this malnourished orphan needs to be nursed and nurtured. I must find the idiot-self creeping about in the infrastructure of my soul. I am the only one who can take it out from its cowering, hiding places and hold it in my arms and warm it. It is I who must give it permission to cry. I must tuck it safely into sanctuary, listen to its questions about complexities, and defend it from harm until it is strong. Self of my self, this abandoned child is very much a part of me.

In complexity, at the same time, I must love that part of David's self which has all these years been unattended.

There is also a part of him that is vulnerable to addiction, a part that overworks to achieve the affirmation it never achieves. I must love him at the very same time that I love myself. Charity like Christ's must be given in the middle of my own hurting. Ever concurrent, love stretches toward God and man.

This is my Good Friday service.

I have been staring out of the windows this morning. This study is that solitary place—a room of one's own— about which Virginia Woolf once wrote (and which she proposed essential for the development of any hypothetical modern "female Shakespeare"). Necessary to me, certainly, for the development of my own existence, both professional and private, although I know it will not render me Shakespearian. Calm gray walls and subdued gray, nubby carpet spin a cocoon of shelter for my energetic mind. Seven books were written before there was any physical space in our home where I could close the door to ensure creative privacy.

The second-floor windows are bare of curtains, and during working hours I lift my eyes to watch the cycling world. The leaves curl and fall. The first snow powders the yard. The daylily border births green mounds. The strawberries blossom in ring-around ground covers beneath the trees. A sparrow walks tight-toed on an oak limb. The geese fly across pewter-washed skies. Often I gaze unseeing on the familiar paraphernalia in my desk organizer—files, a packet of tissues, a stack of Chapel of the Air donor bookmarks, a phone message notebook, an imprinted Holiday Inn tablet, a list of people for whom I am praying. One art postcard leans crookedly, although I straighten it constantly, a pen-and-brown-ink reproduction of Fra Bartolommeo's sketch, "Two Angels, One of Them

Blowing a Trumpet, the Other Holding a Staff." Its sepia tones ease my eyes when I am writing and unknot my tangled brain. But I am not working this morning.

This is one of those rare days in my life. Nothing crowds its beginning or ending or crunches its middle. There is nothing I "have to" do, no place I "have to" be. No one is coming home. It is now eleven o'clock. Still wearing my favorite, ragged velour house robe (which has comforted me for eleven years, my adult "blanket"), I have been hiding in my upholstered wing chair for three hours of uninterrupted thought. Today I have time enough to face facts and to chase truth. Some low-lying, unidentifiable panic has been worming within me, chewing and gnawing. *What?* I wonder. *What is this prickly anxiety?* A memory breaks the crust, the memory of David floundering in the offshore waters of Jamaica.

"He's having trouble," I say to the woman lying beside me, both of us stretched on towels on the Caribbean sand. I am watching David swim back to the boat moored hundreds of yards from the island. His strokes are slow—a cramp? The old summer softball charley-horse that annually immobilizes the same muscle? A premonition, an instinct of danger—he has only halted, but I can feel him pulling. "He's having trouble," I repeat, even though my eye can't see him splashing or flailing. I scramble to my knees and reach out instinctively with spread fingers. I want to cry "David!" but how can he hear me? I want to run into the sea myself, but a tail-end bout with mononucleosis has weighted me and I am exceedingly slow in the water.

Robby Levy, our host in Jamaica (one of the laymen who invited David to preach in a church in Kingston), leans over the side of the moored yacht. He perches on the edge, dives into the Caribbean, swims beside my husband the short distance to the dangling ladder and ushers him to the rungs. They climb—far-off diminutive figures—David first, Robby behind. On my knees still, I monitor exactly when the two men disappear safely over the top of the rail. With unutterable relief, I flop back onto my towel.

"What happened?" I ask after swimming back to the yacht myself. "Are you all right?" David answers, "I don't know. I just ran out of steam."

This memory has provided an emotional symbol. My low-lying panic today is like the one I felt while sitting help-lessly ashore. My husband is drowning again, but this time there is no Robby Levy standing ready to dive into the sea and to swim alongside him. Now, instead of being a pan-icked observer on shore, I feel like I am going under as well, drowning quietly, swallowing waters that keep lapping over my head.

For the last months I have been facing the cold, hard realities of my relationship with David with as much truth as I can bear. David has been working hard at not being a workaholic for years, and the terrible actuality is that not much has changed. Sixteen-hour workdays are still the rule, day after day after day. In addition, the fragile financial condition of our ministry feeds into David's work compul-sion. The more shaky we are, the less staff we can afford, the harder he works to compensate.

The reality I must accept is a truth that I have been fending away from me: My husband is likely always to be a workaholic, to die a workaholic. At this moment, there are no indicators forecasting improvement. I can no longer allow myself to be deluded with the promises of a better day. David is likely never to change. I must con-sider: Can I bear the pain of being the wife of a workaholic for the rest of my life?

I know I am helpless to salvage my husband. All my cries and shouts have gone unheeded. Perhaps I have not screamed loudly enough. Perhaps I have not made enough commotion, splashing and pounding the waters. It is true. I have been mostly silent. I have refused to become a nag or a harridan—haranguing, bitter, sarcastic. I have too much pride. Nor have I allowed myself to see how far from shore we have drifted. It is wretched to admit to myself that I am not cherished enough to be heard. It is humiliating to face my own lack of cleverness, that I am not smart enough to outwit this danger. But the greatest reality I must face right now is my own drowning. An inexorable undertow is sucking me. I am tangled in seaweed, the waving, slithering brackets clutching my ankles and knees. Some sort of fugue-state, some unintentional acquiescence to my own demise, is colluding with the pulling waters.

Loneliness, I can see now, was the first danger sign. Victor Frankl, the Viennese psychiatrist, notes that many wives whose husbands suffer from what he termed the "executive's disease" flee to stupefying alcoholism. One news columnist, examining the growing incidence of alcoholic housewives in upper-middle-class strata, tagged this problem "the lonely disease." The loneliness with which I have been dealing is in great part due to my husband's neglect. I understand (with unusual tender compassion for me, one usually so judgmental) why some married people are vulnerable to sexual infidelity. Simply, union heals disunion.

Confusedly, there has been no chaos in our union. A series of chronic complaints, of ongoing unresolved arguments, of grudging silences, of obvious miscommunications—any of these might have been indexes of trouble, might have instigated change. We live in harmony, David and I, a joyful working team. We share a common central purpose for life, advancing the kingdom of God. But despite the outward harmony, the purposeful dedication to serious goals, we are not connecting in these middle years. I have adapted my life to my husband's work addiction. That very adaptation somehow allowed his compulsions to grow. Our mutual disabilities, David's addiction and my cherished wifely illusions, have been subterranean waves in an underground cavern slowly eroding the sandstone. My lie has been that we have a perfect and happy marriage.

My first choice is to decide whether or not I am going to drown along with my husband. Today I know that I am not strong enough to pull him to safety. I also know that if I stay in these depths any longer, I will go under myself. As a matter of self-preservation, dripping and drenched, I must find a safe shore.

To resign myself to the drowning pool because David is swirling away from me is a wasteful desecration of my own life, not an act of consecration. The widow's pyre is not for the Christian. I must begin to function in a way that will protect me. I must define an existence parallel to my marriage, but designed to meet the imperative requirements for my own health.

I cannot change David. Instead, I must, to the best of my ability, salvage myself. Surfacing, I begin to cough, to gag, to spit out the smothering waters from my lungs. I choose, this morning, not to drown alongside him. Terror screams in me. I tremble toward a shoreline. I do not know if this is an act of courage, abandonment, or ruinous self-centeredness. In terror I kick my feet free.

Another memory rises in this long day of thinking. In 1982 I traveled to Jordan, Israel, and Lebanon with a small group of religious leaders at the behest of Queen Noor, the American wife of Jordan's King Hussein. Our purpose was to learn something about the deathly convolutions of those three countries. We had spent the morning interviewing

Arab students from Birzeit University who graphically re-counted torture at the hands of Israeli soldiers. Expended shells of cluster bombs were shoved into my palm; they were imprinted MADE IN USA. "Why does your country sell these to the Israelis?" A young man insisted I answer; he was the age of one of my sons. Arab mothers, their grief and hatred provoked daily, declared outrage: "The little children pick them up to play!" We interviewed the mayor of Jericho, dining al fresco in the watery January sun, cold in our coats at tables set beneath an arbor of grapevines. He wore a white suit, in romantic Hollywoodish contrast to his dark hair and olive skin and flashing black eyes. Hooked over the chairback, a cane. His legs had been crippled by a political car bombing.

From my balcony each morning I greet the Arab guide who tosses me flirting bouquets of compliments—"A new morning! And a beautiful woman!" He throws kisses with his fingers; he bows. But now, it is late afternoon, and my tour group has gone on to Tel Aviv for dinner. Needing quiet, needing a cessation from emotionalized conversation, I stay behind. I incise the day's emotion and weep over the city.

Overwhelmed with the implacability of ancient race and clan hatreds, like a Jewish mother, like an Arab wife, a blanket covering my forehead, a winding wool binding my chest, I rock and keen. I mourn the broken dreams of new lands and cities rising in the wilderness and of hopeful people starting again, beginning over, fleeing to sanctuary. Tears also drop over our own lostness, David's and mine, over our torn ideals of urban ministry lying like crumpled papers on dirty streets, kicked and trodden by careless pedestrians. Are we not part of the broken, once-hopeful believers? Do we not know something of failure?

A Scripture tunes itself in my ear. I hear a narrator's voice that informs all my life's experiences, no matter how far I wander. No matter how deaf I wish to be, this signer interprets ceaselessly for me. "Esau have I hated, Jacob have I loved."

Esau is now a dispatriate on the West Bank, his ancient water rights pilfered through the modern pumps of high-rise plumbing. Jacob, spoiled by permissiveness, is acting outrageously to the plaudits and claims of a world audience. The Arab students, ages fifteen and sixteen, are being taken into custody and tortured by the Israeli military, by other young men ages nineteen, twenty-two, and twenty-five, whose grandparents were once victims of pogroms and other atrocities.

Why, Lord? Although theologians have expostulated, I have never been satisfied with God's preordained favoritism: Why this preferential foreknowledge? All my life I have been a victim of favoritism, of reverse favor. My wearisome burden is that of approval. In guilty compensations, I bend toward the disadvantaged. Privilege embarrasses me (although I notice I do not hesitate to enjoy it).

"You love me more than you love David," I pray, amazed at my own leap in logic. My words are an accusation. I feel God's pleasure. I know His delight. But He is silent with my husband, a God of emotional absenteeism, a God of deferred promises. Will David always be an outsider on the rim of the insiders' circle?

God relates to my husband in silence like the Jewish rabbi in Chaim Potok's book *The Chosen,* who looks at a son's genius and knows that suffering is necessary to prevent the spoiling of particular brilliance. Yet God smiles on me; His words dance all around. I hear the whisper in the whirlwind, see splendor laughing in the grasses, and know the supernal as it flashes itself before my mortal eyes. I feel weighted with His favor—and wounded by preference.

The sun is at mid-afternoon on this, my thinking day. I remember my past accusation, but what has Jerusalem to do with this life, this moment? Memory again pushes up symbol. Injustice! I had cried, mourning outside the ancient walls for the world over the unending hostility of the human race against itself. But I really mourned (as we always do perhaps when we think grandiloquently that we are distressed over international cataclysms), I mourned mostly for my own loves, over the displacement of my own husband.

"What is that to you?" asked Christ of His disciples who were concerned about the future of their fellow apostle, John. "What is that to you?" I hear the question asked of me this afternoon. Knowing suddenly bypasses feeling, and I answer myself: How God loves His children is God's business—even when my husband is the child. I know at this moment that I must allow God to work in David's life in God's way. If I believe intellectually in a sovereign God, I must conclude that He will do what He will do. All my good wifely intents may only be interference.

This is my spousal relinquishment: I cannot do my husband's living for him. If I do, he may actually reach his future later rather than sooner.

Today, truths roll together—and bump. I understand that in some way, I, the intuitive, introverted, feeling-proficient female, have become the substitute for David's own female self, his anima, to use the Jungian terminology. He, highly developed in the traditional male characteristics—that is, the organizer, the administrator, the authoritarian—functions for me as my animus. Anyone observing our outside selves would judge that I am a strong, independent woman with a career and ministry of her own. They would commend David for being the kind of supportive husband with enough ego capacity to encourage his wife's full development. I certainly feel that way about him.

Our mistakes, however, are deeply interior, hairline flaws with great damaging potential. I have abdicated to my husband my own maleness: "Oh, David is the organized 'workamaton' in the family. He's the detail person." Without consciously understanding my pattern, I have abandoned whole areas of personal inner development. Being too feminized, I have allowed my husband to become, in many ways, my male self. Some of this is an inadvertent defense to the feminine-disapproving church culture in which I was raised. Looking back, I can actually detect an unexpressed sigh of safety as I hid in my husband.

The converse is true for David: "Karen can pick up social nuances I don't even know are happening." Busy with increasing executive responsibilities, he abdicates his feminine inner development to me, his sensitive, affective wife.

This is a complicated discussion to be sure, but it can best be illustrated in the way we handle stress. When faced with painful incidents, David just works harder; he exercises more of his male characteristics. Acting out my own overfeminization, I take into myself his woundedness. A complicated spiral develops. As I carry his pain within me, his feelings become more and more atrophied. That adaptive capacity which pain forces upon us to avoid harm is underdeveloped in David, increasingly so due to my well-meaning collusion. Because I am so full of my husband's pain, I have had no room to recognize my own.

Today I am convinced that what I am doing, as mistaken Christian charity, is basically a pagan approach to loving. Thornton Wilder adapted the ancient legend of Alcestis, queen of Thessaly, to a play, *The Alcestiad.* Her husband, King Admetus, is dying. The gods have decreed that he can be saved by the offering of another life for his own. The queen offers herself as the substitutionary atonement. Line by line, his pain becomes her pain; his suffering becomes her suffering; his death becomes her death. "Take my life," Alcestis, now dying, says to him. "Be happy! Be happy!"

I can see now that this is pagan because it is a pre-Christian concept of sacrifice. Christ is the only one who should take another's pain into Himself. His is the only substitutionary atonement. To mistakenly carry another's pain as though it is my own, to take it for the sake of love into myself, is not only a form of subtle arrogance (I am attempting to do what God only should do), it is also sin in that it actually interferes with the way of God's will for that other. I can love. I can help to hoist another's burdens. I can make the harsh way gentler. I can perform sacrificial acts of joyful service. But to take another's emotional pain into myself actually prevents pain from accomplishing its work.

I must look at David's increasing outcastness and hear Christ's question, "What is that to you?" I cannot see tomorrow. I do not know the ending to our story. "What is that to you?" I must let David's present and future be David's present and future.

This morning I asked starkly, "What if David never changes? Can I bear the pain?" This afternoon I know that I believe intrinsically in the sovereignty of God. Consequently, I must acknowledge that He has designed my marital union for His purpose. The beauties of it, the brilliance of it, the very aching flaws of it are all exactly chosen for my further becoming. Workaholism is in some way a gift to me. I also choose to believe that David's future is in God's hands. I vow at two o'clock to honor what I doubted I could bear at eleven o'clock. I vow to honor the marriage covenant.

This paradoxical task seems to me to be the first task at hand: Concentrating on what is good and beautiful in our marriage at the very time that I mend what has fallen into disrepair. I must remember who it is who is lover and cherished companion and friend. I must resolve to refuse the temptation to focus any rancor or bitterness that rises from neglect upon my husband. Christ calls me to follow Him, to take up the cross of loneliness and pain and to follow Him along the difficult way—a way that does not cast blame, that does not judge, that is not arrogant or rude, that is not irritable or resentful. This, of course, is the way of love, the way of patience and kindness that rejoices in the right, that bears all things, believes all things, hopes all things, endures all things. That never ends.

My great concern is loving David; my great concern is loving myself. I know I will not care for him well until I learn to care for myself well.

For the sake of the kingdom of God on earth, for the sake of my children, for the sake of all that is good in our marriage, for the sake of the love I bear for the man, I will cherish this union—for better, for worse, for richer, for poorer.

Perhaps this is the moment above all other moments in my life when I am most married. This is the moment of clear-eyed rationality when I stake my fate in sovereignty's unknown plans. When I throw David's future away unto God.

Independence

$\mathcal{I}$n July 1989, when David and I found ourselves in future-wary Hong Kong one month after the June 4 Tiananmen Square massacre, we took advantage of international relief contacts and visited one of the refugee camps on the outskirts of the city.

I found these refugees to be very different from the ones I had seen in Southeast Asia in 1980. That earlier group was traumatized, desperate, often suffering starvation, displacement, and genocide. The recent group was well nourished and there were many young families with robust children.

Compelling similarities remained, however; one was that segment officially labeled "unaccompanied minors." All minors in this category arrive without family, either sent away from home deliberately or separated from their parents.

I remember Jubilee Camp, a former police barracks, a maze of grim cubicles rising four floors high, with a population of around six thousand refugees. Here, as I was walking through the courtyard, a little hand slipped into mine. I looked down into the black eyes and bangs-blocked haircut of a little child, her shy smile showing front teeth rotting from malnutrition. She had chosen me, for that moment, to be a friend. Wherever I have traveled, throughout the camps of the world, from the earthquake victims in Guatemala barrios to the political refugees of Southeast Asia or Lebanon, children have slipped their hands into mine.

This reality of unaccompanied minors took on a new form when a little girl, a neighbor's child, came to church with us one Sunday. She appeared on our doorstep, as she does every now and then, having dressed herself, ready to go to church. She often attends Sunday school, then joins us for the adult service. David has seen this child play with the kittens in the garage or sit and giggle with her friends on our front stoop. He made the arrangements for her to attend Sunday school. My sons have seen this child— they're often the ones who inconvenience themselves to make sure she gets to and from church, and they are often the ones who sit beside her in the worship service.

But I, well, I've had busy eyes. I had been traveling, speaking in conferences, hostessing a video project about Russian Christian immigrants, and my recent church attendance had been interrupted. This Sunday, however, our small neighbor sat beside me in church. She came down the aisle, searching the faces of worshipers, looking for someone familiar, and she found me and sat beside me. When it was time to sing a hymn, I tapped out the words and notes in the hymnal as I have always done for my young; she, in an early-reading stage, did the best she could. When the offering plate was passed, she took a crumpled dollar from her pocket and put it in. She listened to the sermon and watched as I marked our progress down the worship bulletin.

When it came time to take communion, we stood in line, my neighbor and I, waiting our turn at the communion rail. She slipped a small hand into mine, her small warm flesh cupped within my own hand. She reached out for me, the way children do when they are uncertain, when they don't know what comes next or where they belong. They touch, grab a pant leg or fistful of skirt, take the hand of the nearest sympathetic adult, so steady, so immovable. Big people know what to do, how to make it work, where to stand, when to kneel, what to say. She went to the railing with me and knelt. The pastor placed his hand on her head in a customary prayer of blessing for a child.

Then my eyes were opened, my busy eyes, and I was deeply moved. For truly I was in the presence of an unaccompanied minor, a child without spiritual parent or next of kin, growing up in this refugee camp world; a child who gets up on Sunday mornings, dresses herself, shoves a dollar in her pink snowsuit pocket, and runs to a neighbor's back door in order to be on time to go to church. She sang the hymns and listened to the sermon the best she could. Then she went to the communion railing, her little hand suddenly thrust into mine, not to take communion but to receive a blessing. She is an unaccompanied minor in the spiritual sense. Blinking against sudden tears, I saw her, I who have been busy with the world's needs, the faraway world's needs.

This incident makes me wonder: How many unaccompanied minors are there in my neighborhood? How many children are without spiritual parents or next of kin? The refugee camps far away come close when I remember to search for those who have a lonely spiritual bent, orphans of a sort in their own loving homes.

Who is my neighbor? The answer to that question is the gift this child has given to me. My neighbor is very near, across the back yard, beyond the garden and the next-door basketball court. She is beyond the brush pile. She lives in the blue house on the other side of the wooded lot. I can see the swing-set, one seat tilted, the paint rusting. There is the kitchen window. In the summer a plastic swimming pool makes ring marks on the grass.

Who is my neighbor? My neighbor is often the one I do not choose, but who chooses me. She is the one who slips her hand into mine.

One of the reasons St. Mark's Episcopal Church is a safe place for me is that David and I have attended for the last year and a half without being asked to do anything. No one knows who I am and, furthermore, no one much cares. This is wonderful for me. I have been left alone to sit in a church pew, to be moved to tears during communion, to work out my own salvation with fear and trembling. No one interferes with my personal labor or asks me for spiritual counsel or requests that I take charge of anything.

For all my life, since childhood, I have worked in some way in a church. When I was in grade school, I didn't attend Vacation Bible School; I helped in Vacation Bible School. In junior high and high school, I assisted the woman who ran the Pioneer Girl program at my Baptist church. I sang in my father's youth choirs, babysat in the nursery, planned social events for our high school youth group. At eighteen, I married a minister, took over a Sunday school class, the junior high Pioneer Girls, the youth program, and began opening our home in what became an unending round of hospitality.

We moved into the inner city, planted a church, and I became the senior pastor's wife. I can't recall what I didn't have my hands in during those ten years. We wrote our own curriculum because of the demands of urban multi-ethnicity. I helped conceive full-length dance worship dramas. We designed outreach programs for the mixed racial neighborhoods in which we served. I led women's growth groups, formed an artist module, served as an elder. All of this was good in many ways, but any absence of responsibility came only during the scant few months of my life set aside for recovery from four terms of childbearing.

Suddenly, at St. Mark's, I was in a church that left me alone to consider my own needs. The very least I could do was speak at Deanery Day.

"What's a Deanery Day?" I inquired of my new rector over the phone. He explained that deaneries are geographical divisions within dioceses to which certain towns and the Episcopal churches within them are allocated. The local priest who had contacted me had been elected to oversee the activities of the deanery; he was therefore the dean. Then Rick Lobs expressed pleasure that I'd been invited to speak at a day set aside for the women of the deanery. Evangelicals within Episcopalianism are often looked at askance by more liberal members of the denomination. This dean has not been hospitable to theological conservatives. My rector, himself a strong evangelical, a man devoted to Scripture and an excellent homilist, thinks this bodes well. He forecasts that there won't be a large gathering of women, perhaps thirty or forty will gather for a morning of spiritual insight and a luncheon.

The attendance forecast has been correct. I slip into the front row of the Episcopal church in nearby St. Charles with my rector's wife, Donna Lobs, wait through the preliminaries, then stand to speak. Arranging my notes on the lectern, I feel the floor solid beneath my feet, take a deep breath, then raise my head with the smile that hopefully says to the audience: I am in control of myself and of my material and it is nice to be here.

To my amazement, while glancing over their faces, I see that my rector has slipped into a back pew. Rick Lobs has come to hear me speak and sits, very noticeable to me in his clerical collar, behind the small group of women. I am startled by his presence. Even though I'm employing tried-and-true material, I struggle to gain my confident speaking pace and not to lose my way in these familiar notes. I stumble in my delivery and attempt not to allow my befuddlement to show. I look directly into his eyes and am surprised to see encouragement there. As I continue (having regained my composure), I glance now and then in this man's direction, only to read approval in his gaze, pleasure at my speaking, and eventually, intense listening.

I finish, make casual conversation over lunch with the women, accept profuse compliments from the dean, and discuss the writings of Frederich Buechner with a small group. All appears normal; I have done well, people are pleased. But while driving home, I realize that for some reason, I am shaken to my soul.

In the late afternoon I receive a phone call of commendation from my rector. It is all too much; I am unaccustomed to male approval. Favor unstrings me emotionally; my soul is all jangling, like a harp where the musical ligaments have been suddenly unwired, which have finally snapped under pressure.

A load of pain buried deep within me (of which I have been completely unaware) comes rushing up to the surface. To David's innocent coming-home question, "How did Deanery Day go?" I respond with tears. Both of us are surprised and confused by the searing sharpness of this emotion. I know it has something to do with my damaged relationship with male ecclesiasticism. Sympathetically, my husband listens as I attempt to talk it out.

A good portion of my life has been given to a teaching ministry that has taken me all over the country and Canada. In a way, I come alive when I take my place before an audience. I work hard to be a conscientious communicator. I pray fervently, and I am often gratified by obvious effectiveness. However, there are many men who have made it a point not to be present when I speak.

Pastors introduce me for conferences in their buildings and then mysteriously absent themselves from the auditorium. In a missions-emphasis week in a church in the South, the entire male staff, after welcoming the audience and greeting me, slipped out the side doors. Friends of mine, finer speakers than me, have endured the indignity of rows of men demonstrating their disapproval by pointedly exiting as they spoke. Women editors often support me when I speak at publishing conventions, but the male executives of publishing enterprises rarely show, even when I'm sponsored by their houses. When I'm a plenary speaker at a major convention, other speakers (almost always all men) are too busy, schedule committee meetings, or catch late suppers. Sometimes I receive apologetic excuses, but most of the time significant men are conspicuous by their absence.

"How does this all make you feel?" asked a friend who is a clinical counselor. For years, I didn't think anything about male support (or its lack), but after a while there began to be a cumulative negative impact. "Well," I replied to my counselor friend, "it makes me feel as though I am not considered a ministering peer, that I am not important enough to give thirty or forty minutes to hear. It makes me feel as though I am not worthy of professional courtesy."

I have been mute about the discourtesy, accepted it as my lot as a woman, been careful not to speak in situations where the spiritual leadership is uncomfortable with extending an invitation to a woman. ("What does your pastor think about my speaking?" I inquire. "Your church governing board?") I have attempted not to become indignant.

The next day, another phone call from my rector—an additional thought. Then in the afternoon, a formal handwritten note of commendation arrives in the mail. These affirmations thrust me again into painful emotion. My soul is sliced open by kindness, and I cannot staunch the weeping.

For years, due to my profession as a writer, I have been pondering the power of symbols. I consider the power of symbols this afternoon and the psychological impact upon me of a male in a clerical collar. It's obvious that a man in clerical garb regarding me with favor is a monumental symbol to me of the church corporate. The trappings of liturgical ecclesiasticism (which have not been part of my plain church past) freshly signify to me in some way the parent church. Through the favorable commendations of a clergyman, garbed clerically, some kind of profound approval has been mediated to me. This I suppose is important because I, of all people, am surrounded by clergymen. I am the wife of an ordained minister. I am the sister of an ordained minister. I am the sister-in-law of an ordained minister. My father, ordained, was a minister of music. I am used to ministers. I am not awed by their positions. If anything, I take them for granted. Yet I can detect a self-protective habit of looking over my shoulder in regards to my role as a woman within evangelicalism.

God knows that healing of some kind is needed in my inner person. Something is wrong between me and His church. More wrong than I know.

I spend the next wakeful night in tears. Again. I hear the inner words, "Call Rick. Call Rick." I think of a thousand reasons why I can't impose upon him. The major reason I discover is that I don't know whether or not I can trust him. In fact, I do not trust him. I look carefully at this reality about 2:00 A.M., and I sense that I am very careful about trusting any men in spiritual leadership. If so—if this is true—doesn't that indicate that trust has been broken in some way? Or perhaps it has never been established?

Two days after Deanery Day, still emotionally unsettled, I finally call the church office and make an appointment to see Rick. Not intending to lose control, I weep over the phone. This loss of composure angers me and my voice constricts. Silence while I struggle for calm. I attempt to explain why his male presence, his phone calls, his affirmation have all unhinged me. I know I am botching my explanation. Silence. Extremely sober, in clipped phrases, I finally make an appointment, hang up, and feel wretched about all the loosed emotion. A few minutes later, the phone rings. It is Rick: "I thought I should call you back. Sometimes, when there is a lot of emotion, we don't say things the way we want to say them. I need to know if I responded to you correctly." I am gracefully given a chance to correct my sloppy communication. I am deeply grateful for this extended gentlemanliness.

Asking for help when I am so needy is not easy for me. It is not easy at all. I have little experience in beggary. But

I find myself that week in the little office that juts above and behind the sanctuary on the second floor of St. Mark's old parish chapel. I receive an hour of uninterrupted listening. I receive the ministrations of oil, Scripture, and prayer. *There,* I think to myself. *Now. Now, I'm all right. I'll never have to go back.*

I am not ungrateful for the attention. I realize that this is the first time since childhood where my pastor has not been related to me by blood or marriage. *A good lesson to learn,* I think. I have become the recipient of what all the men in my life have offered to so many others in so many ways—pastoral care.

Emotional pain often lodges in some part of our bodies and then yowls. I am beginning to see that this ice-pick pain is not going to go away.

I press my forehead and nose against the airplane porthole, grateful for this window seat. I let the tears course down my cheeks, glad that the gentleman next to me cannot notice my obvious distress. Upon takeoff he fell asleep. I am flying to California to honor a half-week of speaking commitments.

"Beverage?" inquires the stewardess. I have already discreetly wiped my tears in anticipation of the refreshment cart.

I consider this psychological phenomenon: I am really hurting. The source of all this is still a mystery to me. It has been weeks since Deanery Day, and I am often unaccountably sliced afresh, bleeding tears in private moments. Yes, I must accept the fact that this is no incidental discomfort in my life: it is not a momentary eruption that will soon go away.

"Chicken or pasta?" inquires the hostess, passing the meal trays.

It will be helpful to apply the rule I developed while working in ministry with hurting folk: The past cause is as severe as the present dysfunction. Often, those of us who attempt to be helpers view only the symptomatic distresses of other's lives. This rule of thumb has helped me deal patiently with people whose therapeutic journeys often take years.

I now apply my own insight to myself. To feel this much pain means that there has been a commensurate cause. I am far enough along in my self-examination to suspect that there is probably not just one source to my flowing river of hurt, but a whole complex of streamlets feeding into the major arterial waterway. What amazes me is the question I ask over and over: If I am hurting to this extent, how could I possibly have allowed myself to become so damaged?

The plane lands at John Wayne Airport. I've arranged to rent a car so that I can take a day to visit some relatives in the area. I actually navigate the notorious Southern California freeways—with tears coursing down my cheeks—a highway map spread across the steering wheel. Sunglasses, ubiquitous to what I consider this far country, are the camouflage behind which I hide the tears. I know enough about psychological health to know that it is important to drain this excess emotion. This trip is as good a time as any. All the while I am cross-referencing road maps with the notes of my great aunt's phone directions, I am also rummaging through my flight bag for Kleenexes to wipe my cheeks. I toot the horn of my rental car—a presumptuous Cadillac has too closely challenged my lane. One part of me stands objectively outside and demands: How can you be so emotionally incompetent right now and so intellectually competent at the same time? Another part of me wants to throw back my head and laugh at my ridiculousness as I change lanes, swerve in front of traffic to make the right exits, check my blind spot, all the while analytically examining my excessively harmful emotions.

My adeptness at thinking simultaneously on two levels is demonstrated on this journey. I meet with relatives, honor my speaking commitments—one for a woman's weekend retreat at First Presbyterian Church in Newport Beach, then another midweek engagement at the Crystal Cathedral in Garden Grove—autograph books, manage home crises by phone, and enjoy dinner with old friends. All the while I am still hurting inside. I can actually press against the physical point on my sternum where all this psychological woundedness has centered. Each moment I am alone, I allow the pain to surface and let the great mysterious grief of it all leak and leak and leak.

On the return flight, settled into seat 16F, I again seriously consider what has gone awry. In a way I detest the self-fixation emotional pain forces upon me. It makes me feel too self-focused, too internalized. "Oh, just a glass of water with a slice of lemon, please," I respond to the steward's inquiries. This time I take the pasta salad. I pass on the movie headset.

If I continue hurting like this, I can foresee a developing breast cancer or eventually succumbing to my maternal family's predilection to heart failure. Either of these responses could become my body's way of coping with this localized expression of psychosomatic pain. I decide that the major calling of my life for these days, until I find some emotional resolution, is to be utterly intentional about my own healing process.

I, too, sleep in flight, my head refusing to stay still, bobbing intermittently, sliding aslant from the tilted headrest, the motion waking me. I jam a pillow against the window and wedge the side of my face into this steadying corner. In wakeful moments the analytical side of my mind continues assessing: I must deliberately collaborate with the Great Counselor, the Holy Spirit, and allow Him time to teach me the sources of my own dilemma. I must find outside help when I need help and be obedient to integrating the truths I learn about myself along the way.

The United Airlines plane touches down at O'Hare, this airport where so much of my life is taken up with departures and arrivals. I wait at the baggage claim and consider for the umpteenth time how convenient it would be for me to travel only with carry-ons. But too many suitcases have been toted through too many terminals, and a sharp pain in my right elbow, officially diagnosed as "luggage elbow," inhibits my lugging capacities. It aches if I hook it under my body when I sleep curled on my side. Shooting pain occurs if I pick up heavy items, a gallon milk bottle, for instance, in the wrong way. Physical exercises have been prescribed for me, and my physician has matter-of-factly instructed me not to drag bags around airports.

I stack my baggage onto the rental cart and suddenly think: *If I am taking care of my elbow because it is hurting, shouldn't I naturally take care of my psychological self because of this unrelenting pain I am feeling?* I exit through the sliding doors, dodge taxis and limousines in the first traffic circle, and pull the cart onto the outside perimeter to wait for my pickup ride. For the first time in my life, I decide that I must become my own priority. I watch for the luggage rack of the station wagon to come creeping through the sluggish traffic. For the first time in my life, I give myself permission to ask, "What is healthy for me today? What is healthy for me?"

Right now, I know that the healthiest thing for me to do today is to reach home.

***

I dream that I am walking in a procession with a crowd of people. I have a sense that I am hiding myself in this crush of folk. Suddenly, a great circle of light shines down on a large engraved insignia set into the road, and the group parts around it. The brightness draws me, however, and I decide to take the risk of being seen and noticed. Stepping out of the throng, moving deliberately into the center of the light for the sake of standing in the heavenly radiance, I find myself in the very middle of the emblem.

When I wake I realize that the medallion in the road in my dream is an enlarged version of the motif imprinted on the front of the worship service cover that I glance at Sunday after Sunday. It is an artist's rendering of the symbol for the Gospel of Mark—a stylized lion.

I dreamed that four angels protected the nave of St. Mark's—one behind the altar, two on either side, and one facing the altar at the crossing, the place outside the communion rail where the aisles intersect. The holy forms shimmered softly in the shadows. A low hum, like the rapid thrumming of something in constant motion, sounded steadily like an organist softly pressing a tuning note in a major scale. The impression of this dream did not fade into forgetfulness after waking as most dreams do. Closing my eyes for prayer, the outline of the four angels, like the delineation of neon signs, glows behind my shut eyelids.

After dreaming this unusual dream, I decided to spend an hour in prayer one afternoon in the chapel of St. Mark's. At first I knelt in a back pew. When no one bothered me, I approached, by increments, a pew nearer to the front. Mustering additional bravery, I finally edged into the gap left by the open gate between the communion rails. No heavenly forms appeared, but the quiet seemed to rush at me. I closed my eyes and the outline of the angels glowed behind my lids with unusual clarity. Serenity surrounded me and, most importantly, the ice-pick pain in my breastbone eased.

Thomas Merton has written about city churches that

"are sometimes quiet and peaceful solitudes, caves of silence where a man can seek refuge from the intolerable arrogance of the business world. One can be more alone, sometimes, in church than in a room in one's own house. At home, one can always be routed out and disturbed. . . . But in these quiet churches one remains nameless, undisturbed in the shadows, where only a few chance."

The solace of this peaceful quiet was so satisfactory that I took Merton's recommendation seriously. "Once you have found such a place, be content with it, and do not be disturbed if a good reason takes you out of it. Love it, and return to it as soon as you can, and do not be too quick to change it for another." I began to pray once a week for an hour and a half, in all seasons, kneeling at the gap in the communion rails, in the shadows and quiet, mostly undisturbed, and imagining that I was surrounded—before, behind, beside—by four angels. It became a remarkable prayer journey.

At first, ten minutes seemed like an hour and a half. My mind wandered. I would get sleepy. Was this a worthy prayer effort? In time, the ninety minutes seemed like ten minutes. After months, I learned to cease in my efforts, to become utterly stilled, and to allow prayer to inhabit me. In a way, I became a receptacle that contained the prayer or received the prayer. Often I experienced physical and psychological solace. Remembering Merton again, "When prayer is sanctified by Divine grace, the whole soul is drawn toward God by some incomprehensible power, sweeping the body with it. . . . Not only the soul, not only the heart, but also the flesh becomes filled with spiritual comfort and bliss—joy in the living God."

I always wonder, however, about subjective spiritual experiences. I am wary of my own predilection to pretensions. Most of the time I accept these unusual "showings"—prophetic dreams, the inner word of instruction, a symbolic daytime picture from the subconscious mind—

with gentle skepticism. (I am a historic evangelical after all—one of the most rationalistic of the Christian confessions.) I am well aware of the dangers of undisciplined subjectivity; it can lead to arrogance, on the one hand, or to heresy, on the other.

Consequently, I have imposed personal measurements on my subjective experiences of the supernatural. For me, one of the validities of a subjective spiritual experience can be measured by the amount of surprise that accompanies it. If I have designed the imaginary event, it is of my mind; if it surprises me, it comes as a gift and can be of the divine. It must not offend Scripture, orthodox doctrine, or the traditions of the historical saints who have made the pilgrimage before me. It must lead me into a deeper desire for God or into a clearer understanding of myself before God. Also, I have learned that when the Holy Spirit is attempting to guide me with subjective spiritual experience, He will accommodate my caution by verifying the guidance with additional data. I have learned to pay attention to that verification.

Consequently, because I am so cautious about my own subjective understanding, I have told no one about my dream of the angelic presence in the sanctuary of St. Mark's. It is my own internal knowing to hold secretly.

My afternoon today has been rich with joyful prayer. A warmth suffuses me, and I am flush with the presence of God. I give nothing in terms of practical energies (except a tithe) to this church body. Consequently, it is a joy to spend time praying for the staff and people of St. Mark's.

Without looking up, I feel Kendall sit down on the step beside me. She is a woman with whom I am working as she rehabilitates from a background that has included occultic, satanic rituals. Holy things have been so profaned for her that to walk into a church evokes great terror. Crossing the threshold alone evokes memories of black chants and unholy curses. Because she lives with us and has observed my weekly appointment to pray at St. Mark's, she has suggested that without others but myself around, perhaps she will be able to work through her terrors more easily.

So now she sits on the step beside me, facing back into the nave. She is rough looking, this person who has survived the streets, but when I look at Kendall, I see a womanliness that she has hidden from the world, a soft-heartedness. Even while she wears the inevitable tight jeans, scuffed shoes, and black jacket (leather if possible)—which is most of the time—I find that I am filled with an unaccountable love for her. Following this gift of God's love into the bypaths of the world often leads me to amazing human conjunctions.

There. I am done with prayer. I rock from my knees onto my stair-seat. A slight tremor—an anointing of some kind I think—has touched my body for the last fifteen minutes. I smile at Kendall whose eyes are open, serious. "Are you OK?" I inquire, remembering that what is sweet and powerful and holy for me is often terrifying for her.

"What is it?" she asks, her voice low, raspy, gruff. "Every time I sit beside you I begin to shake. It scares me. Something very powerful is here. I'm sure something very powerful is here."

I attribute this to Kendall's terror. At the same time I too am convinced that something very powerful is here. I throw a smile her way and gather my purse, Bible, and prayer notebook. I slip on my shoes, which I usually remove, not because of prescriptions to holiness, but because the hard edges of the soles often catch uncomfortably under my body when I stay in prayer positions for a time.

We reach the black doors. They must be twelve feet tall and curve at the top in a Gothic arch. The hinges groan rheumatically outward. Kendall stops, turns around, and looks back toward the sanctuary. "Oh," she says. "Did I tell you I saw an angel up there?"

"You mean the little cherubs that decorate the hanging lamp?" I ask casually. I have told no one about my dream.

"No, no. A great big guy in that corner, the left-hand corner. He was just standing there one day when I came in here. 'Bout eight feet tall. Scared me to death. I thought, I'm not gonna mess with this guy. No, sir. You gotta believe me. I thought to myself, 'Not gonna mess around at all.'"

My legs cramp as I kneel before the altar. I shift my position across the step, lean my back against the left-side gatepost, and wedge the toes of my shoes against its opposite companion. It is winter, and the nave of St. Mark's chapel is unheated, so I am wearing my warmest coat, a tacky old fake fur. I often have chills in the air of the old stone building. But I am learning that the soul must be enlarged more and more to accommodate one's God. Consequently, I am diligent at keeping my spiritual promises. This cold afternoon I shift again into a huddle, my forehead pressed to my knees, and suddenly I feel something small and hard beneath my palm. The carpet is patterned, threadbare here and there at this close examination, but I find a shriveled berry, fallen from some floral arrangement and overlooked by the custodian and vacuum cleaner. It had rolled out of sight and into my grasp. This is my prayer berry, I think, and laugh at the childlikeness of this idea.

My prayer journey here in the chapel has convinced me that I am but a novitiate of the soul. All of my work, my work of writing and of spiritual exercise, are but child's play. When I offer my efforts up to my Papa God, I am a chubby-fisted toddler, finding and holding up a smooth pebble, a perfectly colored leaf, a plucked flower.

I have written five books this last year; this accomplishment gives me satisfaction in that I am finally disciplined enough to perform up to speed and nearly on schedule. I return to Papa again, feeling favored, with my scribbled lines on construction paper, with my bunched clay figure cast hard in the sun, with my name printed in big block letters on ruled lines—KAREN.

"Ah!" He exclaims, kissing me. "Look what you've made! Look what you've done all by yourself! How wonderful! How beautiful!"

He, after all, is God and I am but a child with sweaty face and bright eyes, holding forth a bauble, some gewgaw in my fist. This realization of His infinitude and my finiteness is a freedom; it releases me from the agony of vaulting creative ambition. I will still do the work at hand and grow to the best of my ability and strive for the artistic edge. "See! See!" I will cry, but my leaf will always wither and crumble. I cannot cast stars in the universe. I cannot spin protozoa from imagination, nor split the microcosm into infinities.

I hold the shriveled rust-colored berry between my fingers and roll it with my thumb. *This is my prayer berry,* I think. My prayers too are like this. Although I am striving with mighty effort; I know that it will be years before I truly will be of any use to God and to His world through these initiate disciplines of hours of silence, of devotion. My spiritual efforts are shriveled, mostly unbloomed. I plop the berry into the pocket of my coat and pull the collar around me against the bitter chill of the sanctuary.

I finger the hard knob, hidden among the wool fluffs that scatter in the seam of my pocket. I am a learner, a journeywoman into the spiritual life. There is so much I don't know about prayer. There is so much I want to know, but I also want to know by experience. I am hungry for primary spiritual knowing. I am not satisfied with other people's living as a substitute for my own.

A new thought thrusts itself into my mind: *Perhaps this berry is a symbol of something else.* Perhaps I am the shriveled berry, life lambent within me, waiting to flower like the late spring rosebush in the garden, waiting for prayer to water me so I will bloom and God will say (instead of "Ah! Look what you've done!") rather, "Look what you've become. How wonderful! How beautiful!"

What kind of bloom will I become? I wonder. Certainly, a pristine, white, multi-petaled rose, a climber hopefully, everblooming. Instead, into my mind intrudes the image of a wild, exotic jungle flower, red and orange and tinged with purple! The symbol arrives so unexpectedly and is so contradictory to what I had thought it would be that I laugh—aloud—in the sanctuary of St. Mark's. What does this mean, this amazing unconstructed inner picture? Can it be that my spiritual being is not the ordinary, garden-variety spiritual being? Is it—or am I—something unruly, untamed, rare and lush? "Mains," I say to myself, "you have a whacko creative imagination. Don't tell this to anyone. Better yet, just forget it."

The next morning I wake from sleep, go downstairs, and find a new plant on the dining room table. Kendall has been assisting a close friend of mine, a designer, as he sets up booths for trade shows. Late last night, after finishing their tasks, they decided to bring one of the leftover decorations home as a gift for me. It is an exotic orange-and-red bird of paradise, suspiciously like the one that had come popping out of my subconscious mind.

This is a funny incident to me, and simple, but it is also the common gifts that bear straightforward spiritual meanings which we humans choose to ignore so adroitly. Julian of Norwich found profound meaning in something as small as a common hazelnut resting in the palm of her hand:

> And in this he showed me something small, no
> bigger than a hazelnut, lying in the palm of my hand,

as round as a ball. I looked at it with the eye of my understanding and thought: What can this be? I was amazed that it could last, for I thought that because of its littleness it would suddenly have fallen into nothing. And I was answered in my understanding: It lasts and always will, because God loves it, and thus everything has being through the love of God.

A berry is in my coat pocket, and it reminds me of a truth that I believe God is attempting to convey to me. He has made the true me more exotic than I know. I can only praise Him fully by finding and living in my true self. John Keats has written, "A man's life of any worth is a continual Allegory, and very few eyes can see the Mystery of his life." I am learning to plumb the mystery of my own being—rather, my Creator is insisting that I do so.

I look at the lush bird of paradise, orange and red-lipped, exotically blue-purple at its deepest center, blooming out of context on the oak table of my Chicago suburban home and I think, *How surprising!*

The tables for the vestry meeting are joined together to create a spacious rectangle. The vestry is the governing board of an Episcopal church, and after much prayer I have agreed to serve a three-year term. I walk through the glass-paned doors this cold February evening into the narthex of the new building that has only recently been finished. Unaccountably, I feel as though the double doors have slammed shut behind me. A low-level anxiety stirs; church governing boards have been either the source of much frustration or the source of excruciating pain in my checkered pastor's wife's past. Moreover, I, more than most lay people, am not ignorant of the amount of volunteer time I am committing myself to if I am going to serve this congregation well. I am nervous about fitting all this into an already overcrowded existence.

The improvised board table is surrounded by men (most of whom I really do not know), two other vestry women, and the rector, who presides as president of this council. Despite the presence of the two women and the fact that my rector's wife has recently been ordained into the deaconate (and actually wears a clerical collar), functioning officially and visibly in worship services on Sundays, this does not feel like friendly territory. I note my feeling that I am an alien in a foreign land and consciously observe quiet inward maneuverings to protect myself.

By the time the meeting is over, particularly after the new vestry appointments have been announced, I feel that I have entered a prison. The steel doors have slammed behind me, and an incarceration for a sentence of three years' duration is ahead. It is fitting, I think, that in Episcopalianese, the senior lay official of the vestry is titled "the warden."

What have I let myself in for? Why in the world did I say that I would serve?

I leave my first vestry meeting in a state of suppressed but frank rage. Several commission chair positions had been vacated by the retiring vestry class. Two were potentially interesting, areas where I felt I could make significant contributions. One was the Hospitality Commission. Since my book *Open Heart Open Home* deals with a philosophy of scriptural hospitality and has sold hundreds of thousands of copies, resulting in my conducting seminars and workshops on the topic across the country, this seemed like a natural appointment. There was another vestry member, however, already positioned and excellently equipped to take this chair position.

The vacant commission that most attracted me was the one called Spiritual Life. This was kind of a collection center for the odds and ends of church affairs. The former commissioner had been puzzled as to how to frame it since its mandate was vague. Due to my experience as a pastor's wife in inner-city church planting, however, I had quickly and with little mental energy already conceived definite ideas as to how this commission could be profitably administrated to function in a growing church like St. Mark's. In fact, because my travel schedule was still heavy, it was probably the only commission I could comfortably administrate without major attendance conflicts. In short, because of its very ill-defined mandate, I could naturally design the commission's function around my major areas of interest—spiritual life, utilizing the gifts of lay people, developing small groups, worship and prayer. I could easily schedule the Spiritual Life responsibilities around my complicated travel, broadcasting, and writing schedules.

Anticipating a misappointment, I had already officially discussed this over breakfast one Saturday morning with the senior warden. The one vacant commission I did not feel appropriately suited to lead was the Youth Commission. I thought that I had strongly stated my preferences and hesitations.

Tonight, however, I have been assigned the Youth Commission. In my estimation, it is a disastrous match. I leave for home infuriated, call the warden, and in no uncertain terms let him know exactly what I think of this assignment. It is not one of my better moments.

As far as I can tell from our conversation, little thought has been given to gifts or experience. People have been assigned to spots simply to fill positions. This is a philosophy of church life I abhor; David and I have worked all our professional lives to build the programs of the church around the gifts of the people, not to cram the gifts of the people into the existing programs of the church. After hanging up the phone, I lie in bed angry at the system, infuriated with myself for getting into such a predicament, and mad at my rector (who certainly must have had some input in the commission chair assignments). How can I possibly tolerate three years working in an area that does not motivate me? Shouldn't I just resign now and save us all further grief? But how awkward and incongruous to say a prayerful yes and then to retract one's commitment. What is God doing in this? A yawning chasm of suffering opens in me. Incensed rage gives way to anger that vents itself in tears.

Generally, in our marriage, David lets me fight my own battles. But after a day of my wallowing (again) in inordinately painful emotion, my husband suggests that we make an appointment with Rick Lobs and that we both go and talk things out. The whole vestry incident has obviously shoved me back into some old woundedness. The last thing our family needs, with its intense unending, deadline patterns, is the added stress of three years of mom and wife coping with perpetual conflict. So we sit in the rector's office, with the senior warden of the vestry also present, and talk things through. I leave feeling calmed, my rector is distressed, and now David is angry. We are heard, yet nothing is altered. I am even told (nicely) that I could still resign from the vestry appointment with grace.

I go home, spend a week considering myself, and then write a memo to my rector.

Dear Rick:
     I have finally localized the source of my rage. Let me walk through it quickly.
     When David and I started to work with blacks at Circle Church, we joyfully invited a black family to our home for Sunday dinner. The husband, Abraham, was a working man from the Cabrini Green housing projects, and we wanted badly to honor him by inviting him into our lives for a meal. We lived in the Old Town Triangle where parking was at a premium. Consequently, we grabbed any place our Volkswagen Bug could fit. On this Sunday it happened to be near the

back entrance. In order to enter through the front door, we would have to walk around the block. So, as was customary for us, we took our guests up the back stairs. In our innocence and with the greatest of good intentions, we couldn't have done anything worse. Abraham was used to being called "boy" and to being sent to the back door. To his credit he stuck with us, and it was only three months later that we discovered our terrible error.

This is what, during those years of the 60s and 70s, blacks taught us to call "nigger" issues: areas of painful vulnerability that well-intentioned whites innocently trigger because of inexperience or ignorance or because of systemic or institutionalized racism.

The churches of my background refused to use women in any policy-making or governing roles within the church. Women were relegated to the church kitchen, to the training of the children, to the missionary society, and to women's groups (obviously they carried 80 percent of the function of the church, but they were excluded from the power structure).

David and I basically created Circle Church together. Our gifts are utterly complementary. But when the governing organizations were formed, enough old-line thinking lobbied for a male-only board. David fought this tooth and nail, and finally four women were invited to serve in a temporary way as we all took time to determine from Scripture whether or not women could function as elders. In essence, that was a two-year process in which the elders met weekly and which finally became a time in which I weekly had to defend my very nature as a woman, how I felt women were gifted to function, what God had called them to be, and how they were of equal value to men. That was hard on me, but it focused my mind and exposed me to misogyny and to what many women have experienced in more profound and damaging ways in their lives as a regular course of fare.

What I now realize (as of this week) was most damaging to me was the unstated attitude of negation. That is, I could do the work of the church (co-initiate its very formation; partake in the discussions regarding its philosophical undergirdings; design curricula for a racially integrated Sunday school; invite people into my home for breakfast, lunch, and dinner; even write a best-selling book on hospitality; counsel/mentor/disciple; integrate the arts into the life of the church; supervise and plan weddings; etc. ad infinitum), but in these men's minds, I could not use my chief gifts (speaking/teaching; oversight/shepherding; decision making) in the authority structure of the church. This in its own way is an nigger issue.

In addition, my spirituality (which was burgeoning during these years) was extremely suspect to these men. If I laid on hands for healing, I was charismatic. If I testified to the existential drama of God in my every day, I was too experiential. According to Scripture, a woman didn't do this/she didn't do that, and in my inner heart, I knew I could do all of those things. They were gifts God had given me and was calling me to use. In other words, God was calling me to dramatic growth, and these men were holding me to a kind of subtle spiritual stasis. This tension is extremely schizophrenic, and it causes evil damage in the soft soul.

At any rate, we four women finally became approved elders at Circle Church—perhaps the first, if not the only ones in the whole denomination. I never really worked through the pain of this issue. David and I resigned and went through the convulsions of dislocating, becoming public religious leaders, raising children, salvaging and revitalizing an old-line broadcast. My father was slowly dying. There were many more pressing things to attend to than some bruised feminism.

I found, however, that I was now one of ten to twenty significant women who began opening up much of evangelicalism to the gifts of women. We have all spoken on platforms no woman had previously spoken on. We are serving on boards that have been all male. For several years I was one of the rare women's voices broadcasting regularly on conservative national radio. We used a term in conversation last week—"Someone draws the lightning." So this handful of women got the dump—how else can I say it? One woman recently had a row of gentlemen walk out on her to make some sort of point—rudeness perhaps. We have taken all this, I think, with surprising grace, have swallowed bitter pills and are now reaping the fruit of painful labor—respect, a changing atmosphere, more and more openings for that younger group of women beginning to emerge, and increasing opportunities coming our way. Most of all, I believe that Christ's Spirit is represented more completely when women's voices are welcomed to function in all capacities within His body.

Obviously, the commission appointment felt like a nigger issue to me: "Now that we've got your commitment, you gotta do what we tell you, girl. Back to the kitchen and the kids." Or at least it opened up for me the great unresolved exclusionary issue in my life related to my being a woman. The vestry incident happened to be too close to the old pain. In addition, I do not have enough trust toward the men on the vestry to maintain what in psychological circles is known as object constancy. I could not say to myself, "I know the personalities involved enough to know they would not deliberately pull a sexist bushwhack on me. I know Rick and can trust him." I felt as though you, Rick, in particular, had observed my spiritual abilities over the last few years, had found them lacking, and then plugged me into the very best place just to keep me out of the way. It was Karen Mains and the white male club again, and I have paid so many dues in so many ways, I just didn't have it in me to do it again.

Nor was I aware of the deep shame I have absorbed regarding my being as a woman. There is a profound and subtle self-loathing in me I have sucked from evangelicalism, from the nonverbal signals (no women on the platform, no women staff, no women on the decision-making councils) which nevertheless proclaim: No Women Allowed. I understand that the discussions during the years of Circle Church when we were hotly debating women's roles were demeaning in that I was forced to debate my own value before God, to prove to a judging committee that our gifts and abilities as women were acceptable. Being helplessly thrust into an old pattern during my first vestry meeting evoked this shameful embarrassment I feel at being female. It has come boldly forth in real pain.

OK. Now, I'm in touch with my issue. Give me a week and I will look rationally at this appointment. Everything still feels raw, but obviously it's time for me to start working on this. No better place to work it out than in the home territory.

Well, the amazing emotion of all this has settled, but I am still surprised with the intensity of my feelings. In prayer (Is it healthy for me to stay / I do not want to debate or cope again with "the woman thing" / Have you really ordained that I am to serve here / My entire life is given to your Kingdom work / Do I need to do more?), I hear clearly that I am supposed to serve on the vestry. Stop hiding and step into the light shining on the insignia that represents St. Mark's. In prayer I also feel clearly that I am supposed to function in Spiritual Life, not in youth. Finally, thrust into a tension I am incapable of resolving, I throw up my hands. A vestry retreat is scheduled for this weekend, but I have had a previous speaking engagement on my calendar for several years and am unable to attend. "God," I pray, "You take care of this mess, please."

When I return home on Sunday, I receive a phone call from the senior warden. Another vestry member in my class (who had been assigned Spiritual Life) was as uncomfortable with his appointment as I had been with mine. He felt his gifts were better placed in the Finance Committee. Consequently, he was moved to finance, I was moved to Spiritual Life, and poor orphaned Youth was sort of line-itemed under my already vague job description.

Thus the complications are neatly resolved. Someone can be trusted, this One who is always trustworthy. I sleep untroubled. I dream that I am following a path in a wood filtered with sunlight on a lovely summer morning. The path comes to a glen in the middle of which is a lodge. A large group of people step out to greet me as though they had been awaiting my arrival. One of them, a man who attends St. Mark's and whom I knew years ago in high school, holds up a bouquet of woodland flowers tied with ribbons for me. I am delighted with this gift, deeply pleased by his thoughtfulness. Kindly, he places one arm around my waist and ushers me into the crowd, and they welcome me warmly.

My journeys through the world's refugee camps have been a travelogue in feedings. Refugees stand in line for bread. In Thailand, I poured frothy and warm milk into hundreds of faded pale pink, green, and white plastic glasses for Cambodian children. Tin cans were held up for dried beans in drought-stricken Kenya. In tin-roofed huts, in thatched open shelters, in cement-block hovels—all over the globe—great kettles of rice steamed for hungry stomachs.

I also go to the communion rail for bread. I am a psychological refugee, exiled here in this safe place, St. Mark's. I take communion twice a week, once at Sunday worship and again early on Wednesday mornings at a small healing service. If I could, I would receive it every day. For me, partaking of the Lord's Supper is more than a solemn act; it frequently becomes a moment of unaccountable spiritual reality. It is like the wardrobe through which I step into the land of Narnia.

Since early adulthood, since serving in the pastorate of Circle Evangelical Free Church in Chicago, I have known the near presence of Christ with spiritual clarity—especially during communion. A touch presses between my shoulder blades (when no one is near); my hand shakes slightly when I guide the common cup to my lips; my body trembles quietly. I am always glad to hurry back to my pew where I can kneel, bow, hide, and receive the sacrament into my deepest being. The wine burns for moments in my throat. Yet these physical sensibilities are only signs. Most importantly, I am acutely impressed with the closeness of Christ, my "most courteous and dear-worthy Lord."

I found safety in the nave of St. Mark's parish chapel in Geneva, Illinois, without knowing I was even seeking sanctuary. I attribute this feeling of safety to the frequency of communion. To be able to participate weekly is to receive a balm that heals the wounds of my psyche, offers solace for emotional distress, strengthens my very ligaments and bones, and comforts me spiritually. But then I began to realize, as I had suspected earlier in my life, that I am also susceptible to sacramentality. I am one of those spiritual types who experiences God mediated through all of life: in materiality, in the natural, created order, in everyday events, in ordinary time. Every moment is potentially pregnant with the holy. "The Lord is in this place," is my frequent heart's cry.

For the ten years of my life preceding my attendance at St. Mark's, Christ had been my ultimate relationship. A teaching speech that I deliver frequently concentrates upon the scriptural metaphor that Christ is the bread of life. "To whom do you go to first when you are in crisis?" I ask my audiences. "Who is it who will never abandon you when all others forsake you? Upon whom do you daily feed?"

"Christ is the ultimate relationship," I proclaim. This has been utterly true for me. I have been captured by the present-tense Jesus. His historicity was not nearly so pregnant for me as was His immanency. For a decade of my life, He had essentially taken from me (in one way or another) mother and father and friend and husband—all other relationships. He had insisted that He be the beginning and ending of my being as well as all of my in-betweens.

But this Wednesday morning I suddenly realize that I cannot receive the bread unless I take it from a man's hand. A *man's* hand. This spiritual blessing does not float to me by some ethereal disembodied means. In this church, a man's voice speaks the startling words which, proceeding down the rail in serving, become a voiced round: The body of Christ . . . The body of Christ . . . The body . . . of the body . . . of Christ. A man's voice speaks this haunting phrase.

I do not trust that man (nor, it seems, any man in spiritual leadership). I do not trust the complications of cross-gender sexuality. I cannot bear any more vulnerability, nor do I want to cope with theologized disapproval attached to my femaleness. I am choosing not to risk being devalued any more by men in spiritual leadership. Moreover, I know some of this man's particular frailties; I know that he is not perfect.

So I cannot receive the bread, the body of Christ, unless I take it from the body of another—from the very hand of the man who brings me blessing. The oil pressed in the form of a cross on my forehead is pressed there by the flesh of another. I can feel the very bones in the hands of the man who presses them lightly to my head as I kneel in prayer. Human warmth is part of the sacramental touch that so unaccountably brings healing to my displacement.

On Wednesday mornings I sit in the choir loft, a short dozen or so people scarcely filling the five half-pews. I am stunned with reality. This is the body of Christ; these paltry few people in this small byway. I do not receive the bread or the wine without them being prepared for me by others—

the women of the altar guild—or offered to me by another—this Episcopalian priest. The body of Christ brings to me the body of Christ.

In this very sanctuary of St. Mark's, in this safe place, my subconscious mind once tossed to the notice of my conscious self a graphic picture of the reality of my neediness. I was a starving, fragile refugee. I was surprised. I am still a starving, needy refugee, but I am surprised no more.

I am seeing myself these days, coming to know my own refugeeness. Composed outwardly, I am nevertheless privately pleading for bread, my cup lifted empty. No beggars in the world are any more so than me. I exist in great psychological and emotional poverty. In a very real sense, I too am an unaccompanied minor.

This morning I leave the little choir loft and walk to the communion rail. I kneel, most grateful for safe havens, for sanctuaries to which displaced persons can flee, where in quiet they can listen for the rumble of the bread trucks and hold out their hands. I am grateful for all the world's unharrassed hideaways where the thirsty can wait their turn in line for a dole from the water barrels.

Like refugees throughout time, I too hold up my palms, begging and imploring for food. I hear the rhythmical pronouncement down the line: The body of Christ . . . The body of Christ . . . The bread of heaven . . . The bread of heaven. A man's voice speaks the words. I hear his low tones approaching. I feel now the swish of the robes as he pauses before me. Quickly, I glance up into his eyes. He nods slightly. I bow my head again and lift my crossed palms. I take the body of Christ from the body of Christ. I receive the bread from the hand of a man.

I stand before the window in my room in the Hilton and look out across the night city, to Grant Park, to lampposts doing sentry duty above park benches, to Lake Michigan with a few bright lights shimmering upon it. "Why do some words go straight to the heart?" I wonder. They are like a spoonful of honey, sharp with sweetness on the tongue, after a diet of gruel. A word fitly spoken was given to me tonight. With one sentence, I have been granted a temporary working visa.

I am waiting for my roommate, Jeanette Yep, and I may soon go to bed before she arrives. Jeanette is an InterVarsity staff worker, an area director in northern Illinois. I'm waiting for Jeanette because I want to chew over today's events. She and I were part of a team of InterVarsity staff and trustees who have planned and moderated a hands-on presentation of the issues of multi-ethnicity currently challenging campus ministries. The board was divided into three teams and then transported onto various campuses in the Chicago area to dialogue with students: to Northeastern on the northwest side of the city where there is an InterVarsity chapter with a strong Hispanic outreach; to Northwestern in Evanston, a Big Ten school where the chapter has attracted many Asians; and to Chicago State, an inner-city, primarily black, commuter campus.

Being a part of the multi-ethnic teaching team, working with bright and good minds, has invigorated me. I also believe strongly in the importance of the discussion. In the twenty-first century, for the first time, racial and ethnic groups will outnumber whites in the United States. This browning of America will alter everything in society, from politics and education to industry, to values and purchasing patterns, to religion and culture. In the days ahead, we will be testing the meaning of the Latin slogan engraved on U.S. coins: *e pluribus unum* ("one formed from many"). By the year 2000, 50 percent of our college campuses will be multi-ethnic. Comprehending the implications of multi-ethnicity, of coming to difficult terms with its demands, is a major factor in determining the success or failure of Christian

108

groups seeking to engage university cultures or a changing American society with Christ.

Jeanette is late, so I crawl beneath my covers. Tonight I feel forcibly expatriated from the city-state of racial issues and tensions; as though I had been weighed and found wanting in the urban balances; as though I had been exiled to the homogeneous backwaters of suburbia and evangelical theology as interpreted through a WASP ideology. Circle Church, where we pastored, underwent intense racial conflict and eventually split along black and white lines. But these IV trustee discussions have moved me—there are faint stirrings.

The word fitly spoken came tonight after our team's reading of a script tracing InterVarsity's evolving fifty-year commitment to multi-ethnicity. This participatory forum on multi-ethnicity was challenging in its demands and implications; it was hardly the traditional study of the quarterly corporate financial statement. I anticipate some negative reaction. Comments from staff and the executive council, however, indicated overwhelming enthusiasm: "Finally, the IV board is doing what we need a board to do!"

I am often the recipient of compliments, and I am canny enough to know that too much praise is like too much candy. But some words need to reach the soul. They are God's words spoken through another. Sheldon Nix, the young African-American heading up the difficult Black Campus Ministries division (and, as always, with inadequate funding), stood quietly beside me and said, "I have never seen you in action, but I want to tell you that I am impressed."

Yes, I've been standing in the suburbs, a child of the sixties, looking back nostalgically to the demonstrations, the placards, the community feeling of accomplishing something together of significance. For ten years at Circle Church, everyone, black and brown, yellow and white, worked hard toward establishing what we then called an open church—a worshiping communion where people of all races could be safe and feel valued. I had accepted the fiat of denaturalization. But recently, as recently as this weekend, I discovered that I was lonely for the old places, for the old arguments and combats, for the literacy of pain and struggle surrounding this crucial social issue.

I've come near to the city limits again, remembered the smell of grit on hot summer sidewalks, heard the eager blare and hurry of the streets, the lyricism of urban jive. A familiar demanding energy has quickened my emotions. Today I have been walking shoulder to shoulder again with people who know their way through back alleys, in and out of public housing cul-de-sacs, and through the neighborhoods where all the street signs have been vandalized. I read again the lingo of graffiti.

Tonight I know that I can still speak the language and not nearly as haltingly as I feared. I remember the cultural customs. The street idioms are all fresh, stored whole in my mind. An African-American male, checking out my city-state passport, has just stamped it: AP-PROVED. It is only a working visa for temporary employment. But for now, for tonight, for one in exile too long, it is enough.

"I'm looking for a spiritual director," I explain to the voice at the other end of the phone line.

"I'm sorry," the receptionist replies. "Everyone here at the Cenacle is full—oh, wait. We do have one woman available. But she will only be here for four months."

Perfect, I think to myself. If this is an unsuitable arrangement, then I will have a natural means of termination.

Eugene Peterson, the writer and Presbyterian minister, looked directly at me across a table this last February at a meeting of fellow writers and commanded, "Karen. Get a spiritual director." I laughed and told him that it wasn't quite the voice of God. But almost.

Almost enough, that here I am in early April making this phone appointment. I have finally chided myself into action: "Oh, Karen. You're making too much of this. All you really need is someone who loves to talk about prayer."

A week after the phone contact, I find myself parking the car in the Cenacle lot in Warrenville, ten minutes away from home. I walk across the little bridge that spans the lagoon. Cenacle is a Catholic retreat center that specializes in providing opportunities for those seeking silence, a place for small-group retreats, and seminars for spiritual renewal. On several occasions I have reserved a small room in order to spend two or three days in solitude and prayer here, but I have never requested the available spiritual guidance.

Sister Lois Dideon meets me and leads me to a small room. I learn that she is a nun who has been the director of training novices for the whole order. At the end of July her plan is to assume the responsibilities of superior for the Cenacle retreat center in Houston. One of her specialties is spiritual direction, and she actually trains others to be spiritual directors. Spiritual directors are a part of the Catholic tradition. In the simplest of terms, they are soul friends, accomplished in the travails of soul-knowing, who stand beside others in their spiritual pilgrimages and assist them in achieving proficiency in the practice of gazing Godward. Some Catholic seminaries offer advanced degrees in spiritual direction.

She and I settle into chairs. The windows in the room face eastward, and I look out onto a bright green lawn. Lois is about my age, her short hair graying slightly. She exudes an air of inescapable, but quiet authority. "Why have you come?" she questions me. "Why do you seek spiritual direction?"

A volume of answers waits for me to open. I have a hundred reasons, any of which would be sufficient. "I need

111

someone of spiritual skill to walk along beside me as I journey deeply into prayer. I need to learn to be a contemplative in the middle of my activist life!"

She laughs, "Well, it's true that all contemplatives are not found in the cloisters. How do you define contemplative prayer?"

I think for a moment. "I define contemplative prayer as a life of prayer out of which all activity springs, rather than a life of activity which is so full we are forced to pray."

"That's a good definition," she replies. "I think I might define contemplation another way. I would define it as a life centered in Christ."

At this moment I know we are on sure footing with one another, I the daughter of evangelicalism and she, a Catholic nun, trainer of novices, caretaker of souls. Of course, true contemplative prayer is a prayer life in which the focus is Christ and more of Christ—"I saw Him and sought Him: I had Him and I wanted Him."

"How do you experience God?" she asks of me.

"One way is through unaccountable waves of love," I reply. Since I experience God in all of life, her question is hard for me to answer. It's hard to give a nugget response when, in fact, spiritual gold richly veins my very being and daily living.

"Oh, I see. Sensible consolations."

"Sensible what?"

"Sensible consolations. Experiencing something of God through the measurement of our senses."

It is Catholic terminology, and I am delighted with its archaic freshness. But I have a feeling Sister Dideon does not quite approve of experiencing God only through "sensible consolations."

We talk for an hour and a half and make an appointment to meet again. It is late afternoon, and I am rushing off to prepare dinner and then meet my sister-in-law. We have plans to attend a lecture at Wheaton College by Madeleine L'Engle.

I walk out of the little meeting room, up the stairs, through the chapel where before I have prayed alone. My feet pound on the plank bridge; it echoes hollowly beneath me. I am buoyant. I stop for a few seconds to watch the afternoon sunlight filter through the trees, to catch a translucent beam resting on the rail in the palm of my hand. I observe the ducks waddling about on shore; they are fatly content with their own state of grubbing, wallowing, and wading.

Why am I now so lighthearted? I wonder and know the answer: This is the first time someone has listened to me talk about what is dearest in all the world to me—my own soulish journeying. For a whole hour and a half! It is one of the first times in my life when I have not had to worry about the spiritual state of the one beside me, or be concerned about talking too much about myself. It is one of the rare moments in my life when I have not been worried about boring a less spiritually inclined listener or confusing them with my own subjective realities.

I have a guide—if only for a few months. For these brief weeks, I am no longer an unaccompanied minor.

I wake with a sense of profound well-being. Again, a young man has come to me in my dreams. After dreaming about him, I am always left with a sense of wellness.

The first time he appeared to me was during a weeklong spiritual retreat I took alone in California. Friends had arranged a rental cottage on the grounds of Mount Herman, a Christian conference center. My plans were to take two days for prayer and silence, then spend the rest of the time reading and blocking out chapters for my children's book, *Tales of the Kingdom*. Instead, during the first night, then night after night, the young man came into my dreams. My two days of silence stretched into four, then five, and finally six, in which I fasted and rested continually in profound contemplative prayer. Julian of Norwich once so aptly described this kind of moment. "But when our courteous Lord of his special grace shows himself to our soul, we have what we desire, and then for that time we do not see what we should pray for, but all our intention and all our powers are wholly directed to contemplating him. And as I see it, this is an exalted and imperceptible prayer; for the whole reason why we pray is to be united into the vision and contemplation of him to whom we pray, wonderfully rejoicing with reverent fear, and with so much sweetness and delight in him that we cannot pray at all except as he moves us at the time."

He was tall, the young man, well formed and trim, somewhere in his early thirties. In the first dream, I was beginning a journey, and he assisted me into the car. The driver's door slammed closed, and the young man leaned outside, stiff-armed against the ledge of the rolled-down window. His fine, dark hair fell in a thick lock across his forehead. He tossed it back, bent closer, his blue-gray eyes looking earnestly into mine. "You are everything I have ever wanted spiritually," he said before I started to drive away. "You are everything I have ever wanted spiritually."

In this fashion, tenderly always, but without any sexual connotations, without any physical improprieties, he has come to me in my dreams over these last years. Most of the time, he never speaks but only gazes at me. I read honor in his glance. I am surprised. I read regard and admiration. I pause during sleep and wonder at it. Always I wake from these nighttime visitations with a deeply rooted sense of well-being. Sometimes it feels as though a single satisfactory tone has been struck on the great gong of my soul, which hums although I wake and am dressing and even though my day is filling with clamor and chaos. All I need to remember is the young man's eyes and a peace enfolds me softly.

114

He has come so frequently, six or eight times a year for the last four or five years, and the dreams have such a positively profound effect upon me that I consult with Leanne Payne, the director of Pastoral Care Ministries and my unofficial spiritual mentor.

"Well," she says, "your male-self is certainly wooing you."

My male-self?

I consider her words, the words of a spiritual counselor wise in these subjective matters. I think about them slowly, over and over. There is no need to rush into the meaning of this. Time will take its own time telling. One day, certainly, I will understand who the young man is who keeps appearing in my dreams and who looks at me with such affectionate regard.

But who (or what) is my male-self? What does he want of me? Why is he wooing me? For what? Why does he gaze at me so tenderly? Why is there such a profound effect of wellness after I look into his eyes?

"Did you ask his name?" my spiritual director inquires. We have been talking about the young man who comes to me in my dreams. Sister Dideon has been trained as a psychotherapist, and out of this expertise she has affirmed that this indeed is my male-self, the animus that I need to complement my female being, the anima. This psychological concept of the male-within-the-female and the female-within-the-male was developed by Carl Jung, but it has always seemed exceptionally scriptural to me. "When God created man, he made him in the likeness of God. Male and female he created them, and he blessed them and named them Man when they were created" (Gen. 5:1–2).

We are again in a quiet room. No phones interrupt. No teens intrude, needing information as to the whereabouts

115

of misplaced items. No one can find me here. My spiritual director sits quietly in her chair. She is in street clothes, wearing sturdy flat shoes. She has placed a missal of some sort on the table beside her. "Some women," she muses, "fall in love with their own animus." I wonder if all these women see a young man as attractive as the one who appears in my dreams. If so, although I am not tempted to this extreme, I can nevertheless understand their affection.

My spiritual director and I have talked significantly in our few sessions together about maleness, about how it becomes disassociated in our female selves and how easy it is, when this happens, for some women to become attached to a man who symbolizes their own lost male characteristics. In a sense, they see in him the male half of their uncompleted female selves. Although this might be categorized as "falling in love," they have fallen in love with their own projected, unrecognized selves.

"All love is of God," she explains. "Love for any human or from any human is always a gift from God. It is what we do with it, how we use it, or misuse it, which determines whether it is holy or sinful. But we would never know love of any kind if we did not receive it from its first source, God."

Much of the spiritual guidance this woman has given has verified my solo learning. I have chosen, at what seemed to be the incessant prodding of the Holy Spirit, to develop friendships with certain men. I refused to close my heart to God's love for them, but at the same time I have vowed that nothing sexual would occur between us; certainly, there would be no flirtatiousness in my demeanor. The consequences have been several rewarding and what I consider "safe" cross-gender friendships. How good it is to hear from some other person that I have not been in error. After an intense search of Scripture, (I have memorized that treatise on love: 1, 2, and 3 John), I have come to the conclusion that in God's eyes it is as unholy to withhold love from any human (including all the men in my life—my husband, my co-workers, my professional colleagues) as it is to wrongfully sexualize affections outside of marriage.

I describe to her what I analyze to be the source of much of my misplaced self, symbolized by this young man who keeps wooing me in my dreams. I talk about the negative split between the feminine and the masculine in evangelicalism which, because it has been theologized, is therefore exceedingly difficult to confront. I talk about what I have detected as a fear of the feminine in my own ecclesiastical circles; of the terror of women functioning within the authority structures. I talk about what I consider a harmful division between male and female camps illustrated by well-meaning, but to me distressing, recommendations that men stay with men (teach one another, counsel one another, socialize with one another) and women stay with women. "Doesn't this division create the very hunger for the opposite sex that it is attempting to correct?" I ask. "Doesn't Christ set another model, a better model? That of a new family of mothers and sisters and brothers—all who hear His Word and do His will? Isn't this new order supposed to relate to one another in all charity and with purity?"

She smiles at me. Her role is to keep me thinking for myself, not to teach me her answers. I am gobbling up the time. There is so much to talk about and I only have a few weeks left.

"You know," she says. "When the cloisters were opened after Vatican II under Pope John, I was a young nun. At that time, we were told that within the space of our lifetime we would fall in love, oh, perhaps as many as seven times.

"Well, I was appalled. Here I was, a young woman who had taken orders and given myself to Christ. I then had a limited vision of how God's love is poured out in His community, the body of His Son.

"At the same time, we were given very clear instructions as to how we were to proceed if and when this should

117

happen in the mix between celibate men and women in these communities. We were to address this with the other party openly—to bring what was hidden to the light so it would be divested of its subterranean power. And we were both to have a spiritually wise confidant outside of the cross-gender friendship to whom we were to go for counsel and accountability."

This feels so much healthier to me than the system in which I find myself. I heard a religious broadcast recently in which two men, Christian leaders, were discussing the dangers of cross-gender relationships. Their conclusion was to have little or nothing to do with the opposite sex other than their own wives and to watch out for those women who were basically temptresses. Unfortunately, this told much more about the men than it did about the women who were so troublesome to them. It said that they had not reached a level where they could relate in all purity to the opposite sex (and particularly to those whose own sexuality was broken). Frankly, I would have respected their comments much more if they had been self-aware enough to admit this. But alas, they weren't.

"Yes," I reply to her original question. "I did ask the young man his name."

"What did he answer?"

"His name is Eddie Bishop."

We both laugh. It is a rather presumptuous name.

"How interesting. Bishop—a spiritual authority in the church. And then such a contrast, the diminutive given name, so familiar—Eddie."

"That's not all." I say. "I asked the young man about his first name: 'I suppose Eddie is short for Edward.' He replied, 'Oh, no. It's the shortened form for Theodore.'"

Theo—of God. Bishop—a spiritual authority in the church. From what have I been restraining myself? What kind of internal, awkward split has this unrecognized refusal to integrate my whole self imposed upon me?

118

Jung (in what I consider his own conflicted way) emphasized that for spiritual and psychological health a person must have a harmonious and friendly relationship with his or her unconscious. I suppose this has been the greatest work of my middle years. Through the insistent initiation of the Holy Spirit, I am being forcefully guided to make rapprochement with my inner, deepest center. Again, Julian of Norwich, that great mentor from the past, so aptly expresses this spiritual truth, "We can never attain to the full knowledge of God until we have first known our own soul thoroughly. Until our soul reaches its full development we can never be completely holy."

The young man appeared to me in a dream again last night. We were in a large crowd of people in a meeting hall. I noticed him standing at the edge of the group. His eyes sought mine. They looked at me with longing, with a question in his expression. He wants something of me, I thought in the dream. I smiled and he smiled back in return. Tall and handsome, he was about thirty-three years of age.

"I knew you at Circle Church, didn't I?" I asked of him, surprised recognition in my voice.

"Yes," he replied. "We knew each other then."

The meeting we were attending continued, but I was aware of him without looking in his direction, the way we are conscious of someone in a room who is obviously watching us.

Suddenly, he ran over to me, knelt beside me, put his arms around me, clung desperately, pressed his curly head to my breast and wept. He wept and wept. *How embarrassing,* I thought. In front of all these people.

Then in the dream, I reconsidered. No. This is a soul in deep pain. I don't care what people think.

119

I embraced him tightly in my arms. My body shook with the effect of his sobs.

On Sunday, I slipped into the new nave, surprised by how many people are already gathered because of this being Easter morning. I have offered to arrange for certain vestry members to lay on hands and pray for St. Mark's clergy between services. All three clergy agreed to meet early in the new nave before the second service. Early enough, I figured, so that there wouldn't be many parishioners in the pews, and the prayer gifts would be conducted semi-privately—an important condition for me. But now, with so many already in the pews, I nervously think that this will hardly be a private act of ministry.

The clergy in turn, the curate, our associate priest, and the deacon, Donna Lobs, kneel at the rail. By the time our rector, Rick Lobs, kneels, I am unconscionably distressed. I'm wearing a pink tailored suit and it feels neon-lit.

Long ago, I sought the Holy Spirit and He found me. One of the effects of that dramatic spiritual encounter was that I was left with a mark of power rushing through my hands at solemn holy moments, particularly when I lay on hands in prayer. This, I was informed by those more in the know than myself, was often a sign of the charism of healing. I have employed it carefully in private or small gatherings, or carefully hidden this ability within a group of people laying on hands. Frankly, I have always had a horror of making a spectacle of myself. I have never desired to be a spiritual lightning rod. Consequently, I am exceedingly uncomfortable this morning, intensely self-conscious in this act of charity (which I have boldly suggested), even though I am surrounded by other vestry members.

Rick kneels at the rail last. I lay a hand on his back and the other against his sternum. Quietly, in a way that no one

120

can possibly see, he moves the front hand aside. I fight for stability through the entire morning liturgy. By the time the Easter service is over and we have sung the last glorious hymn, everyone else has ascended into resurrection, but I have descended again into the grave.

"I have had an inordinate emotional reaction," I report to my spiritual director.

"Let us be careful when we use the word *inordinate*," she cautions. "In God's timing all things are ordinate. He uses all the unsettled conditions of our life to teach us what it is He needs us to know. Now tell me what has happened."

The triduum, the three days of Easter holy week, had certainly been unsettling for me. First of all, my grandmother had died two weeks earlier at ninety-one years of age. She did not have a Christian burial (even though her instructions as to her funeral were clearly written and given to my sister and me—which dress hanging inside-out in her closet to use, the kind of ceremony, the grave plot purchased and waiting beside my mother's). At my aunt's wishes, she was cremated instead and her ashes, I am told by my sister, whose husband conducted a small memorial service, are contained in an urn by the fireplace in the living room.

Also, David was speaking at the graduation ceremonies of a Bible school in Canada, and I confess that I had sorely missed his being beside me. There have just been too many sacred holidays celebrated on my own.

Plus I am always susceptible to the holy seasons. This weekend has forced upon me the spinning rounds of an emotional roulette. The loaded chamber happened to discharge on Easter Sunday.

In addition, as a spiritual activity, I had watched again Franco Zeffirelli's film *Jesus of Nazareth*. The eyes of the actor portraying Christ looking out from the television screen captivated me, seemed to stare at me alone and left me unaccountably disturbed. All weekend in my memory, I kept seeing that amazing, penetrating gaze of compassion.

My spiritual director smiles and quietly asks, "What did you feel when your rector pushed your hand away?"

Oh, everything. Abandonment. Rejection. Not being good enough. Being a silly woman in a bright pink suit. I know, I say to her, that if Rick had knelt at the railing in jeans and a street shirt and had adjusted my hand, I might have thought (or even said, depending on my mood) "You turkey. What's up? Have I done something wrong?" But vested, on Easter Sunday, with my feelings so exposed, grieving David's absence and the loss of my grandmother, I was vulnerable. This laying on of hands, the shaking that comes through them, this power I have not sought or appreciated, always feels to me like a symbol of my essential oddity. The man in vestments pushed my hand aside, and it was as though the whole church, the looming institution of it, was saying to me that I was too strange, too unacceptable, too odd to ever be of worth to it.

"Have you talked about this with your rector?"

Yes, we've talked. To him it was nothing. It was as though he was brushing away a mosquito. The problem is not with him; the problem is within me. If I have any reason to be angry (and believe me, I was angry) it is not that he moved my hand, but that at some point he didn't express to me his opinion that this style was perhaps inappropriate to the Episcopal way of doing things. (Yet I think maybe he did say something a while back, but it was so cloaked, I didn't hear him.)

At any rate, while I was not singing the last hymn on Easter Sunday, a picture thrust itself into my mind of the idiot-self inside me.

"What did you see?"

An idiot-child sitting at a table with other people. Its head was totally bald and lolled to one side. It was drooling and seemed to be six, seven, or eight years of age—but that was hard to determine, it was so emaciated and malnourished. He was a little skeleton of a ragamuffin, wearing a torn undershirt without sleeves in some kind of homespun dull gray fabric. Cold, bare-armed, without leggings of any kind, barefoot. He turned his sad, huge eyes on me and smiled sweetly. He was sitting at the far end of a long table with a rough bowl before him filled with a thin, weak gruel.

"How do you feel about the child?"

I—I love him. I love him intensely. It's how others feel about him that bothers me. This is my idiot-child, the idiot-self of my self.

"How do you think he feels about you?"

He loves me.

"Can you get closer to him? Can you close your eyes, see the child again, and will he let you sit beside him?"

I close my eyes and relax in my chair. I see again the picture of the idiot-child who had presented himself to me as I stood shaken at St. Mark's, struggling to control the rising dam of my emotion that threatened to loosen itself on Easter Sunday morning.

Yes, yes, I can get close to him. I am sitting beside him on the bench. I have put my arm around him. Poor little thing, so cold, but now, now a warm radiance seems to be emanating from the little body. That soft glow is growing, filling the space between us. I can no longer see the other people at the table, but this warm light is enfolding the two of us. We are in a circle of the child's luminescence alone together.

"Can you ask him his name?"

In prayer, in silence, I ask the child to tell me his name. No, no—I can't—oh, wait. I hear that he is the Christ child.

"Yes," says my director. "That is what I heard also."

This idiot-self, this unformed being, is in some part the Christ child that is within me. Can it be? Can it be that the young man who has come to me in my dream is more than my excluded male-self? Is he also Christ? Has He been attempting to woo me because an essential part of my identity in Him has been expelled from my adult development?

123

"What does the laying on of hands represent to you?"

Oddity. I feel freakish. I don't want people to see this spiritual power. I don't understand it, and I don't know how to use it. I do not want people to know how strange I am—because I will be unacceptable. Unacceptable to the church, to evangelicalism. To further complicate matters, this is all packaged unacceptably within a woman's frame.

"What else does the laying on of hands represent to you?"

I am quiet. I am listening. I wait for the answer to rise out of the deepest part of me: Spiritual authority. It represents a spiritual authority that I am afraid of having.

"Yes. Now what I want you to do is to take this Christ child with you whenever you go to the communion rail."

I do. The Christ child within me, the oddest part of myself that I have hidden from the eyes of others, I take along to receive the bread and wine. Whenever I lay on hands, embarrassed by the holy force that flushes through them, I will ask the Christ child to stand beside me. This act will be an intentional humility. I will come to terms with the fact that He has framed me strange, that this strangeness is a likeness of Him and that I must learn to love it, not to hide it away in the dungeon of my being. I must accept my oddity and accept the fact that most of the theological world will never understand what it is that God has made me to be.

On Easter, my idiot-self always rises. The gospel too is a foolishness. Christ Himself is strange to us, a stranger in His own created order.

Christ's eyes have been watching me. His gaze has been mediated to me through countless means. They are eyes of love and approval. "You are everything I have ever wanted spiritually," He has said. I have rejected not only a part of myself, but a part of myself that is Christ. I will be a stranger to myself no more. From now on, I will look at Him and He will look at me.

Reconciliation

$\mathcal{I}$am staying for the week with a friend who owns a five-hundred-acre farm/ranch/retreat center near Galena Territory. The bunkhouse is my creative center, and my computer sits in readiness. The paper in a neat pile is curled officially behind the printer. The reference notes wait self-importantly in my notebooks. But all creativity and inspiration are sterile because (despite myself) I have gone deeply into the moment. Moments piled upon moments; days upon days. The shining that lies always buried beneath the created order has risen, translucent glory. I am distracted, discombobulated by radiance.

I was awakened this morning by a peacock crying, his call strangled like a tortured child retching. He strutted above my head along the crest of the bunkhouse. I fixed coffee. The cry again! Why would anyone think of peacocks as a Christ symbol? The crested head, perhaps. The thousand majestic eyes opening when the great feathers fan. Perhaps the cry, its agony echoing in the air. But who would want twenty of these creatures? Flannery O'Connor raised peacocks. Did she hear Christ crying?

On the deck with my coffee, I watched the hills, rolling, misty green from morning rain, like low Appalachian ranges. Cattle grazed the meadows, hiding and seeking in damp foggy patches. I followed the peacock's cry, taking the still-warm mug, and I turned the outside corner of the bunkhouse just as the obstinate creature descended down the opposite side. All I saw was his crested crown above the roofline. The kitten who follows me whenever I emerge from my hideaway snaked friendly around my ankles. Sitting in the swing, I pushed; toes up, toes down. Brushing a crusty cicada shell from the seat, I heard the music of the seven-year infestation sawing from the trees in the valley. Jumping to my lap, the kitten curled, uncurled, rubbed white cat hairs against my royal blue cotton pullover, and paw-pushed softly on my thighs. A woodpecker hammered in a tree down by the barn. Workmen, early at their tasks, pounded on the half-finished big house my friend and her husband are building next door.

The two children, precocious young girls, have read my Kingdom Tales books and are entranced by my presence, respectful; which nevertheless does not prohibit them from interrupting me with a hundred apologies, not wanting to intrude as one of them said, "On your inspiration." I suspect their mother has given them a lecture.

Yesterday the world came to my bunkhouse door. I opened it to find a disreputable-looking character standing outside with bulging plastic sacks of muddy garden vegetables in his hands. "This is for that woman what gave me wood last winter." His t-shirt was filthy with a raveling hole torn above his navel. Teeth were missing. His hair had been shorn. I sent him over to my friend at the big house.

Later the children were selling fund-raising candy. I bought two chocolate bars. When I returned later in the afternoon after a walk, a vase of irises was on the table with a note from the eight-year-old. "Fresh from Great Park [the idyllic setting of my children's book]. Enjoy. To the Kingdom! To the King!" [quotes from my book].

After a while one of the children (profusely apologizing regarding my inspiration again) needed to get a baseball mit out of the storage closet. I looked out and saw the pet lamb, Lamby, following on the heels of the children's aunt, her arms full of giant spring irises. The farm dog followed them both. It was an enchanting entourage.

My friend apologized for her children's interrupting me. But it was not these little ones who were prohibiting my writing progress. They honored me with their avid interest to (albeit surreptitiously) watch a real author working. It was the world, the whole antic caravan of it parading before my windows, my working space, turning somersaults, juggling cherry blossoms and wild blooming rose bushes that interrupted me. I could not stay inside. "Look! Look at us!" the flock of roller pigeons cried, performing aerobatics in the air above the barnyard and corral. Their wing tips reflected the high light. They looped precisely, scudding on the winds, their undersides showing. "Now watch this!" I watch, my mouth open. "And this!" The drum rolled, a fanfare. "You have eyes to see," the divine ringmaster cried. "See!"

So I gave up. Today I have taken a walk and am now collecting eggs, robbing the nests as I enter into the mysterious quiet of the clucking fowls. To me, henhouses are mysterious, like prayer huts. At the barn, I greet the lady who does the chores here. She, sun-crimped and grizzled, wearing pants and boots on her husky body, chugs away on the tractor. I go horseback riding on the trails that wind through pasture and forest and across stream and up and down hills. I have been undone. The computer remains silent, much to the disappointment of the children who think I should have a book written by the end of the week. But I cannot for I am watching. Watching.

Sometimes I wake out of ordinary time to find myself in extraordinary time. Most of our lives are lived as outsiders to the moment, perhaps even as observers. But few of us walk into the reality that is beneath the reality. These days have been extended moments, piled upon themselves, which have drawn me into their center. I am aghast with my wastefulness but have given myself to this temptation. I am in the moments, immersed deeply in the mystery of being; God breathing through His created world over my shoulder. I am of them and in them and they in turn—cat and cicadas, nodding grass, clover and vetch—acknowledge the exquisite being of me. I look at God in His created things. He is looking at me. We are like lovers who cannot keep eyes off each other. We touch eyelids tenderly. We brush cheeks. We kiss the back of fingertips. We notice each other glancing across the crowded rooms. I will not neglect to see Him when He shows Himself to me.

Back at the bunkhouse, a voice calls, "Karen?" It's my friend's brother, a missionary returned for extended leave who is married to the woman with irises in her arms and the lamb at her heels. I have not seen him for thirty years, not since high school. He is handsome still, trim, and reminds me of his father (whom I also have not seen for thirty years). Having served a mission organization in Africa, he is home in the States recovering from a troublesome fatigue syndrome. A leash dangles in his hand; he has been walking the dog. "Nancy wondered if you could come for dinner tonight."

I spend the rest of the afternoon in the sun on the deck, watching. How can I explain to the children that this too is the work I have to do? I go for dinner, walking past the big house to the guest quarters. I am completely rested in time as we three sit above the valley and talk about our lives, what we have learned, how we have served God, and what we know about whom we know. We eat a cold salad supper.

I go to bed and awaken to the peacock's raucous cry at five o'clock in the morning. I know what my work is to be. I fix coffee, walk a half-mile to the main highway, walk two miles down the road to an overlook where I can sit and watch the sun rise. Slowly it pierces the hazy half-lighted, dew-heavy fields. When I return, I find the classical music station from the University of Iowa, just over the Mississippi River in Ames, and then amplify it so the bunkhouse shakes with the symphony. I step out onto the porch deck again and face the valley.

The eyes of God are around me. I am watching Him and He is watching me. I pull my chair into the new light, and plop my bare heels on the rail. I let the world go

130

through me, heart and soul, flesh and bone: the wind in my hair, the "little fellas" (bugs and ants), the noise of it all, the damp secret shade of it, the tantalizing whispers that undulate in the air, the wonderdome sky. My molecules are drenched, saturated with this watching. My soul hurts from bearing the beauty of this knowing. My spirit and the sweet green spirit of it all are one. My being is invaded with this being. I am watching the world today and am utterly content. I have only one concern. Only one concern. Will I live through it?

Two aging sisters appear on the screens. The Spiritual Life Commission is sponsoring a film viewing with accompanying discussion questions for interested parishioners over the Thanksgiving weekend. Three monitors have been positioned in the narthex, and some twenty-five people gather in three small groups in front of the television. The subtitles read: "The sisters are the model of charity, spending almost all their time and their limited income on good works."

The film we are watching is the Academy Award-winning foreign work, *Babette's Feast*. This is an enchanting visual parable, adapted from a short story by Isak Dinesen, about very religious sisters (Martina and Phillipa, named after Martin Luther and his close friend, Philip Melanchton) who live in an isolated fishing village on the Danish coast. Their father was a priest and a prophet, the founder of a religious sect, which in the years since his death has grown older in age and fewer in numbers.

The two sisters work hard to serve the disciples of their father and to keep the memory of his teachings alive, but as the years progress the aging disciples become more fractious, cantankerous, and querulous. Jealousies arise. Old grievances are not forgotten. While they still gather weekly to sing the old hymns, to listen to the founder's teachings regarding the Scriptures and how to live with each other, they have forgotten the beauty and harmony of their former spiritual condition.

Into this simple setting comes a younger woman, Babette Hersant, a refugee fleeing the civil war in France. She has been sent here by a former voice coach of one of the sisters, the famous opera singer, Achille Papin. The woman's own husband and son have been killed on the streets of Paris. Will they give this woman sanctuary? Will they allow her to be their servant?

For fourteen years Babette serves as housekeeper to the aging sisters, cooking nothing more exciting than the traditional boiled codfish and the uninspiring ale-bread gruel. Nevertheless, the sisters prosper under Babette's management, and the villagers come to love and respect her. She is exceedingly frugal, creative in market bartering, and ingenious in food preparation. Martina and Phillipa are freed from the household responsibilities to devote themselves to more charitable work.

In time, the centennial anniversary of the founder's birthday approaches. The two sisters prepare to celebrate this occasion. "We shall serve a small supper followed by a cup of coffee," say the two sisters.

But Babette has another idea. Her only tie to France for the last fourteen years has been a lottery ticket, which a good friend in Paris renews for her yearly. A letter comes informing her that she has won the lottery, a ten thousand franc prize. She asks for permission to serve the founder's celebratory meal, to buy all the provisions, and to prepare it exactly as she pleases.

The film, which to this moment has been a study in plain and simple lives, lingers now in loving visual tribute to the sensual exquisiteness of the food preparations. Babette, who unbeknownst to the sisters is a culinary genius, spends her entire ten thousand francs on a most

132

remarkable meal. The ten elderly disciples, including the sisters, are joined for the celebration by General Lorens Lowenhielm (who as a young man had been a suitor of one of the sisters) and his greatly aged aunt, a member of the landed gentry. This makes twelve celebrants in all.

The villager disciples are extremely skeptical about the lavish preparations, fearful of being seduced by a materiality that is beyond their ken. They vow to each other to eat the prepared menu but to not speak a word about the food or the drink. The general, however, knows how rare and exquisite the gifts are, and course after course, wine after wine, he interprets the great artistry of the chef. "Oh, a real amontillado! True turtle soup! Blenis Demidoff! Cailles en Sarcophage!"

As he exclaims over the food and as the disciples eat together (keeping their vow of silence about the food, but increasingly enjoying it nevertheless), their hearts are warmed toward one another, differences are forgotten, old grievances become joking matters. Once again, around the celebratory table, they become people who are living within the precepts of their dead founder's wishes and desires. They are no longer bitter, old people looking only toward death.

The general makes a toast. As a young lieutenant, having just won a riding competition, his fellow officers treated him to a dinner at Café Anglais in Paris. The head chef, a woman of great renown who had invented the remarkable dish Cailles en Sarcophage, was reported to have the ability to transform a dinner into a kind of love affair, a love affair that made no distinction between bodily appetite and spiritual appetite. He had eaten her menu then. He is eating the same menu now.

Then the general, a man who in his middle years has been torn by a question of the rightness of his youthful decision to seek power and position, reaches his own inward reconciliation. He accepts the fact of God's grace. Quoting one of the founder's favorite psalms, Psalm 87, "Steadfast love and faithfulness will meet; righteousness and peace will kiss each other," he then explains what he has concluded during this remarkable meal, "We come to realize that mercy is infinite and we have only to wait with confidence and to receive it with gratitude."

Forgiveness is offered among the old people. Two embattled parties, an old man and a woman, kiss. The evening ends with coffee and liqueur, with songs around the piano. Then the general and his aunt finally depart in an open, horse-drawn carriage into the cold December night. With the two smiling sisters watching from their door, the eight remaining disciples join hands and dance around the village well as they all sing a hymn of blessing. "Alleluia!" shouts one of the old gentleman. It is a word of true praise.

After the guests have departed, the elderly sisters realize that their cook has spent all her money on the celebratory meal. "Dinner for twelve at the Cafe Anglais costs ten thousand francs," Babette explains to their amazement.

"You should not have given all your money for us! Now you'll be poor for the rest of your life."

With the stacks of dirty dishes crowding the tiny kitchen, with her new copper pots hanging from the ancient wooden beams, Babette is deeply satisfied. Her work has been done well (and amazingly, interpreted for all correctly). She also knows the sisters' lament is not true. "An artist," she explains, "is never poor." She then quotes her friend in Paris, the great singer Papin who once sent her to this isolated shelter: "Throughout the world sounds one loud cry from the heart of the artist: 'Give me the chance to do my very best.'"

The credits roll and the three television monitors go gray. We now break for a "small supper followed by a cup of coffee" and then gather again for group discussion. The discussion questions prepared by a Spiritual Life coworker asks: "With which character in the film do you

134

most identify? The two sisters, Martina and Phillipa? The disciples of the founder in the isolated fishing village? The outsider, General Lorens Lowenhielm? The culinary artist, Babette? The aging opera singer, Achille Papin? Choose one, then explain to the group why you identify with this particular character."

Each time I view *Babette's Feast,* I am accosted by its profound meaning. To me it is a parable of the way in which the artist, freed to do her best, can impact the body of Christ. I realize that throughout my years of service to the church—all my life—I have been restrained due to the accustomed fashion of serving ale-bread gruel and boiled codfish. With whatever meager means are at my disposal, I am always attempting to create celebrations that become love feasts where the physical and the spiritual meet and fuse together as holy. "Babette," I reply in answer to the discussion question, without a pause. "Definitely Babette."

This is the first time I have ever put myself in the category of the artist. I understand artistic yearnings, read and view and listen to the works of artists intuitively, easily interpret their meaning, long for artistic reconciliations within the institutions of Christianity. Out of this understanding has come the formation of the artists' colony here at St. Mark's with its four natural divisions: the visual artists, the dramatists, the writers, and the musicians. I have always considered myself a writer and suspected that my abilities are woefully underdeveloped. But I have never before labeled myself with that singular terminology. I have never said the words, "I, too, am an artist."

But I identify so deeply with Babette in the film. I understand her service to lesser artistic understandings, the kind of spiritual submission required to do this well—a discipline of limitations that must be accepted joyfully less it cause harmful damage to the inner senses. I understand her longing to spend everything she has on one grand, ultimate act of creative love.

135

Deep within me, so entrapped in muteness that I hear barely more than a muffled choke, there is a strangled cry stemming from artistry of some kind. Some undiscovered kind. "Give me," it pleads. "Give me, give me," it begs. "Please. Give me the chance to do my very best!"

Cantate Domino means "Sing to the Lord," and Cantate Domino Sunday is the day the Spiritual Life Commission set aside to honor the artists and musicians of our parish. This is the second year that our artists' colony has sponsored an exhibit of their works. The colony originated with my encouragement, and I have nurtured the concept of the exhibit (borrowed from a past Circle Church tradition). Even though I personally handled the administrative details for this event—sending out invitations, cataloging the registrants, supplying bulletin announcements, making endless phone calls, notifying the Property Commission of our need for the portable (but heavy) divider to be moved into position for displays, writing and typing the Cantate Domino bulletin insert—I have not had a moment to look, to really look at the works that have been mounted.

I walk alone past the tables and wall hangings. This is wonderful! What a rich display! A large, stained-glass window hangs on a wall. There are watercolors, cartoons, imprinted original designs on t-shirts, homemade baskets, needlepoint, pen-and-ink sketches, photographs, quilts, excellent calligraphy, oil paintings, complicated church models, weavings, pen-and-pencil illustrations, painted wooden boxes, dried floral arrangements, a variety of hand-tooled crosses, and printed book cover designs. I notice handpainted Easter eggs by a new artist, one not even listed in my registration. They are enchanting!

This is everything I wanted it to be—not an elitist collection, but a spontaneous response to an invitation to display the works that have been formed out of individual ability and the great gift of creativity that God has granted to them. "You have an abundance of workmen; stone-cutters, masons, carpenters, and all kinds of craftsmen without number, skilled in working gold, silver, bronze, and iron. Arise and be doing! The Lord be with you!" How we honor God when we create out of that giftedness, when we affirm the struggle to make beauty! When we as a community bring forth gifts, when we combine our talents, God's multiplicity is displayed, as it is here.

I believe strongly that artists are the prophets of society (good or bad prophets), that in general they are disenfranchised by the church. Extending invitations like this is soulishly healing for them and will eventually challenge any congregation that has courage or vision enough to integrate the artist and his or her works into the life of its body.

John H. Westerhoff expresses what I deeply believe in an article titled, "What Has Zion to Do with Bohemia?" He writes: "The function of artistic expression is to illumine and draw us deeper into life's depths. The arts incarnate our experience of mystery, wonder and awe and thereby aid us to encounter the holy or sacred. . . . They remind us that faith precedes theology."

Religious life and artistic life should go hand-in-hand. Spiritual meaning often begins with feelings and moves to intuition and then to cognitive analysis. Religious thought cannot be separated from religious experience and our personal encounter with the spiritual, with that ultimate mystery that we struggle so to explicate, with God the Almighty, but it is nurtured, articulated, and shared through the forms that best communicate mystery—dance, painting, music, sculpture, poetry, and drama.

Over and over this morning, in the crush of enthusiastic viewers, I heard people exclaim, "Are these all St. Mark's artists? I didn't know we had so many creative people." Oh, no? But I knew. I knew! Creative people are everywhere, under rocks, behind doorposts, in the pews. They only need one insistent invitation that says, "Arise and be doing!" Any church that provides this, that blesses and nurtures its creative community, is blessed in return. When the artist is freed to bring his or her unique inner vision to the church, just as the musician is freed to lead the congregation in praise, we are all brought nearer to discovering the creativity in our own souls that reflect the Creator God. Not only this, we are also better enabled to ponder the ineffable mystery.

I walk from piece to piece, brushing the fabrics, the wood, the frames with my fingertips in a sort of unconscious form of blessing. Rectangles of late afternoon sunshine fall on the floor, like ephemeral boxes of light stacked across the red carpet; glamour glints off the purples and maroons, the soft pastels, the greens and blues on the stained glass, on the quilts, on the paintings. It is so quiet and I want to enjoy the luxury of the beauty of it all, the success of an idea being more remarkable than its originator dreamed. I sit crossed-legged in the sun and with the evidence of all these works before me, lift my hands and thank God that He has made us in His image.

This project has exceeded my expectations, delighted the members of the parish, and positioned its artistic members in the middle of approval. It is good; it is very good. I consciously empty the tension, will the tightness caused by stress across my back and hips to drain. I roll my head, press an ear to a shoulder, then the other ear to the other shoulder, and suddenly hear that inward word I have learned to identify so surely due to years of practicing a listening silence. I know that voice, as familiar as my mother's once was to me, or as recognized as my husband's.

I am aware, gently but suddenly, of the presence of my Lord. His in-this-moment nearness is as real to me this afternoon of Cantate Domino Sunday as though He had taken on flesh, drawn me by my hand up from my knee-crossed position to His standing side and spoken the words

138

out loud. I hear them distinctly whispered to my soul. "Thank you," says the inner word. "Thank you."

"Oh, props," laughs Frank Griswold, bishop of the Episcopal diocese of Chicago. My arms are filled with the separated sections of two flag stands and two rolled banners, all of which keep sliding away at odd angles as I attempt to shake his hand. As the awkwardly shifting poles continue to keep me from making hand contact, I smile and agree, "Props."

I am setting up the last of my "props" for the special eucharistic service we are holding this evening in honor of the bishop's visit to our parish. A private dinner is to be served for St. Mark's vestry and clergy at the home of our junior warden, and then everyone will convene at the church building again, joining with the congregation. Bishop's visits are traditional, in that the bishop attempts to attend every church in his diocese at least once a year. Due to the fact that David and I are in a variety of churches ourselves, I feel intense empathy for the professional side of those visitations, meeting an unending myriad of strangers, eating countless dinners or dessert offerings, making interminable repetitive chitchat. I want to create a special occasion, to give a gift of beauty to the bishop and his wife.

A grand scheme has been fertilizing itself in my creative mind for more than a year: an event that would include visual richness, provide opportunities for our dramatically gifted folk, and introduce liturgical dance in some small fashion, all contributing to one motif—a celebration of the Word.

Wednesday afternoon last week I flew home from meetings and in five days—with dogged effort, much preplanning, and much imploring for divine aid—all the elements have come together. The fifteen-page script, a reader's theater for five speaking voices and one narrator, was written in five hours Thursday morning. The script's Scriptures trace the Word of the Lord coming to the Old Testament prophets, then coming in the flesh as Christ, the Word. When we were in the pastorate at Circle Church, experimenting with ways to enhance the reading of Scripture in our worship services, David and I utilized a variety of spoken choral renderings. It feels good to once again employ these old (and most effective) reading techniques.

I have contacted an interpreter for the deaf to sign certain parts of the reading as a means of conveying additional visual and emotional impact. With her aid, the congregation can consider what the Scripture from Colossians sounds *and* looks like. The solo liturgical dancer will become a physical picture of outward joy representing the inward celebration that should go on in our hearts when we consider this great and profound gift. I integrate a precedent from the Hebrew holiday Simhat Torah into the writing. Simhat Torah is the holy day in Jerusalem when the Old Testament lectionary readings are completed for the year and the new reading cycle begins. The sacred scrolls are lifted high and carried through the streets to the Western Wall in great celebration, with Jewish men dancing, shouting, singing, and weeping in procession.

The script is approved by the rector Thursday afternoon, duplicated, then practiced for the first time Friday evening under the direction of one of the members of our artist colony who has professional theater experience. I spend Friday gathering the original fabric worship art of Marge Geiser, some fifteen wall panels that have been designed for her church as illustrations for the pastor's sermon series. Along with these artistic interpretations of Scripture, we will mount some thirty of her pulpit cloths. Marge meets me at College Church in Wheaton, where her beautiful work is stored in a dusty garret above the worship sanctuary.

140

On Saturday morning, members of the Property Commission assist me in placing four large hangings in the nave. Two brilliant blue panels with the raised emblem of the Lion of St. Mark in their centers and with stylized Scriptures from the Gospel of Mark delineated in fine gold braid, all exquisite in their artistry, hang on either side of the new organ. Twin deep royal blue panels with *Hosannah!* and *Alleluia!* inscribed in gold lamé, fall long on either side of the high wall of windows facing west. By Saturday evening, the narthex and nave are filled with visual glory and will serve as a surprise for the congregation as it arrives on Sunday.

We hold rehearsals Sunday afternoon for the liturgical dancer. For this first effort under my supervision, I want to emphasize movement rather than rhythm and music. She will dance accompanied only by her own tambourine. Appropriate costuming is determined—a black leotard top and full skirt, a multicolored, striped fabric scarf interwoven with gold threads for a waist girdle, and the tambourine tied with colorful flowing satin ribbons. The dramatists practice the reading again. By Tuesday evening (except for the last props I am juggling in my arms when I meet the bishop) all is in readiness.

The private dinner is enjoyed; the congregation gathers. My signer has not as yet arrived. A marked script has been delivered to her previously. The readers are vested in black cassocks. Waiting in the narthex in the crush of arriving people, I pace—to the side, the front, and the back doors. A St. Mark's old-timer grabs me at this nervous moment to inform me that one of the fabric banners is hanging over the fire extinguisher. I apologize and promise never to do it again. Quickly, coolly (in case the interpreter for the deaf does not arrive on time), I begin to redesign the script in my head. Suddenly she is beside me, wearing an ankle cast. I slip her into the cassock I had reserved for her and briefly coach her on exactly where to sit, when to take her

141

place on the stage, and where to exit. This twenty-minute celebration is to be performed before the processional that traditionally initiates the eucharistic service.

Much to my pleasure, we begin on time. The readers, in formal black, march at a deliberate pace down the aisle, take their positions, and hold the black choir books containing their scripts in readiness. I pound with a wooden mallet on the last pew. This deep sound from the back calls the congregation to attention, stating that the curtain has risen. On cue, the choral reading begins. Twenty minutes later it ends with the congregation joining in a responsive reading:

> Leader: Praise to Christ! Praise to Him who comes, who has come, who is coming, who will come again!
>
> People: Are you He who is to come, or should we look for another?
>
> Leader: But you Bethlehem Ephrathah, out of you will come for me one who will be ruler over Israel, whose origins are of old, from ancient times.
>
> People: The woman said to him, "I know that Messiah is coming; when He comes, He will explain everything to us."
>
> Leader: Jesus said to her, "I who speak to you am He."
>
> People: "Come, see a man who told me everything I ever did!"
>
> Leader: When the Son of Man comes in His glory, and all the angels with Him, He will sit on His throne in heavenly glory. Then the King will say to those on His right, "Come, you who are blessed of My Father; take your inheritance, the kingdom prepared for you since the creation of the world."
>
> People: This is He who comes, who has come, who is coming, who will come again!
>
> Leader: The Spirit and the bride say, "Come!"
>
> People: And let Him who hears say, "Come!"

Leader: Give praise! Give praise to Him who comes,
    who has come.
All: To Him who is coming, who will come again.
    Come Lord Jesus! Come!
Leader: The Word of the Lord!
All: Thanks be to God!

Everything goes without a hitch, and (given the amount of time we have had to pull this event together) I am exceedingly pleased with the overall impact. I have loved giving a gift to the bishop and to the people of St. Mark's. Even more importantly, we have been able to employ some underused skills of certain talented people in the congregation—the dramatists, a director, the liturgical dancer. I have been able to make another significant statement regarding the place of arts within the life of the church.

I go to bed tonight deeply satisfied, hardly tired—rather, euphoric. I am deeply grateful for the opportunity to use my underdeveloped gifts, abilities I had just begun to discover when we were in the pastorate at Circle Church and which were blooming due to the freedom for expression there. I am sincerely grateful for the Spiritual Life responsibilities, and lying abed I ruminate on other events I have been able to design in my two years of service, a kind of creative counting out.

There was the icon exhibit, for instance, in which we mounted some thirty to forty icons on loan from a publisher, designed an adult Christian education class on the role of icons as a worship and meditative tool in Eastern Orthodoxy. Then we set up actual tours on three Friday nights to Orthodox churches in the Chicago area where we were able to view the iconostasis, traditional screens made of separate icons that divide the space between the altar and the congregation. Here we carried on a significant dialogue on the meaning of Orthodoxy with Orthodox clergy. These rich evenings were ended with conversations and laughter (and the complications of dividing the common food bill) around tables in Greek restaurants.

I think with great pleasure on the children's recital. First, we displayed collections owned by the children of the church. My associate worker and I wrapped forty to fifty empty boxes of all sizes with slick white paper from a printer's roll. The boxes provided different levels to display baseball cards and prized model airplanes—the whole panoply of wondrous accumulations which children cherish! Borrowed red bunting adorned the display tables, and red and blue helium balloons lifted the eye.

Second, every child in the parish was invited to perform in the children's recital late Saturday afternoon. The idea was that they were welcome to do whatever they wanted to do. It was a wondrous event that honored the special abilities of each child. One boy performed a hoola-hoop routine (with his dad sitting on the edge of the stage to lend moral courage); a little girl clogged. Children played violins, sang duets, and mouthed popular recorded music. The performance that still stands out in my mind is that of identical twins, robust boys of eight, bouncing on two pogo-balls to a choreographed routine—with their nine-months-pregnant mother sitting in the front row.

I love to provide these opportunities for children and adults to use their gifts in the church. I am grateful that this position at St. Mark's has given me the chance to use my gift of utilizing other people's gifts! Indeed, when I am designing these affairs, inviting body-life participation and empowering the gifts of the laity, I am in a state of near bliss.

So the bishop's visit went well, and I am pleased. Drowsy now, I begin to drift into sleep. But before unconsciousness completely overtakes me, one trailing thought flits across my mind, like the liturgical dancer in her black leotard and black skirt, striking the tambourine. A quick word in passing ends this fine evening. I remember it the next morning. "Think what you could do if you had all the time you needed."

<hr>

Sometimes the car, parked in the driveway, is the only place where David and I can have a serious conversation without casual eavesdroppers or frustrating interruptions.

"You aren't delighting in me," he says.

We are having one of those intense conversations now.

"You delight in other people more than you do in me," he continues. It is an accusation, not a matter-of-fact statement.

Is this a symptom of some modern malaise? I wonder. How many husbands today accuse their wives of the same kind of negligence; not the negligence caused by over-attending to children, nor of being caught up in housework, but of having interests outside of the family's life that are consuming, fascinating, and utterly fulfilling?

Yet the truth, I must admit, is: I'm having a wonderful time. Joy rises constantly in me, a soaring bird. My energies and resources are expanding through all the administrative tasks at St. Mark's. I have never felt stronger physically. The emotional pain that once weighted me is mostly gone. Constantly surprised by my own burgeoning capacities, I am discovering that I love executive responsibilities. I am intrigued and challenged by oversight. I have a proclivity for management. People, it appears, love working with me, and I am fascinated by solving the puzzles of fitting people where they best belong. Most amazingly, I am told that I have a facility for conflict resolution!

Since the age of eighteen when I married David, I have been part of a tandem. At first it was Karen Mains, the wife of David Mains. Then it became David and Karen Mains. For brief periods, I was then known as Karen Burton Mains. But now, for the first time in my adult years, I have been functioning for an extended period without riding the marital bicycle-built-for-two. These days I am Karen Mains. I have uncoupled my identity from my husband's enough to discover my own heretofore unferreted being which exists apart from my life of mothering and wifing.

The truth is: A cycle of love now enfolds me. I give out to the body of Christ in this local church community, and love (sometimes what feels like waves of love) is given back to me. Favor is proffered to me; consequently I easily return it in kind. I do delight in this community of faith, in the joy of my accomplishments among God's people. Mostly I delight in watching others flourish. After years of loneliness, I am euphoric in these relationships.

We look out the front windshield, faces forward, eyes staring. The weight of our conversation is so overwhelming, the subtext so potentially explosive, that we dare not make it heavier by looking into each other's eyes. Neither of us knows what the future of our words portends for us.

"You delight in other people more than you do in me," he says again. "You're eager to be with them. Your conversation is filled with tales of folks from St. Mark's, with stories about your acquaintances and your plans. I actually think you don't want me in these parts of your life."

David's accusations are true. I have given up attempting to pull him into my world. It is easier to accept his overwork, protest it no more, speak only when the opportunities rise. Not being able to change David's compulsions, I have made a joyful place for myself, and I am delighting in unaccustomed at-homeness. In a sense, I do not want to make a place for him.

"You're right," I say. "And I'm sorry that this has brought you pain. I do delight in my friends and in my personal activities. I have found places of my own where I am wanted, appreciated, and loved. I have friends who are interested in my interests. I do delight in them. Perhaps I delight in them because they also delight in me."

I turn to look at my husband, this world-changer, this man with an ever-evolving strategy behind his eyes. Now his eyes are filled with pain. Compassion tempts me. The old patterns woo me: Make it right. Take away his pain. Say it isn't true. Say, "Of course, I delight in you." But I know it may be another ten years if I do not grab this opportunity now. Life being the hazard that it is, David and I may not have another ten years. I must speak the truth as I see it.

"I think I do delight in them more than I delight in you," I continue, groping to explain what I have been tongued-tied through the years to make clear. "And now you feel the pain of this. And I'm sorry that you're hurting. I am very sorry. But listen to me very carefully . . ." *Kindly, kindly,* I remind myself. Speak the words without accusation, without anger. Find the love you bear for him, even as you speak.

"You're only feeling now, David, what I have been feeling for a long, long time. For the last twenty years you have delighted in your work more than you have delighted in me. I often have been lonely for your attention. I have attempted to speak to you about this, but you wouldn't hear me. Perhaps some of that was my fault, in that I couldn't find the right words. I think you're feeling some of the pain—only some—of what I've been suffering all these years. I have not intended to harm you. I would never, out of vindictiveness, intentionally wound you. But perhaps this is the only way God could show you what I have experienced these long, long years."

He is silent. Listening. He doesn't defend himself or counterconfront. His body is stiff on the other side of the car, fortified against me.

I continue gently, as gently as possible: "I haven't wanted to exclude you from my life in any way. A thousand, thousand times I've reached out to take your hand to pull you into my world—as I have willingly walked with you into your world. But you wouldn't be pulled. So I decided that I could be overwhelmed with pain, like the pain you're feeling now, and become disabled, or I could go on with my life. I decided to go on and live as fully as possible. I have given God my half-a-loaf marriage and have accepted that reality. Perhaps it is even absurd for me to expect more. I have chosen to rejoice in what is beautiful between us and not to focus on the negative. I am accepting the realities of our union. I love you. I love you deeply. I will always love you.

"I cannot, however, I cannot before God be half a woman. I cannot, with life passing so quickly, wait for you any longer. So I decided, within the framework of what is good in our marriage, to go on and be everything God wants me to be."

Truth is the distance that separates me from my husband now. We are both stunned with its magnitude.

Groping for the right words, I go on: "Of course, I delight in these people. They're giving to me what I need. They are there when I hurt. They applaud my gifts in areas that aren't meaningful to you but which are meaningful to me. They approve of who I am, not just of what I do. In their company, I feel as though I'm no longer lost. They value me. Because of them, because of each of them, I am no longer lonely. And I have been very lonely."

David turns in the driver's seat toward me. He looks directly at me. There is still pain in his eyes. The silence between us grows. Wounded by me, the person in all the world who loves him most, he nods. His voice is low, "I hear you."

I have never loved my husband more than at this moment of painful encounter, at this risky moment of truth with its unknown consequences.

"David," I say, still with the physical space between us. "We have the whole rest of our lives before us, however many years God may grant. I don't want to delight in others more than I delight in you. I am more than willing, in these middle years, to work primarily at this marriage relationship. I want to make these our very best years together. But

148

I don't want to work on it alone. I will not do it alone. I promise I will match you step for step, effort for effort. I promise I will work to delight primarily in you if—IF—you work to delight primarily in me."

He hears me, this my husband, my scheming strategist of the grand designs, my field marshal, my master planner. I have been as kind as possible, but firm. I have spoken the truth to the best of my ability. I know most certainly and with a kind of accompanying astonishment that I finally—finally—have David's total, undiverted, unequivocal attention.

At four o'clock, my customary early hour, I rise this Friday morning, the day of St. Mark's women's fall gathering. I sit on the screened-in porch, a sweater pulled over my faded-blue sweat suit, my Day Runner and a cup of coffee nearby as I mark the rising day, crisp and sunny and cool, a brisk October dawning. Knowing that only a few details remain to be completed for the retreat, I go over my lists. Three more centerpieces need to be arranged for Saturday's luncheon tables due to an influx of late registrants.

One of the greatest terrors in my life is double-bookings, promising to be in two places at the same time. I regularly go over my travel calendar with a fine-tooth comb, cross-reference it against my at-home planning calendar, then check everything with my personal Day Runner and, finally, against David's three-year calendar with the month-at-a-glance pages. Very infrequently, embarrassing glitches do happen. This year there have been two double-bookings, and I am rigorously reexamining my office systems.

Two weeks had passed before I could inform the committee working with me on the fall gathering that I (or my secretary) had double-booked my schedule. During the time I am supposed to act as chairperson for the October retreat for St. Mark's, I had also accepted a speaking engagement in the Baltimore area. After fourteen days, my self-recrimination began to settle, and I decided to look on this latest faux pas as a test of my administrative capacities. I divided the responsibilities according to time/events and chose a woman to be a leader for each section. The theme for this year's retreat is "Turning Life's Losses into Gains."

My schedule for this day folds out on the calendar pages before me: throw a load of laundry in the washing machine, pack, go over my teaching notes for Baltimore, time my ten-minute address for Wheaton's homecoming chapel, dress professionally in something that will wear well for today's platform work and for evening travel, arrive at Edman Chapel at 9:45 A.M., speak for homecoming weekend, come home and complete the last three centerpieces, fold dry clothes and move laundry along, meet with my committee person in charge of food at St. Mark's at 3:00 P.M., set up for tonight's meeting, demonstrate the place settings on one table for the luncheon tomorrow, meet with Betty Parker, who will take the committee chair baton from my hand, leave from the church at 5:00 P.M., drive to O'Hare, park, and be at the gate ready to fly out at 7:45 P.M.

All goes according to the morning schedule until I park the car in the lot behind Edman Chapel, leave the keys in my ignition, and lock the door. By the time I discover my error, the chapel has cleared and there are no friends to whom I can appeal for help. But a kind of foreordination has covered me. One of my sons locked the keys in his car a couple of weeks earlier. I know exactly what to do. I find a pay phone, call the Wheaton police, and request assistance. Then I stand waiting in the parking lot and make a decision about my emotional state.

My children tease me about one of my major life themes. "Now you have a choice," they copy in imitation sing-song, chanting the words in recognition to each other. "Mother always said, 'You can choose to make this a good day. Or you can choose to make this a bad day.'" My home-coming talk went well—at least there is time to savor that moment. I decide to exult in this forced half-hour of consid-eration, and as I watch for a roving police car, I deliberately enter into the awareness of the glory of this autumn day. A batter of yellow, umber, gold, and orange maple leaves, spiced with sunlight, seasoned with glad cries from college students to one another, sweetened with the fresh fall air—all these are mixed in the day's bowl. I lean back against the hood of my locked car and feed.

The policeman arrives. "No woman could be more glad to see a man than I am glad to see you!" I announce truthfully and apologize for taking up his important time with my stu-pidity. He is gallant, pronounces absolution, sticks his jimmy between the car window and the door, and as a formality warns me that this might break the lock and the Wheaton Police Department won't be responsible. I tell him to go ahead. In two tries the car door is open and my lock is intact.

I drive home, arrange dried, curling, broad-leaf dock in three medium-sized paper sacks, the tops rolled down and sprayed all over with shellac to make them stiff and shiny. I tie a band of printed chintz around each bag, knot and pin together three oversize soft bows, then load the remaining boxes of supplies—maroon paper luncheon plates and nap-kins, printed programs, twelve new cream bed sheets for tablecloths, an iron, and ironing board. Then my overnight suitcase, my hanging garment bag, and my briefcase go into the car. Ginny Yeck, my food expert, meets me at the church. Kicking off my heels, I hang up my red suit jacket. We pull the serving table for tonight into place, lug chairs into small-group discussion circles, and iron cloths. I set one table as a sample how-to and am delighted with the ef-fect. Two larger centerpieces, overblown and wild, go on the table for tonight's dessert buffet.

Betty Parker arrives, and one last time I go over the typed schedules, check off any last-minute changes, review the responsibilities of each chairperson. Virginia Vagt will act as emcee. Amy Harwell, a gifted communicator who in her professional life is a business-woman with her own private consulting firm, will speak for twenty minutes. Then a reader's theater group will perform a section from Ginny Newitt's original script, "The Garment Mender."

Betty Parker, confident and efficient, shoos me off to O'Hare. Despite rush-hour traffic, I arrive in good order, park, cart my luggage to the gate, and settle into my airplane seat. I realize I am slightly smug about my competency (ignoring the awkward paradox that because of incompetency my body is winging toward Baltimore when my emotions are still attached to the fall gathering in Geneva, Illinois).

In Baltimore I am met by a welcoming committee. The two women apologize to me as they drive me from the airport that they had promised some 300 registrants, but due to the fact that this is their first community retreat, there are only 175. I understand completely.

Only after being ensconced in my motel room do I realize I am exhausted. I crawl into bed, aware finally that fatigue is spreading to the very marrow of my bones; I am so weary my body aches if I roll over. I remind myself that one of the reasons I took on the responsibilities for the women's retreat ministries at St. Mark's was because I so often fly into conferences, do my thing, reap the harvest of other women's hard behind-the-scenes labor, and fly out, trailing their glory behind me. Public living is dangerous in that the temptation to gather too much credit unto oneself is indigenous to success. There is nothing more leveling than the reality of doing the thankless grunt work. However, I never intended doing both at the same time. I turn out the light; my feet are cramping. I get up, swallow some calcium capsules, crawl groaning back to bed. I sleep fitfully, exhaustion deep-creasing my muscles, my bones lie heavy, as though weighted by leg irons.

152

The next day I know that I am in physical trouble. Having spoken once, and while the women are in workshops, I am led to the youth pastor's office where there is quiet, a couch, and a clock on the wall by which I can monitor a cat-nap. I am so tired I can hardly lift my knees to climb the stairs. I wonder: *How can I minister to these women when I can't even pray for them?*

In the middle of my third speech, the last, that inward word comes to me as distinctly as though I had heard it out loud: *You are made for the giving and the receiving of love.* Emphasis is on the last half of the statement. *The receiving of love.*

Suddenly I see the women who are sitting before me. I see love in their eyes as they look up at me. I have spent years protecting myself, wrapping my heart with plastic and spraying it with teflon so that I wouldn't succumb to the allure of celebrityitis. Suddenly, tired and weary and holding to the podium for the strength to go on—no longer the competent wonder-woman-administrative-genius—I understand as I never have before that there is a mutual exchange that must occur in ministry. These women have as much to give me as I have to give to them.

Continuing with my outline, my voice functions from habit, but my mind is actually repeating to myself the inner words I have heard. I open myself to these people sitting at my feet; they are hungry for spiritual reality, longing for practical truth, and at this moment they are receiving it from my shaking hand. Their wave of favor embraces me— these women who because of my fatigue are being so inadequately taught—and I consciously let love into my aching body.

I am made for the giving of love. I am made for the receiving of love.

I have considered this Maryland meeting a glitch on my schedule, proof of my need for still-to-be-improved-upon efficiency. Now I begin to consider that perhaps I haven't double-booked myself; perhaps it is God who has designed this dysfunction. Perhaps it is He who has something to teach me, something profound that I need to hear.

When I am functioning efficiently, inner reminders are often lost in the middle of lists, plans, time lines, and agendas. It's when the microchip in my brain glitches that instruction comes. How often, like the apostle Paul, I kick against these goads, privately fuming at my own inabilities. But it is in the pauses that I am forced to reconsider. It is in the bad moments of my life that I must choose to learn the opportunity that hides at its deepest center. When my inadequacies rise, rebelling against my carefully constructed external persona then—then—God can get my attention.

It is He, I suspect, this wily ancient rascal, who is responsible for my double-booking. He is never terrified that I will unknowingly promise to be two places at the same time. But then, He wouldn't be, would He, this everywhere-present One?

You are made for the giving and receiving of love. I remember these words as I sit in my living room Tuesday afternoon after my weekend retreat in Baltimore. I am due to fly out early this evening to speak at a spiritual life emphasis week at Biola University in LaMirada, California. Rick Lobs is sitting on the church pew by the fireplace. The old, terrible fatigue that I fear, and which disables me at mysterious times, coils and lurches now, turning me in the vise of its ghastly grip. "Maybe you shouldn't go on this trip," he suggests.

I had called him an hour ago on the phone. "Do you think I could possibly take private communion before I go? I won't be able to attend eucharist tomorrow morning—and I don't have the energy to see anyone." I dread seeing anyone in my drained condition; the effort to be friendly, kind, conversational appalls me. All my resources are being mustered to get myself ready to drive to the airport by 4:30 this afternoon.

"Shall I bring the elements to you?" he kindly offers. I am again surprised by his pastoral availability and as usual, most uncomfortable with the necessity of imposing upon his busy schedule. I know that I flirt with brinkmanship, skidding overscheduled on two wheels around the rim of a canyon of chaos. Speeding along and feeling strong, then things are very good for me, but when I slide over the precipice of my energy at unaccountable moments, things are horrid. The meetings in Baltimore have tipped me precariously near the brink.

I hear again that insistent inward reminder which I suspect I have been making a habit of disregarding. *Let my love reach you through this my servant.*

Looking at this man, who has so unbegrudgingly interrupted his day, I think how cautious I have been about any emotional attachment regarding him, how exceedingly hesitant about the dangers of cross-gender relationships. But now opening my prayer book, receiving the anointing of oil and the laying on of his hands, hearing his voice read the Psalms and lift to God in prayer, I realize that I am a walled fortress with a moat of water twenty feet wide surrounding me. I have been too self-protective.

As I once received the bread from this man's hands, I now intentionally receive love as it is mediated to me through this human form. I am so needy I must pause to attend to the inward word that keeps repeating itself over and over in me like an annoying scratched record. *You were made . . . You were made . . . for the giving and receiving . . . for the giving and receiving . . . of love . . . of love . . .* I open myself to allowing God to incarnate His love to me by this means, by any means He chooses.

"Perhaps you shouldn't go," Rick says again, "if you feel this bad." At this moment, I feel like a shattered mirror, haphazard pieces scattered on the floor. I feel like a child in adult skin, shaken and frightened and incapable of big-people responsibilities. I am a little girl needing a Daddy. I want to crawl close to this man's protective side and hide. Instead, I gather my dutiful self together and stand, "No, I need to go, and I'd better get moving or I won't make my plane."

For this month David and I are having an "airport marriage." David is in transit across the country conducting The Chapel of the Air annual fall pastors' conferences. Our plan has been for me to drive to O'Hare, park the car, meet him at his United Airlines arrival gate, give him the keys and car location, and then catch my flight to California.

Wearily, I check my bag at the United counter and when I scan the Arrival/Departure monitor, I find that David's flight will arrive ahead of schedule. He will disembark from Gate C3; my flight leaves from Gate C7. In the immense dual terminal system at the United hub in O'Hare, to have our gates so close together (even in the same terminal) is proof to me of divine compassion.

Handing over the keys and the parking ticket, I realize how good it is to feel my husband's embrace. The wonderful familiarity of his body, the soft wool of his dress sport coat. Sitting together, catching up during our extended time (twenty minutes instead of ten!), I take his hand and press the back of it against my forehead and cheek. "I am exhausted," I report. "I've done it again, gone beyond mere fatigue."

"Oh, Doll," he says sympathetically, "I'm so sorry. Will you manage this trip? How many times do you have to speak?"

I am filled with regard for David in more than just a wifely way, but as a spiritual peer, I consider him a man of enormous stature. His integrity and fidelity to God and to me are remarkable. I have always been proud to be his

156

wife. David's visionary quality, his capacity to choose significant arenas of function, his ability to communicate truth in a motivational way, his passion for the Kingdom still cause awe in the visionary, cause-driven, professional communicator sides of me.

But—sitting hand-in-hand in this terminal at O'Hare, waiting for my departure call—I realize that I have in some subtle, subterranean way closed myself to his love. Perhaps it is all those minuscule paper cuts from workaholism. Perhaps I have reactively, automatically protected myself from receiving more. Perhaps it was the long four years of my father's dying which instructed me all too well that death is the end of every cherished human relationship. Perhaps I have been preparing myself for what I consider the inevitable widowhood ahead. Perhaps all these goings, these leavings and many absences, these minor losses and endings that constitute the travel style of our days, these little deaths have demanded that I not live in a constant state of separation anxiety. So I have closed an emotional door for the sake of self-protection, and closing the heart to any love closes it always, in some strange way, to all loves.

Receive My love through this My servant, your husband.
Intentionally, at this moment, I open myself to David's love, and it warms me physically; it reaches the aching muscles. We are funny together, laughing about our transit marriage, sympathetic to each other's travel tiredness. David enfolds me tenderly with care and concern, and I, allowing God's love to be incarnated to me through my husband, receive it into my being.

You are made for the giving and receiving of love. I think about this as I stow my baggage and crawl into my assigned seat. The two seats beside me are empty in an overcrowded evening flight. *Why don't any of those people move back here?* I wonder, looking down the aisle at all the passengers jammed into the steerage of the fuselage before me. Nonsmokers will think I am in a smoking row, and no one behind me, preferring cigarettes, will move into a seat beside me. This again is evidence to me of divine care. As soon as the plane is in the air, I grab pillows, flip up the two armrests and stretch across the three seats for the duration of the flight. Crawling beneath the wool airline throw, I feel a flannel infant blanket of God's love enfold me. I sleep deeply, the sleep of healing.

You are made for the giving and receiving of love, I think, when on Thursday I walk into the gymnasium for the morning session in which I am to speak. A group of men and students are standing at the front praying, and I slip into the circle, slide my arms around the waist of the folk on either side of me. Suddenly, I realize that Ken Medema, the Christian concert artist, is standing to my right. We haven't seen each other for seventeen years. "It's Karen Mains, Ken," I whisper, not wanting to interrupt the prayer but, due to his blindness, wishing for him to know who has moved beside him.

"Oh, Karen," he says when we are done praying. "When you whispered your name, it was like a bolt of lightning went through me."

I am speaking this morning on a topic I have never taught before, the fact that we are a body of Christ, a community of people who must help each other become all God is calling us to become. In his amazing spontaneity, Ken sings and plays the piano, his song about the God Search. Still weary despite my long sleep, I am sitting on the platform. By now I know that the shattering going on within me is more than a physical breaking. Something in my basic identity is being cracked. The words of the song reach me, something about being lost in a wilderness and being met by a stranger.

"Her eyes, her hands, her feet, her fragrance, were the eyes, the hands, the feet, the fragrance of God. It is Karen," this bold man sings. "And God has met me in the meeting with her."

158

Let My love reach you in this song, in the inner sight of this man, My servant, I hear.

Jill Briscoe's topic on Thursday afternoon is titled, "Running on Empty." I am empty right now, crushed and poured out. She and I have breakfast together on Friday. I consider Jill one of the amazing women of contemporary Christendom. She leans over the table and says in an off-handed comment, "Karen, you have such an unusual quality of love about you." At this moment of extreme frailty I need to hear it.

That is good to know, particularly from Jill. I have worked hard at loving other folk, but now I am aware—I am being made acutely aware—that I must make a 180-degree shift and allow the love of Christ's body to touch me, to pour over my head, to wash my interior being like a sea, to drip into the wounded cracks and crevices of my whole parched self.

Months ago, having no idea how strategic a personal retreat would be at this time, I decided to take advantage of some friends' invitation to stay in their condominium in Long Beach, often loaned to people in Christian ministry for rest and recreation. Around three o'clock Saturday afternoon I unlock the door with the keys that were mailed to our Wheaton offices. Exhausted, I tuck myself to bed and sleep the sleep of the dead until I rouse myself about nine o'clock at night. Pulling back the curtains from the window walls that face the shoreline, I am stunned by the lights of the city shimmering in a crescent arc along the bay. The moored ocean liner, the *Queen Mary,* sparkles just offshore. I am lulled by the warmth of the air. Propping my feet on the balcony rail, I take my prayer journal and begin to assess: What in the world is going on in me?

You are made for the giving and receiving of love. I have heard that inner word and know that this is not just a psychological notion. It is the sure inner instruction of the Holy

Spirit that often rises in me. The source of it is divine truth because it is insistent, very distinctly formed in my inner ear, utterly convincing in itself that it is from God, carrying authority, persistent in my memory, producing a sudden change in my outlook. If it is anything like the other words of truth that have been spoken to my interior soul through the years, this will have a profound influence on the rest of my life.

I have been in error, somehow dividing love into human and divine camps. I am beginning to understand now that when it is holy love, there is no distinction. All love is of God. It is what we do with it that makes it holy or unholy; how we use it or misuse it.

"Beloved, let us love one another; for love is of God, and he who loves is born of God and knows God. He who does not love does not know God for God is love" (1 John 4:7–8). I wonder if this could also be translated (in its intent), "Beloved, let us receive love from one another." Long ago, I concluded that it was an error to withhold love from anyone, and if that is so, then it must be a commensurate sin to refuse to receive appropriate, holy love from anyone.

This is really a kind of arrogance in me. I can give out God's love, but I am too proud (or too lacking in trust, or too fearful) to take it. This stern tutorial under the rod of this insistent Taskmaster which I am undergoing indicates that my Maker considers it time in my life to learn the lesson, perhaps past time. He has been attempting to get my attention for years and has had to allow this shattering in my ego so that I would finally hear: You are made for the giving and receiving of love.

Listening to the sound of the eternal waves beneath me in the absolute quiet of this cloister condominium, I realize that I am finally mature enough to understand the truth about the unity of God's love. When I love one, I in truth love all. When I am loved by one, I in truth am loved by all. Love goes out to someone, then through that person to the whole world and is used in ways we can never measure. That is why it must be kept holy. That is why we must be very careful not to transgress the codes that exist about giving and receiving this powerful gift. It is a fire. It is a wind. It is an earthquake. In its holy power it will help to shake the firmament of the earth.

"I'm sorry," says my husband. "I haven't savored the moments with you." This is a new thought to David. I can see it in his eyes.

We have been reading, David in his book and I in mine. A few quiet afternoons and evenings of this rare week have been given over to a common communion between separate bookbindings. Ever since I was a girl scavenging the stacks in the Wheaton Public Library, I have loved to read.

"What do you mean?" I ask, surprised by this out-of-the-blue pronouncement. I push in my heels on the couch cushions, straightening my spine which has been twisting in serpentine imitations.

"Well, this book has a chapter on savoring the moments, and I realize I haven't savored the moments with you." I can feel his mind computing the information. It's a radical discovery.

"I've always had my own agenda. I've always had something else I was planning. I haven't stopped and enjoyed fully the moments of our shared life together. Forgive me."

I understand in a way not before comprehensible to me; there has always been something else on his mind. A broadcast due. Lists to be counted on the abacus of agendas. Items to scratch off the lists. No wonder I feel as though he looks at me but doesn't notice me. Oh, he sees what I wear and how I look and is appreciative. I take pains to dress well, mostly for David's pleasure. But the *me* of me—the person beneath the epidermis, the inner oddities of me, the passionate complexities—this he hasn't seen. Yes! That is what it is! There has always been a benign inattention, a glancing away behind the eyes, his private thoughts chasing mightily around the legs of all my words. David's consuming plans. The multiplicity of things to be done, of endless spinning worlds to conquer.

Sorrow wells up in me suddenly and overflows. I begin to acknowledge all the lost moments. I have not been given his attention. (He has said it!) The wound in my soul which heals and splits and heals and splits, splits again. I begin to grieve the might-have-beens. Yes, yes, we have lost time. Now with middle life upon us, we cannot capture again the neglected exaltations of all the magic of our God-given human passings.

It is David's admission that fully opens up the pain I have so often denied to myself and now am owning absolutely. His confession is my permission. Maria Ranier Rilke, the poet, wrote, "I feel as though I had been sleeping for years or had lain in the lowest hold of a ship that, loaded with heavy things, sailed through strange distances. Oh, to climb up on deck once more and feel the winds and the birds, and to see how the great, great nights come with their gleaming stars."

I have been anesthetized by these continual doses of inattention. I have succumbed to the chloroform of lifelong refusals:

Can you come? *No, I have things to do.*

Can't you walk with me on the soft grass? Tread the woodland paths and hunt the wildflower seedlings? Watch spring rise in its time-lapse forth-going and not allow it to surprise us this year? *No, I have things to do.*

Can't you howl with me at the moon? Dance fairy rings at midnight and leave behind a morning circle of

162

mushrooms? Watch dew sparkle diamond-bright in the velvet leaves of the lady's mantle and then collect these ephemeral riches? *No, I have things to do.*

Can't you sit in the sun for a moment, just one tiny moment, and lift your face and exult in the down-shaken quicksilver of God's creatorness? *There is so much to do.*

I have been novocained, but now, with my husband's antidotal words, I feel the hollow in my soul where the abscesses puffed and swelled. Benumbed no more, a tingling alive spreads with these words.

The greatest of the practiced arts is to live life deeply, fully. The greatest achievement is to participate consciously in time, to know how precious life's gifts are and that they race before us and are gone suddenly if we do not reach out to grab them.

Long ago, I determined to honor life's gifts. Then I discovered that God is surprisingly in the moments of being. The I Am who declares Himself in the blazing bush on the desert floor blazes forth as real for contemporary humans as for ancient patriarchs—but only when we have eyes to see, when we take time to touch the burning things, when we risk the scorching of our fingers. God is in common time. Much of my life and most of my writing has been a recorded chronology, "Oh see! Oh see!"

Jean-Pierre de Caussade, acting as spiritual adviser to nuns some two hundred years ago, wrote, "Those who have abandoned themselves to God always lead mysterious lives and receive from him exceptional and miraculous gifts by means of the most ordinary, natural and chance experiences in which there appears to be nothing unusual. The simplest sermon, the most banal conversations, the least erudite books become a source of knowledge and wisdom to these souls by virtue of God's purpose. This is why they carefully pick up the crumbs which clever minds tread under foot for to them everything is precious and a source of enrichment. They exist

163

in a state of total impartiality, neglecting nothing, respecting and making use of everything."

Over the years I have become facile at seeing. God reveals Himself in the moments, and I, surprised at first, then delighted by this divine revelation, have become an anxious witness to sacred sharings. I look through the window of my humanity, hoping to see God in the act. I see! It is disconcerting, but wondrous, too, and He winks at me approvingly, "See you have found Me out."

But I have been lonely, achingly lonely for a concelebrator. This man (the husband You gave to me, oh, Lord!) has had an agenda behind his eyes, has been checking off his lists even as he looks at me, has not savored or rolled over on his tongue the succulent time. He has often only responded, "Uh-huh," when I have shouted, "Oh, see! Oh, see!"

So today I grieve. I grieve for time lost but also for all our carelessness. I mourn all our casual trampling of holy happenings. Then, the weight of grief so heavy on this reading day, I put my book aside and retreat to bed, the place where I mourn best in privacy, where I do intense prayerwork prone, where I hide myself from painful confusion between the pillows.

Truth, who has appointed himself my dogged companion, crawls beneath the bed sheets with me, tucks his toes behind my own, embraces me, and whispers in my ear: *This is David's sin, surely, that is so. He has named it, and you accept that naming. This is good. But in truth, let us consider more. Are you not the one given the sensitivity, the wild capacity of risky intuitive leaping, the sound sense to hear beyond other hearings? Is not this your capability and your function and your giftedness? Hasn't your joy not triumphed because, again, you have been asking, "What about John? What about him?"* Truth is always a cold, hard water treatment, like washing your hair in melting ice in the winter season.

Today I was reading *An Interrupted Life: The Diaries of Etty Hillesum, 1941–43*. This is the story of amazing spiritual growth written by a young Jewish woman in Holland who eventually died in Auschwitz at the age of twenty-nine. I remember a paragraph and kick off the bed covers. Grabbing this intruder Truth by the hand, I drag him downstairs to where the book lies halved, face-down, spine stretching. Together we read Hillesum's words, written from Westerbork, a transit camp:

> There is no hidden poet in me, just a little piece of God that might grow into poetry.
> And a camp needs a poet, one who experiences life there, even there, as a bard and is able to sing about it.
> At night, as I lay in the camp on my plank bed, surrounded by women and girls gently snoring, dreaming aloud, quietly sobbing and tossing and turning, women and girls who often told me during the day, "We don't want to think, we don't want to feel, otherwise we are sure to go out of our minds," I was sometimes filled with an infinite tenderness, and lay awake for hours letting all the many, too many impressions of a much too long day wash over me, and I prayed, "Let me be the thinking heart of these barracks." And that is what I want to be again. The thinking heart of a whole concentration camp.

What is that to you? says Truth. David's artistry is his business; it is my own artistry that is my concern. I vow to be the thinking heart of this family's life. I will no longer wait for another. I refuse to be rushed by that dictator known as Schedule, or bullied by that hoodlum known as Deadline. I will know an angel has visited me in the stranger. I will touch Christ when I hold the child whose mother, my friend, fights her personal bedlam of multiple personality disorder. I will clap my hands when the supernatural tumbles, juggles, trampolines, and somersaults into the natural. I will applaud this world wild with glory; God shining.

My children accuse me: "Mother, you see Christ figures in everything." I do! I will! I will not be blind to the visitations; I will make use of everything. Camps need their poets, bards who, with whatever songs they own, can sing about it.

I forgive David. Of course, I forgive.

God forgive me. Let me never again be numbed, half-awake to life. Let me, too, be filled with an always infinite, undying tenderness.

Our son Joel is a film student at Columbia College on Michigan Avenue in Chicago. Columbia is a computer school specializing in technical and performing arts with students mostly from working, lower-middle or middle-middle class families. Film students are remarkably consistent in their hostility toward formal religion. Joel has often described the environment as "dark." During his first quarter of school, one of his film assignments was chosen best of two in his class. This, along with twenty-one other film clips, each about four minutes long, is to be shown in an evening viewing. So I traipsed into the city and sat in an auditorium at Columbia College with my son, the film student, and waited for the viewing.

Midway through the films I began to realize that an underlying theme punctuated a number of these projects. Many clips concentrated on the loss of faith, on hypocrisy in the church, on the damaging religious rigidity of parents. One showed novice nuns sneaking smokes before the altar, another portrayed a mother-son relationship in which she beat him on the head with a Bible. Religion appeared to be uppermost in many of these students' minds. To be sure, the majority of students were products of Catholic Chicago and were hostile to Catholicism, but as I sat in that darkened auditorium I had many thoughts on the way we all wound our young.

On Saturday I return home from a week away to find David and Joel waiting for me. Together they had attended a conference conducted under the auspices of the School for Pastoral Care at the Wheaton Graduate Center. Joel sits with us in the living room, his eyes shining. He of all our children looks most like his father and is the only one of the four to have inherited David's brown eyes. But this son and I are also alike in that we have suffered most from David's addiction to work. It is often Joel, struggling to be forthright, who in these recent years has been my model in the painful process of learning to live honestly.

David is alive with epiphanies. The conference teachings on family dysfunction and some twelve characteristics of ill health are informative tools that are opening his mind, piercing the last vestiges of denial. In this week he has come to understand the causes of his own work addiction, to make essential distinctions between malign intent and the true damage of benign-but-nevertheless-harmful environments. As is so typical of David, he is already applying this information to a broader scope: how the qualities of unhealthy family life can become measurements for the family of God. He is diagnosing the past childhood church in which he was raised and the theological systems that once wounded him.

But it is really last Thursday night when their mutual story begins, my son's and my husband's. While driving home together, David was elated with his burgeoning comprehension, all the pieces of the complicated puzzle of his life suddenly coming together. But Joel was depressed. At twenty-two, he was the youngest attender of several hundred. "What if it's God you're angry with?" he asked his father. "How do you forgive God?"

Not sure how to respond, David nevertheless suggested, "Maybe, Joel, it's not God you're angry with. Maybe you're angry with me. With your dad."

Tears. A choking. Joel began to weep in the car. "You were never there Dad when I needed you . . . you were too busy to play catch . . . I wanted you to come to my games . . . and you always had too much to do." The litany of pain and its accompanying grief ascended. The suppressed sorrow filled the car with wave after wave of hurt.

When they arrived home, Joel went to his room and flopped on the floor. David stretched beside him (thinking that he would never get his broadcast done this night in order to record in the studio the next morning at eight, in order to be at the Billy Graham Center for the last meeting at nine). Finally, the sobs ceased. Joel slept and David stayed, stunned by the reality of all this pain. In the middle of the night, Joel woke again. Another paroxysm of weeping.

"Joel, Joel. Why are you crying now, son?"

"Oh, Dad. I'm weeping for you. Someone in this family has to weep for you. You don't know how to do your own weeping. I'm crying for you, Dad."

Company to my son's grief, my husband finally tasted the dregs resulting from his own abandonment and neglect.

The next morning, by the grace of God, David finished his broadcast, rushed to record it, and then met Joel at the conference. The conference concluded with the laying on of hands and a prayer commissioning for individuals. David was one of the first to go to a prayer station where ministering team members stood in front of the platform, across the front of Barrows Auditorium. He had a noontime appointment and needed to leave.

But where was Joel? Looking for his son, David spotted him, nearly the last in a by now long line. Something within cautioned David about leaving, about slipping out of the auditorium to find a pay phone and explain the necessity for tardiness. *Don't go now. You've not been there in the past when he's needed you. If he looks around and finds you gone* . . . So David waited.

Finally, Joel received prayer. As he began to return to his seat, Leanne Payne, the director of the conference and of the Pastoral Care Ministry, called quietly to him. She had not been functioning as a prayer minister on the floor but had remained on the platform. David watched as Leanne, a fixture in our lives for years and someone who loves Joel, leaned from her standing position and took Joel's wrists. Because of the difference in height, his arms reached to her, outstretched.

Leanne was wearing a lavaliere mike. After a few moments, David heard her laughing. Joel was now standing chest-high to the platform, his shoulders shaking, not with sobs but with a holy hilarity. "Oh, please. Please," said Leanne into her lapel mike. "Don't be disturbed. This is just the gift of holy laughter, and I have received it from this young man."

The two of them were incapable of stopping. Leanne, a woman of great spiritual power and dignity, actually had to be helped to her seat. Joel's head and torso flopped to the platform floor in laughter. He pounded with his fist. The merriment sparked, caught, and rose communally in the auditorium, because laughter is catching. A song started. Attendees (many of them ordained clergy from all confessions) moved into the aisles. A time of laughing had come, a time to dance. Joy breached all the waters of pain and disappointment and splashed them with its anointing. Gladness wreathed the souls of the conferees. My husband, my David, having put aside his pressing agenda, stood at the back of the auditorium thanking God that for this time, this time he had been where Joel needed him to be.

So together, this Saturday afternoon, they sit in the living room and tell me their story. We laugh; our eyes become teary. We marvel at God's work. For truly, this is their story, Joel's and David's, but it is a subplot under-pinning my own confessions. What a fitting ending for any narrative. God's love story is basically a comedic en-terprise. A U-shaped tale retold endlessly in minor or major forms, in personally intimate or in grandly cosmic ways, ongoing throughout all creation. Beginning always in paradise, the plot line descends tragically, falling into loss and sorrow and separation. Inevitably (even when we cannot see the next chapters), it turns, soaring al-ways toward redemption. We lift our heads at the rising, helpless to keep from laughing at the surprise endings. And the laughter is catching. Even the angels shout with rejoicing.

Thus we are strangers no more, displaced persons no longer, no longer refugees without a homeland. Oh, yes, we have drunk the bitter dregs of common sin and pain. Now, finally, we accept our own frailties. We are wounded and have been wounded and cannot keep from wounding our own. But God is a redeemer author. Our stories, de-spite our worst imaginings, keep having these happy end-ings. Across borders, over all these territorial crossings, we reach out, aliens once, but now we touch hands. We em-brace. We hold one another. We cannot keep from laugh-ing. We hear the music begin. And we know. We know. We know that home is not far away.

***

The gymnasium at Asbury, the Methodist seminary in Wilmore, Kentucky, is filled with some seven hundred min-isters and their wives. The choir renders the hymns with hearty enthusiasm and the full singing of the mostly male voices in the auditorium is an exultation. Francis Asbury would have been proud. Participating gladly in this worship led by David Seamands, professor of pastoral ministry, I am

170

seated on the platform, scheduled to speak for the morning service.

Dr. Seamands phoned last year; the board had passed an edict that more women plenary speakers were to be employed during Asbury's annual ministers' conference. After prayer, he had felt led to extend an invitation to me.

Dr. Seamands is a man filled with loving reverence. A former missionary in India, a pastor for twenty-two years of the United Methodist Church here in Wilmore, he is the convener of this ministerial conference. Leaning toward me he whispers, "We're full this morning. Often by this last worship session, ministers find they need to begin returning home. I was a little afraid we would sag in attendance. This is a compliment to you."

How lovely. He has been concerned about my feelings, worried a little for me should the attendance drop. I appreciate this quality of courtliness. The author of the best-selling book (among others), *Healing for Damaged Emotions,* he is obviously psychologically astute.

My topic last night was "The Loneliest Man I Have Ever Met," a subject particularly suited to a conference of ministers. Indeed, I am intimately acquainted with loneliness in most of its guises. I know how publicity, public life of any kind, alienates us from our true human centers. We can become lonely for our own lost selves. I know how sincere spiritual desire divides us from other Christians who can't comprehend the intensity of our longings, or how it drives us. We are alienated from the very folk we seek to serve or befriend. I understand ministry marriages where devotion to the cause of advancing the Kingdom becomes confusedly intertwined with our own blindness. We pass our spouses in the nights of comings and doings. We yearn for guides, for compatriots of the soul's pilgrimage.

Today, I look down toward my husband in the front row of the hundreds of folding chairs that have been ordered in straight lines in the gymnasium. It is always comforting to

171

have him in attendance when I speak. He smiles up at me. The president of Asbury Seminary, David McKenna, is beside him. Before leaving the platform, he whispered to me, "Today, Karen, there will be two Davids sitting at your feet."

Who has cued these kind men on my private sorrows? On the solemn griefs that come the way of women distinguished by God with gifts of spiritual authority, or of prophecy, or of teaching? I am touched by their kindness toward me and intentionally open myself to receive it.

I have chosen a new topic for this morning. In its maiden form it's entitled, "The We-Believe People," and its theme is the interdependence of God's body. I'm using Scripture from the Ephesians 2 passage, "For he is our peace who has made us both one and has broken down the dividing wall of hostility." A communion table stands on the platform, spread with a white linen, set neatly with many common pottery goblets and with baskets containing unbroken rounds of bread. While I am seated, the table interrupts my line of vision.

Because of my astigmatism, or due to a divine reconstruction of reality accessible to me through the eyes of my soul, suddenly the material symbols blur, as though a filter of holy gauze has been draped softly over the whole. Here at Asbury, the place from which revival fires once flickered across a nation, I see with heightened awareness the body of Christ through the body of Christ. For a whole half-hour, as the music of praise goes gloriously forth, as Dr. Seamands leads us in prayer and worship, I look at the faces of those men through the diffused forms of pottery goblets and baskets of bread.

When I rise to speak, I know definitively that we are the body of Christ. A powerful anointing of love wells up within me. I remember Father Zossima explaining, in Dostoevsky's book, *The Brothers Karamazov,* "Brothers, love is a teacher; but one must know how to acquire it, for it is hard to acquire, it is dearly bought, it is won slowly by long labor. For we must love not only occasionally, for a moment, but forever. Everyone can love occasionally, even the wicked can. . . . Love a man even in his sin for that is the semblance of Divine Love and is the highest love on earth."

Now, at this moment, I know a wholeness—I and these fellow ministers, men and women. We all are one. Scripture spoken by my own voice rings truth to my own ears, "But now in Jesus Christ you who once were far off have been brought near. . . . By abolishing in his flesh the law of commandments and ordinances, that he might create in himself one new man in place of the two, so making peace."

When I am done speaking, and as the elements are being served, Dr. Seamands asks the ministers to identify their own needs for healing and to humble themselves by going to a fellow minister to request the laying on of hands. In the hush of communion, the crowd quietly ebbs and shifts. Men and women go to one another, confess their need and seek ministry. They rest in each other's embrace. They bend together in prayer. They exchange the kiss of peace. On the platform, David Seamands turns to me and says, "Karen, will you pray for me?" and bows his head before me.

Surprised, but impregnated with holy awareness, I sense the potential power of this act to weave together the loosely clipped threads of my own unfinished life tapestry. Looking at this mighty, humble servant of God, this man offering to me gifts he cannot possibly know he is offering, I hear Peter cry, "Lord, do you wash my feet?" I lift my hands in this sacramental act that has been linked somehow to my deepest feelings of shame and ostracism and outsiderliness, and I lay them in prayer upon his gray head. We stand together. Elevated on the platform. Before the congregation. In bowing his head before me and requesting my ministrations, he offers health and restoration for my own brokenness.

It is a profound reconciliation. As I reach an inner wholeness, I experience a commensurate outer wholeness,

173

a unity between myself and all others. This stretches far to that tripartite unity, to joinedness with the Trinity.

Standing before the congregation, in the middle of communion and these offerings of prayer, I vow silently before God that I will not in any way break this body. I will not build again the wall Christ has torn down. I will not shout rancor where peace prevails. I will not be a party to disunity when union is rolling down. I am of the Oneness and will not make myself of the twain again. Ever again.

I feel as though I have finally come home. I feel as though I am again with the father who so tenderly raised me, with the sons of whom I am proud and who return my admiration, with my brother whom as an infant I once cradled in my arms and who grew to adulthood alongside me, with friends who cherish and know my oddities but accept me, with my husband who loves me above all others. At last, speaking at Asbury, I am at home.

Tom Dunkerton, the chairman of the board of InterVarsity, and I are opposites. Through the years, we have forged out of our friendly combat a relationship of mutual respect. His recommendation is the reason I am a trustee, and I have been often grateful for his frank guidance to me as the new lady on the block.

At the Madison, Wisconsin headquarters, we interview senior staff as to the job performance of the chief executive officer, Stephen Hayner, a man whose leadership abilities often amaze and delight me. Realizing that I have never conducted an annual performance appraisal, I also realize that I have never had an annual performance appraisal conducted on my behalf. Tom is a hard-nosed researcher out of the Madison Avenue corporate advertising culture. He measures evidential data. I sense the unstated subtexts beneath answers, read hidden emotional contexts.

174

We have dinner together to prepare the report. Tom teases me, "I kept thinking, 'Where's she coming from with that off-the-wall question?' The next thing I know someone's sitting there in tears. What a team! You sure see and hear things I don't see and hear." I too enjoy the give and take of this complementariness.

Upon arriving home, I report, "I have this uncanny feeling I'm being groomed for something. But I don't know what I'm being groomed for. The last thing in the world I want to do is serve as chairperson of the board of trustees for InterVarsity Christian Fellowship."

I realize even as I say the words how ungracious they sound. Stephen Hayner has just, in the most complimentary manner, asked if I would consider allowing my name to be placed before the nominating committee. InterVarsity is a theologically conservative, campus-ministry organization that has been in existence for half a century. In its fifty years of history, it has never had a woman chairperson.

Anxiety rises. What about this frail, artistic self that has only begun to emerge? What about my hard-won reconciliations between male and femaleness? Are they not still fragile? Can I afford to give the energy this position will require of me to manage the inevitable unforeseen circumstances that will need to be managed? Will this responsibility unbalance the hard-earned parity of my marriage? Do David and I have the emotional resources to yet again readjust our spousal framework? I realize I have not once asked the question: Can I do the job?

I seek counsel from others. My rector says, "Oh, you'd be great. What an honor to be asked to serve." (My concern over all the ramifications of this decision hasn't allowed me to consider matters of honor.) Then he says, "You need to understand, Karen, that your gifts in administration and leadership are as strong—maybe stronger— than your gifts in writing." I ponder his words. This is a surprise to me. I mull over a phrase that a friend uses—

"unconscious competencies"—strengths we have that are so familiar we don't know we have them.

The first trustee meeting I oversee is our winter meeting in Jacksonville, Florida. The air conditioning is loud, the configuration of the tables makes the group dynamic awkward. Frankly, the comfort of our working relationship is slightly askew due to the oddity of a woman functioning in this capacity. As suspected, I am deficient in the areas where I expected deficiencies and strong in the areas where I analyzed strengths. In the middle of Friday night, I wake, my head awhirl with details. It is then I hear that firm, inward word, *Everything I have been doing in your life has been preparing you to do the work that I have for you to do this moment.*

I've led small groups, worship services, steered task forces, spoken in countless auditoriums to hundreds and thousands of people, designed meetings for consensus discussions, chaired advisory councils, but I've not moderated a business agenda of such complexity. Though I've briefed myself on parliamentary procedures, the rusty details groan and squeak. As I race to match our business to our timeframes, as I analyze where I need to further brief myself, as I decide whether the business discussion has been enough to be profitable, I hear: *There is an artistry in this as well, Karen. Here there is an artistry also.*

"Well," I say to Stephen Hayner as we evaluate my first board meeting. "It wasn't making beautiful music together. But for a premiere rehearsal with an audience in attendance, it wasn't bad."

He is kind, encouraging, insists that some music has indeed been orchestrated. And I am warmed by his faith in me.

Yes, I think, there is an artistry in working well together, an artistry in modeling Christ's true community—men and women functioning in tandem with mutual regard and trust. There is a profound artistry in respect given, in respect received. There is artistry indeed in all the wondrous resolutions of reconciliation.

176

Tibet
An Enduring Civilization

"Tibet is high and its land is pure.
   Its snowy mountains are the origin of all things,
   the source of countless rivers and streams.
   It is the centre of the land of the gods...."

Dunhuang manuscript,
Tibet, 8th century

CONTENTS

TIBET
A WOUNDED CIVILIZATION

Françoise Pommaret

DISCOVERIES®
HARRY N. ABRAMS, INC., PUBLISHERS

Wto 'all *tsampa*-eaters', so closely is this staple food of roast barley flour associated with the identity of Tibet. But this shorthand description gives little hint of the complex reality and land that lie behind it.

What do we mean when we talk about Tibet? The Tibet of Tibetans in exile? The Tibet of Tibetan culture? Tibet as a geographical entity? Or Tibet as defined by the People's Republic of China? In 1959, a call to resistance that appeared in *The Tibet Mirror* was addressed not to Tibetans, but to 'all *tsampa*-eaters', so closely is this staple food of roast barley flour associated with the identity of Tibet. But this shorthand description gives little hint of the complex reality and land that lie behind it.

CHAPTER 1

LAND AND IDENTITY

Multicoloured prayer flags and white scarves are everywhere in Tibet (opposite), streaming above mountain tops and holy sites. Tibet's conversion to Buddhism is represented in this drawing of a female demon (right), symbolizing the country, with temples placed on her heart and joints, pinning her to the ground and subduing her.

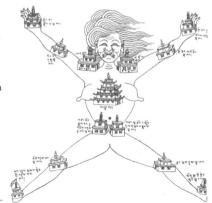

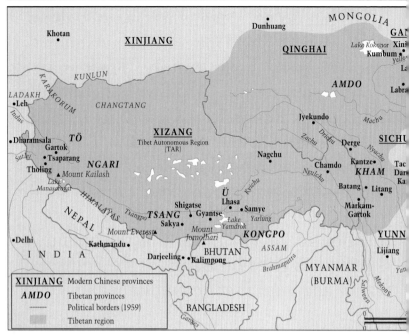

The regions of Tibet

The area called 'Tibet' is a shifting one, varying according to the standpoint taken – ethnic or cultural, historical or contemporary – which is why the few statistics that are available should be treated with caution. It would therefore be helpful at this point to specify the different accepted meanings of the term, and to define the one that will be used in this book.

The Tibetan sphere of influence covers an immense area, stretching from Ladakh in the west to Mongolia in the north and Nepal and Bhutan in the south. Some of these regions, though subject in varying degrees to Tibetan religious and cultural influences, no longer form part of Tibet. A few areas, such as Bhutan and Mongolia, have now gained their independence. In most cases, however, these regions now belong to other nations: Ladakh, Zanskar, Spiti, Lahaul, North Kinnaur, Sikkim and northern Arunachal Pradesh are all Indian; Mugu,

The map above shows the extent of the Tibetan cultural region presently occupied by China, giving the traditional Tibetan names of the provinces and the Chinese names. Tibet consists of a high plateau (at an altitude of about 4,000 m) criss-crossed and surrounded by mountain ranges (rising to 6,000 m). To the south and west lie the Himalayas, to the north the Kunlun, and to the east the Bayan Khara. Neighbouring countries are reached through gorges and mountain passes.

Dolpo, Manang, Yolmo/Helambu, Sherpa territory and northern Arun, meanwhile, are Nepalese.

Though smaller in area, the ethnic and cultural region of Tibet still covers some 3,800,000 km², or an area about the size of western Europe, containing a Tibetan population of just over six million. Making up one third of the surface area of modern-day China (9,600,000 km²), it represents a mere 0.46 per cent of its total population. Within this area, the great provinces of Amdo and Kham (in the north-east and east respectively), U-Tsang (in the centre) and Ngari (in the west) are subdivided into smaller regions, many with their own separate histories, such as Dagpo, Kongpo, Lhodrak, Powo, Derge, Nangchen, Gyalrong, Nyarong, Gyalthang, Trehor and Guge.

It is impossible to speak of the historic kingdom of Tibet in absolute terms, as its frontiers have shifted over the centuries. Stretching as far as Dunhuang on the Silk Road and northern Yunnan, it embraced Ladakh and parts of northern India and Nepal in the 8th century, but by the early 20th century reached its eastern limits at the Yangtse River. But a historic Tibet does not exist outside of specific timeframes. The Chinese language contains no word to designate ethnic Tibet, and similarly, Tibetan has no single term to cover the concept of 'Han China and Tibet'. The Chinese name for China, *Zhongguo* or 'land of the centre', does not include Tibet, and the Tibetans know China by the name of *Gyanak*, or 'black expanse'.

As far as the Tibetan government – in exile since 1959 – is concerned, the name Tibet indicates the whole of the ethnic and cultural region of Tibet, as designated by the term *Bod cholkha sum* –'Tibet of the three provinces': U-Tsang, Kham and Amdo. When using the name Tibet

Chortens (*stupa* in Sanskrit) dot the landscape, reliquary monuments which may be commemorative or protective: those pictured below are at the monastery of Maochok in Lhodrak, at 4,200 m. Varying slightly in shape from region to region, chortens symbolize the mind of the Buddha, and are of course sacred. Like prayer flags, they have come to symbolize an aspect of the Tibetan national identity. The relationship between this identity and

Buddhism is today ambiguous and complex. In the wake of the Chinese occupation and the exile of some of the population, Buddhism has become a manifestation of national feeling – not so much a religion, in the strict sense, as a political declaration and form of protest.

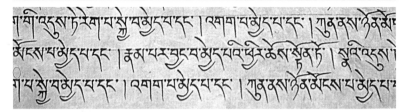

in its general ethnic and cultural sense, scholars and specialists often add the name of the Tibetan province in question, along with its present-day Chinese name.

In China today, the name for Tibet (*Xizang*, or 'western treasure house') is applied solely to the Tibetan Autonomous Region (TAR, created in 1965), with Lhasa as its capital. Its 1,200,000 km² extent covers the provinces of U-Tsang and Ngari, as well as western Kham, with its capital Chamdo. The dismemberment of the rest of Greater Tibet started in the early 18th century, with part of the province of Amdo. In the early 20th century, part of Kham became nominally a province called Xikang, which was abolished by the Communists in 1955. Today, the province of Amdo is divided between three Chinese provinces, Qinghai, Gansu and Sichuan, while Kham is split between Sichuan, Yunnan and the TAR. For the sake of convenience and unless otherwise stated, the name Tibet is used here in the sense of the ethnic and cultural region of Tibet.

The name of Tibet

As is so often the case, Tibet has been known by different names to different cultures. The Western name, Tibet, comes from the Arabic *Tübbet/Tubbat*, which itself derives from *Töpän/Töput*, the name used in the Turco-Mongolian dialect of the Tuyuhun peoples with whom the Arabs had established contacts.

Tibetan script (shown here in a Buddhist manuscript in 'printed' script, from Kachu in central Tibet) is derived from an Indian written language of the 7th century. It is a syllabary using thirty consonants and five vowels. Used for a monosyllabic language with intonations, it has become a complex script which can differentiate between words with similar pronunciations but different spellings. Certain consonants are combined to give different sounds, such as *zl*, pronounced *d*, and are placed as subscripts or before or after the stem consonant in order to differentiate between words. For example, *lha*, *la* and *bla* are all pronounced 'la', but mean 'god', 'pass' and 'soul' respectively. The script is read from left to right, and has no capitals, punctuation or paragraphs, and one word may be made up of two monosyllables. As well as 'printed' script there are also cursive scripts. Books are either written by hand or printed using carved wooden blocks.

The Chinese describe ancient Tibet as the *Tufan* or *Tubo* empire. The Tibetans themselves call their country *Bö* or *Bod*, a name which has two different meanings, according to the context in which it is used. Between Tibetans, it is generally used to indicate central Tibet, with the western provinces of Kham and Amdo known

Tibetan women are hardworking and tough. Even when herding, they continue to spin wool (below), and in legends the spindle is traditionally

by the separate name of *Dokham*. Yet this popular internal usage does not however mean that in a broader context the people of Kham and Amdo do not consider themselves as *Böpa*, or Tibetans. Thus in Amdo and Kham, the term *Gya Bö nyi*, or 'both China and Tibet', implies that both provinces form part of Bö, or Tibet. In relation to foreigners, and especially to the Chinese, all Tibetans consider themselves *Böpa*, or 'people of Bö'. Today the slogan *Bö gi rang-tsen* means 'Tibetan independence', Bö here signifying Tibet in the ethnic and cultural sense. Indeed, as early as the imperial era,

used as a female symbol. Traditional headdresses have disappeared in central Tibet, but are still seen in eastern Tibet, where they serve to identify families or tribal groups (opposite below). Beads of coral, amber and turquoise, which is associated with the soul, are prized by both men and women.

Bö was the name used to describe the country as a whole, as attested by the bilingual stele commemorating the treaty agreed between China and Tibet in 821–22, which stands in front of the Jokhang temple in Lhasa.

Geographical and ecological diversity

Most of Tibet consists of the bed of the sea of Tethys, which dried up 100 million years ago, leaving behind it the numerous saltwater lakes scattered across the country today. To the south, the Tibetan plateau is bordered by the sweeping curve of the Himalayas which, from the Karakoram to northern Burma, separates it from the Indian subcontinent. To the west, it abuts the junction of the Karakoram and Himalayas, while to the east it

Contrary to the popular image of Tibet as a barren plateau, the country contains many different landscapes, changing with altitude. The zone of human habitation rises from 2,800 to 5,300 m. South-eastern and eastern Tibet is characterized by deep, fertile valleys surrounded by mountains. The sloping roofs of the houses in these regions are an indication of the

rises into the mountains of the Amnye Machen, Bayan Khara, Mynak Konga and Minshan ranges. To the north and north-west, the plateau is cut off from Central Asia by the Kunlun Shan mountains and the Qaidam depression, while opening out into the plains of Amdo around Lake Kokonor. The plateau itself is crisscrossed by several mountain ranges rising to over 6,000 m, the largest of which are the Transhimalayas and the Nyanchen Thangla.

All the great rivers of Asia rise in Tibet, and have their own names in Tibetan: the Mekong, Yangtse, Yellow River, Irrawaddy, Salween and Brahmaputra (Tsangpo) all run through central Tibet, while the Indus and Sutlej cross mountain ranges through spectacular gorges before

high levels of rainfall (as in the Gyalrong region in eastern Tibet, above left). In the drier climate of central and western Tibet, the landscape is more austere, with bare mountains flanking broad valleys that are fertile only close to rivers and at altitudes below 4,200 m. Here, villages are often built on the fringes of high-altitude oases (above right), where barley and rape can be grown.

winding across the plains of India and China to flow into the China Sea, the Arabian Sea or the Indian Ocean.

Tibet is not, as is commonly believed, merely an arid, desolate plateau. In most of the country, the altitude at which its people live ranges from 3,100 to 5,000 m, it is true, and nights on the windswept plateau are cold, though the days are very sunny. The region of Changtang in the west and north-west is particularly inhospitable. But in the east and south-east, the monsoon rains manage to cross the barrier of the Himalayas and the eastern mountain ranges, and in the warmer and damper climate, both coniferous and deciduous forests thrive. The north-east is a region of immense pastures and rolling hills at an altitude of

Above 4,200 m is the domain of sheep, goats and yaks, which in summer climb with their shepherds and goatherds to pastures as high as 5,300 m, as at Markyang in the Nyemo region to the west of Lhasa (left). Above 5,300 m is a barren, rocky world where snow may fall throughout the year. Inhabited only by deer, snow leopards and birds of prey, this is the realm of the mountain

4,000 m. Barley is the most widespread crop, but wheat and rape are also grown, and the lowest-lying areas support orchards. As well as serving as beasts of burden, yaks are an indispensable source of both food and materials: even their dung is used as fuel for fires. In the west, wild goats graze the meagre pastures, while the hills of the north-east are the domain of wild sheep.

The origins of the Tibetan people

The Tibetans have a number of different creation myths. According to one of the earliest, dating back to a pre-Buddhist religion, the creator god sent his son to earth to create the human race. There he coupled with a female demon, and the offspring of their union gave rise to the

gods that reign over the wellbeing and prosperity of their territory in return for the respect and veneration shown to them by humans. Peaks above 6,000 m are permanently snow-covered in a mineral world of breathtaking monochrome beauty (right, looking south from Maochok to the 7,300-m peaks of the Tibet-Bhutan border).

six original Tibetan tribes. The most widely believed version, however, is a much more recent Buddhist myth, dating from the 12th century, in which the Tibetans were born of the union of the bodhisattva Avalokiteshvara and a female rock demon, so inheriting the compassion of their paternal ancestor and the ferocity of their maternal one.

But however interesting they may be, these myths cannot make up for the lack of precise scientific data which only genetic testing could yield. Even today, the origins of the Tibetan people remain largely unknown. Theories based on anthropological observations and archaeological discoveries tend to favour multiple origins, with a dominant substratum of Mongol blood.

The extensive racial intermixing and assimilation of foreign peoples (including Turco-Mongols such as the Sumpa and Tuyuhun, the Indo-Scythians, and later the Mongols of Zhang Zhung), which started in the time of the Tibetan empire in the 7th to 9th centuries and continued in later eras, is

evidence of racial diversity throughout history. The exception to this would seem to be eastern Tibet, where western and Chinese analysts today tend to believe the inhabitants are descended from the Qiang tribes. The existence of these Tibetan-Burmese peoples in northern China is documented as early as the Zhou period (1121–222 BC), and they later migrated to the region around Lake Kokonor and to present-day Sichuan, where some of their descendants may still be found. These people share the Tibetan belief of their descent from a monkey, and their use of a white sheep as a sacrificial animal.

While it is not possible to trace the precise origins of the inhabitants of Tibet, the layering of different peoples and the fluidity of their movements bear witness – despite the commonly held views to the contrary – to the accessibility of this region from earliest history. From the 7th century AD, Chinese chronicles refer to the existence of a people called the *Tufan*.

A shared sense of place?

What unites the Tibetan people is their shared culture, marks of identity which transcend differences of dialect and dress or traditional sources of dispute. Characteristic of the whole of Tibet, from the desolate western plateau to the forests of the east, these markers – despite local differences – are sufficiently distinctive to recognized as Tibetan.

What form do they take? First and foremost, they may be seen in the form of a physical stamp on the landscape, rendering it instantly identifiable as Tibetan: prayer scarves streaming in the wind, chortens dotting the roads, cairns marking the summits of mountain passes, and sanctuaries dedicated to local divinities clinging to rocky mountainsides or built against house walls. Houses and villages conform to a common model, based on a strong conception of the opposition of the lower valleys, as cultivated and civilized, and the upper valleys, as

The Tibetan national identity is rooted partly in myths and traditional ways of representing the world. Opposite, a modern painting depicts the three worlds over which three different types of deity reign: *lou* who rule the underworld, seas and lakes; *tsen*, the fierce warriors who rule over the earth; and the benign *lha* of the

celestial realm. Above, a Tibetan creation myth is illustrated in a painting from the Norbulingka Institute, Lhasa. In a cave near the town of Tsetang, a monkey, the spiritual emanation of Avalokiteshvara, and a female demon sit surrounded by their children, ancestors of the Tibetans, who derive their spirituality from their paternal forebear and their ferocity from their maternal one.

untamed or wild. The vocabulary of place is precise: *tö* indicates the uppermost part of a valley, while *me* denotes the lowest reaches. Terms used to denote space that is uninhabited and potentially dangerous all contain the word *ri*. Generally translated in the West simply as 'mountain', *ri*, carries much broader connotations in Tibetan culture. Thus *ri dag* means wild animals, *ri phag* a wild boar, and *ri ma* arid land, impossible to cultivate.

Although domestic architecture varies on the outside from region to region, according to environment and climate, the internal layout of houses remains fairly constant. The only rooms with a fixed use are the kitchen (the room in which daily life takes place), the storeroom, behind the kitchen to the north, and the family shrine. Always placed at the top of the building, this is also the room in which important guests are received. Livestock and grain stores are kept on the ground floor, while animal fodder is stored on the roof. The stove for ritual wood-burning may also be found on the roof, or in the courtyard, along with a shrine to the earth deity.

A collective memory

Tibetans share a communal heritage of myths, of fragments of their history and characters from it, and

Tibetan villages (above) consist of two self-contained worlds set one within the other: the houses cluster together (except in some regions of Kham) to form 'blocks', while at the same time remaining private entities within themselves. Typically, village houses have small windows in their external walls, with larger ones looking on to an internal courtyard which provides shelter from the wind, and where fodder and livestock can be accommodated. The walls are principally of cob or stone, with wood being limited chiefly to eastern Tibet, as in Derge (opposite, below).

even of spatial representations of their land. One of the most telling illustrations of this combines all these elements. A female demon, symbolizing Tibet in its primitive state and covering the land with her body, was vanquished by King Songsten Gampo (620–49). By the method of building Buddhist temples over her heart and along her limbs, he pinned her to the ground and so prevented her from doing harm. With its profound level of symbolism, this is one of the myths that is anchored most deeply in the Tibetans' collective memory. Another myth of great resonance is that of the reign of Gesar, King of Ling.

Because it has been handed down orally, this collective memory has naturally undergone changes over the centuries; but it is also known through written texts, transcribed in a common Tibetan language which has hardly altered since it first evolved in the 7th century. Embracing the entire region, this written lingua franca has encouraged the development and diffusion of a large body of literary, religious and historical texts. Not limited to the borders of Greater Tibet, it also includes the whole area of Tibetan culture. Hence from Amdo, in north-eastern Tibet, to Ladakh, over 3,000 km away in the far west, the same texts can be read and discussed, when at the same time linguistic differences render the different dialects mutually incomprehensible in conversation.

The Tibetan saying 'Every land has its own way of speaking, every lama has his own way of teaching' shows

The principal room, and the only one warmed by a hearth or stove, is the kitchen (below), where everyone has an allotted place according to their social rank and their place in the family. Those of the lowest social standing and distant relatives sit closest to the door. All visitors are offered tea made with salted butter. The walls are blackened by smoke as chimneys are traditionally unknown in Tibet; smoke invariably fills the room, although some escapes through a hole in the roof.

that the Tibetans are fully aware of their diversity but nevertheless feel that it is transcended by the markers of the common identity to which they all belong, to the extent of themselves adopting the epithet of 'red-faced *tsampa*-eaters'. The years of Chinese occupation have served only to deepen and sharpen this profound sense of national identity. Far from setting them in stone, the Tibetans are constantly adapting the basic elements of their cultural heritage, sometimes giving prominence to different aspects according to the requirements of the changing political or ideological context.

Shared beliefs

The shared beliefs of the Tibetans focus particularly on local divinities, including those of mountains and lakes, who ensure happiness in earthly life: these gods have their origins in pre-Buddhist beliefs. With their markedly anthropomorphic natures, the deities may be beneficent or wrathful according to the manner in which humans comport themselves in society and in their natural environment. Highly irascible, these gods are liable to vent their anger in the form of hailstorms or by causing the death of livestock, while at the same time squabbling jealously with each other over the occupancy of springs or other natural riches. Each has his or her favourite foods and chosen partner, and none of them shows any hesitation in being unfaithful or in forsaking their region for warmer climes in winter. They are worshipped in a fairly similar fashion throughout Tibet, with incense burning, offerings of food, alcohol or milk, modest propitiation ceremonies, and occasionally horse races and archery or shooting contests.

Buddhism is viewed by many, especially in the West, as one of the main components, if not the sole component, of the identity of Tibet. Certainly Buddhism is an important factor in Tibet, especially since so many

Mount Kailash (also called Gang Tise or Gang Rinpoche – 'precious mountain' in Tibetan) lies in western Tibet. Standing 6,638 m tall, it is believed to be the central pillar of the universe and the centre of the cosmic mandala. The Indus, Sutlej, Brahmaputra and Karnali rivers all have their source close to this peak, which dominates the Tibetan plateau. A pilgrimage around the mountain – home of Shiva or Chakrasamvara, and sacred to Buddhists, Bönpo, Hindus and Jains alike – is an act of purification. It generally takes three days, but the hardiest souls complete it in twenty hours, prostrating themselves as they go. The pilgrimage is punctuated by prayers and prostrations at sites of symbolic significance, and the journey through the Drolma pass, 5,650 m high, is viewed as a rebirth.

Buddhism, which became the state religion in the 8th century, has undergone changes over the centuries, assimilating native beliefs and evolving the distinctive philosophical and liturgical features that define it today. It is known by various names, including Tibetan Buddhism, *Vajrayana* (the 'diamond vehicle'), Tantric Buddhism and – particularly in the early 20th century – Lamaism. The Tibetan word *chö*, which originally meant 'religion' or 'system of beliefs', has become synonymous with Buddhism. The burning of branches of juniper or pine (*sang* in Tibetan) on mountain tops or rooftops, is a local purification ritual that has been assimilated by Buddhism (left).

●With this essence of the forests of the high mountains, sweet-smelling and duly prepared incense, let us purify the gods above, let us purify the *lou* spirits of the underworld, let us purify the *nyen* spirits of the space between, let us purify our homes, our clothes and our possessions.●

Sang ritual prayer

Buddhists in exile have found unity around the charismatic figure of the 14th Dalai Lama, but the ten per cent of the population who are not Buddhists but Bönpo are undeniably Tibetans, as are the few thousand Tibetan Muslims. Buddhism is fundamental to Tibetan society, but the identity of Tibet cannot be reduced to Buddhism alone.

For most Westerners, the name Tibet means Buddhism and lamas. This image, propagated by many books, is largely true but at the same time should be tempered with an understanding of the specific – and sometimes surprising – philosophical, symbolic and iconographic characteristics of this faith. A product of Tibetan culture, Tibetan Buddhism can be disconcerting both for 'rationalist' Westerners and followers of a 'simpler' form of Buddhism.

CHAPTER 2

RELIGIONS AND BELIEFS

Karma is the result of past actions, and leads to rebirth as illustrated by the great Wheel of Life (opposite). Ignorance, anger and desire are original poisons, symbolized in the centre of the wheel by three animals: the pig, the serpent and the cock. The poisons make human beings fall back into the cycle of incarnations – *samsara* – and hence into suffering. The ultimate goal of sentient beings is to leave the circle and attain Enlightenment. There are several different ways of doing this: to enter into holy orders, to go on a pilgrimage, or to meditate. One of the simplest is to turn the prayer wheel (left).

The pre-Buddhist belief system of ancient Tibet

The Tibet in which Buddhism arrived in the 7th century was by no means devoid of religious beliefs. Indeed, there existed a deeply rooted system of beliefs which

was partly assimilated and partly obliterated by Buddhism, with Buddhist missionaries even penning virtual manuals of conversion techniques, examples of which have been found in manuscripts discovered in the Dunhuang caves.

Our understanding of this religion, known as Bön, remains incomplete. Only a painstaking reading of the fragmentary Dunhuang manuscripts could produce a contemporary portrait of the period when this faith was dominant, the days of the Tibetan empire. Archaeological excavations are still too few, and the study of pre-Buddhist sites and monuments is far from systematic. All the same, it is now possible to discern the broad outlines of this ancient religion. The Bön universe was created by the pcha gods, who lived in the sky, imposed order and delegated powers to their representatives on earth. The

Ancient Tibetan beliefs were organized into a religious system that was probably named Bön, and the priests were named Bönpo. Many Westerners long regarded this faith as nothing but sorcery and witchcraft, but from the 1960s onwards, scholars began to reject this negative interpretation after studying the Dunhuang manuscripts. Above, a deity protecting a territory; on both pages, animals that ferry souls to the land of the dead.

earth was held in place by the mountains, which stretched out the sky like a tent. When humans died, they were guided by animals such as sheep, horses and yaks to the land of the dead. This consisted of a region of suffering and a region of happiness, where, surrounded by their possessions and food, the dead awaited resurrection in a new golden age.

Ages of prosperity and times of calamity followed one another, corresponding to periods when the faith was flourishing or was persecuted.

Priests, known as *bönpo* or *shen*, practised numerous rituals, including animal sacrifice, in order to appease a multitude of divinities who were very closely linked with nature. These gods might be benevolent or wrathful to humans, depending on the manner in which the latter comported themselves. The two most important categories of gods appear to have been mountain gods – the *kula* and the female *mamo* – who protected the lives and power of nobles and the king. Safeguarding stability and order, they brought good health and abundant harvests and livestock. When angered they would abandon the king, causing his death and endangering the stability of his kingdom and the prosperity of his subjects. Major rituals were therefore necessary to appease these life-supporting gods.

Royalty was sacred, as kings were descended from the first king of the creation myths, a *pcha* sky god, who chose to manifest himself on earth in Tibet because it was high and pure. Divination, using a variety of techniques, played an important practical role, dictating important decisions at both a state and domestic level. This highly anthropomorphic religion possessed a rich

The term Bön also refers to a religious school established in the 11th century in Zhang Zhung in western Tibet, and known as Yungdrung Bön. Its founding master was

Tönpa Shenrab, the equivalent of the Buddha Shakyamuni for the Buddhists, but to date there is no documentary evidence of his existence. The term *yungdrung* denotes

the swastika, a Bön symbol. Bön rituals and teachings have retained some elements of the pre-Buddhist faith, but the philosophy is close to that of the Buddhist Nyingmapa school. Above, Bön tantrists in Amdo, performing a ritual with little drums.

mythology which served to bring meaning to its rituals. These myths and rituals were both passed down in part to the Yungdrung Bön school of faith, which came into being from the 11th century.

The origins of Buddhism

Buddhism arrived in Tibet in the 7th century, simultaneously from China and from India, each of these sources offering a different approach to the attainment of Enlightenment. In the Chinese Ch'an doctrine (later Zen in Japan), or 'sudden way', mental or physical activity was an obstacle to Enlightenment, whereas in the Indian *Madhyamaka*, the 'Middle Way', Enlightenment was attained through virtuous actions and assiduous religious practice. According to Tibetan historiography, in the 8th century a great debate took place between these two schools at Samye Monastery. Whatever the form and the reality of this debate, controversy raged, with the Indian 'Middle Way' emerging triumphant, but incorporating elements of Tantrism.

Tantrism is a religious movement which plays a prominent part in both Hinduism and Buddhism. It lays stress on the practice of yoga, on secret teachings founded on texts known as Tantra, which can be understood only when explained by a master or guru, and finally – for its most advanced followers – on sexual symbolism. At this period, it was practised particularly in north-eastern India, Swat (present-day

In India, in 'Greater Vehicle' Buddhism (*Mahayana*) which was prevalent at the time, 'the way of the tantras' (*Tantrayana*) coexisted with 'the middle way' (*Madhyamaka*). The 'great fulfilled', such as Dombi Heruka, seen below with his consort (17th-century painting) were important in their role of passing on the tantra texts to the Tibetan people.

Pakistan) and Kashmir. It was from Swat that Padmasambhava emerged in the 8th century. This Tantric master, of whose life we know very little, was to become a religious hero throughout the Tibetan world, with a golden legend growing up around him from the 12th century.

The Tibetans view India as the cradle of their religion, with many of the faithful making the long journey to spend months or years at the feet of Indian masters in Indian monasteries (it is this aspect of Tibetan Buddhism, incidentally, which enables the Chinese government today to describe it as a 'foreign' religion, imported from abroad). This tradition was interrupted only in the early 13th century, when Muslim invaders destroyed monasteries throughout northern India.

Tibetan Buddhism

Buddhism gradually adapted itself to and imposed itself upon this substratum of an indigenous religion whose beliefs were impossible to reconcile with its own, which were based on non-creation, impermanence and karma, and the importance of actions. While it assimilated several elements, such as local divinities, Buddhism gradually abolished or adapted the more troublesome aspects, such as the myth of creation, animal sacrifices, the attainment of happiness after death, and the importance accorded to earthly life. This was nevertheless a slow process, which probably lasted from the 7th to the 10th century, and it was not accomplished without conflict. As late as the 10th century, for instance, the king of western Tibet, Yeshe Ö, criticized Buddhists who were continuing to practise animal sacrifice.

Padmasambhava – or Guru Rinpoche, 'the Precious Master' – is considered by the Nyingmapa school to be the second Buddha, and he is the subject of a 'golden legend'. This tantrist master, originally from Swat, introduced the use of the ritual dagger (*phurba*), and he is also credited with other teachings intended to subdue hostile spirits. There are many iconographic images of him that make references to his great deeds, either real or imagined; masked dances are also dedicated to him.

In the 8th and 9th centuries, during the period known as the 'first diffusion' or 'first propagation', encouraged by the kings Senaleg and Relpachen, Tibetan Buddhists accomplished an extraordinary feat in the field of vocabulary, either designating Buddhist meanings for terms used to refer to a different concept in the pre-Buddhist religion, or creating Tibetan neologisms as translations for Buddhist terms in Sanskrit. They also compiled the *Mahavyutpatti*, the great Sanskrit-Tibetan dictionary, and laid down the rules of translation in its introduction.

Schools of Tibetan Buddhism

Tibetan Buddhism is today divided into four great schools, some of which are further subdivided into separate smaller branches. The doctrinal differences between these schools are minor, and they all possess the same fundamental beliefs. They are differentiated, however, by the importance that they place on specific texts, and in particular by the way in which complex texts are interpreted through the oral teachings of a spiritual master.

Furthermore, only those who have received this oral interpretation, under certain specified conditions, can go on to transmit it to other disciples. The teacher, or lama, is therefore a supremely important figure, since religious schools grow up around the charismatic personality and

The text of the *Prajnaparamita* Sutra – Transcendental Wisdom – is one of the most important in Buddhism. Tibetan versions may be richly illuminated, like the manuscript below, which depicts Maitreya, the Buddha of the

teachings of an individual holy man.

The school of the Nyingmapa, or 'the Ancients', follows the teachings of Padmasambhava and shares the

future, and a bodhisattva, surrounded by monks (13th–14th century, western Tibet).

philosophy of *dzogchen*, or 'great perfection', with the Bön faith. This school, which is particularly influential in central and eastern Tibet, is subdivided into a number of different religious lineages – Kathok, Dzogchen, Jangter, Peling and Tersar – whose teachers have always maintained a spiritual interaction. The Nyingmapa school follows a large body of tantra texts, translated or developed during the first diffusion of Buddhism but not recognized as valid by the other schools. From the 10th century, by contrast, all schools accepted the tantras translated or transmitted by Tibetan masters including Rinchen Zangpo.

The school of the Kadampa, or 'those bound together by oral teachings', was the first to make its appearance during the second diffusion of Buddhism. Its founder was Dromtönpa, disciple of the Indian master Atisha (982–1054), who had been invited to Tibet by the king of western Tibet in order to spread the Buddhist religion. The emphasis in this school was placed on discipline and philosophy, with the teaching of esoteric tantras reserved for an elite few. With its principal monastery at Reting (founded 1073), the school was absorbed into the Gelugpa school in the 14th century.

The exceptional work above (tempera on canvas, 19th century) illustrates one of the most complex aspects of Tibetan Buddhism. It shows offerings being made in order to please the indigenous deity Begtse, who had become the protector of Buddhism and, in particular, of the Dalai Lamas. Begtse is depicted as a ferocious warrior, here surrounded by offerings of flayed men who represent the enemies of the faith. On the tables are ritual objects, such as sacrificial cakes that have been prepared for the god. Animals both real and mythical stand guard; some are also offerings themselves.

The Sakyapa school was founded in the 9th century by the master Brogmi, who had spent eight years in the monastery at Vikramashila in India. In 1073, his pupil Könchog Gyalpo, of the Khön tribe, founded a monastery at Sakya in the province of Tsang, which gave its name to the Sakyapa school. This school was distinguished by the fact that from the outset it was led by a hierarchy from two families of the Khön tribe, who took turns in assuming this responsibility.

The Kagyupa school, the school of 'oral transmission', considered Marpa (1012–99) and his disciple, the ascetic and poet Milarepa (1052–1135), as their founders. Marpa went to study in India under the masters Naropa and Maitripa, and the esoteric practices of *The Six Yogas of Naropa* and *The Great Seal* form part of the advanced teachings of this school. The Kagyupa are subdivided into numerous branches, some of which, such as the Phagmodrupa and the Tselpa, have now disappeared, along with their oral teachings. Those that are still in existence include the Karmapa, the first school to introduce – in the 13th century – the system of hierarchical succession through a line of incarnations; the Drungpa, very active today in Ladakh; and the Drukpa, present in Bhutan since the 17th century and so closely identified with the country that they have given it its indigenous name, *Druk Yul.*

The school of the Gelugpa, or 'the Virtuous', was founded in the 14th century by the reformist monk Tsongkhapa (1357–1419). Adopting the teachings of the earlier Kadampa school, it laid stress on monastic discipline, philosophy and debate, while reserving its tantras for an elite who were reaching the end of their studies. One of their basic texts was the *Lamrin,* composed by the lama Tsongkhapa. The descendants of this school

Different Buddhist schools may place greater emphasis on the practice of yoga, or meditation, or an intensive study of the tantras or of metaphysics. However, there is nothing to prevent a follower of any school from studying in a monastery or receiving instruction from teachers of other schools, following the example of the Dalai Lamas themselves. This desire to avoid compartmentalizing the schools is epitomized by the slogan 'eclectic, not sectarian', which spread from eastern Tibet during the 19th century.

Sakya Pandita (1182–1251; left) arrived in Mongolia in 1244, at the invitation of the prince Goden, one of Genghis Khan's grandsons. Famous for its scholars, the Sakyapa school became the first to achieve political dominance in Tibet (1260–1350) after the fall of the empire in 852. In the 13th century the Jonangpa school separated from the Sakyapa. Its doctrines were regarded as heretical, and it was outlawed by the 5th Dalai Lama in the 17th century.

Paintings and statues symbolize the body of the Buddha. Some paintings are all the more sacred because they bear the hand or footprints of the holy man represented or of another famous lama. A typical example is this thangka (a painting on rolled cloth: left), which features Dromtönpa (1005–64), the Kadampa master and disciple of Atisha, who can be seen at the top of the picture (17th century).

Milarepa (below, clay statue, 15th century), committed acts of violence early in his life, then repented, and became a great thinker. He is associated with many holy sites, and is traditionally represented as emaciated, with his hand to his ear, singing his mystic poems.

Earlier Western terminology divided the Buddhist schools into 'red hats' and 'yellow hats'. This originated from Chinese classifications that date from the Qing dynasty, but does not reflect any Tibetan classification, has no religious foundation, and is rejected by the Tibetans. Opposite, a lama from the Drukpa Kagyupa school, 19th-century painting; left, Tsongkhapa, founder of the Gelugpa school, and an incarnation of Manjushri with his attributes of a sword and a book. 15th century, White Temple, Tholing.

A monk's life is strictly regulated, and the rituals are an all-absorbing activity (see overleaf). The monks are seated in a precise hierarchical order, with the youngest being closest to the entrance. Some ceremonies begin in the half-light of dawn, with the temple illuminated only by butter lamps. The atmosphere is impressive, even to non-believers. Those officiating wear heavy coats to protect themselves against the cold, but they only put on their hats at specific moments during the ceremony, and in between they keep them on their shoulders.

– dalai lamas and panchen lamas – were to assume a historical role of great importance from the 17th century onwards: in 1642, the 5th Dalai Lama assumed political power in Tibet, and the Gelugpa became the dominant political power.

Monks, lamas and nuns

Contrary to the general assumption in the West, not all lamas are monks, and not all monks are lamas, or gurus. Indeed, the word *lama* does not mean 'monk' but rather 'spiritual teacher', the word for monk being *drapa*. A monk is a Buddhist holy man who has taken vows of celibacy. In Tibetan Buddhism, this vow is obligatory for those wishing to be monks. Monks follow an educational curriculum, but do not necessarily become lamas, or spiritual teachers capable of giving guidance to others.

Monks are under the authority of an abbot, or *khenpo*. They are nonetheless able to renounce their vows of celibacy at any time and return to their former lives. While the rest of society may regret this lost opportunity to progress towards Enlightenment, monks who decide to take this course are not ostracized. The worst sin would be to break one's vows by committing actions that are forbidden to a monk. Monks generally live in monasteries, where they are allotted tasks according to their intellectual, artistic or sometimes even administrative capabilities. Some pursue lengthy studies in philosophy, and after periods of meditation and

•Buddhist compassion has nothing to do with emotion. It is completely objective, cold, and linked to a metaphysical concept. It is not spontaneous, but the consequence of prolonged meditation.•
Jacques Bacot

The words of the Tibetan scholar Jacques Bacot are reflected by the man meditating in his cave (opposite, above). But compassion can also be attained through rituals, as practised by monks, nuns (opposite, below), and this tantrist (left), who is wearing bone ornaments.

learning from the teachings of masters, become lamas themselves.

A lama is a spiritual teacher, but not necessarily a monk; that is to say, he has not taken certain vows, in particular those of celibacy. If he is a monk, he wears a monk's robes, or a form of dress somewhere in between that of a monk and a lay person, and he does not shave his head. Among the Nyingmapa and the Bönpo, in particular, many lamas wear their hair long, tied back in either a bun or a braid. Other holy men, married or unmarried and frequently specializing in rites of exorcism, are known as *nagpa*, or 'tantrists'. Finally, ascetics (*drubthob* or *gomchen*) elect to live as hermits, devoting their lives to solitary meditation.

Nuns (*ani*) are less numerous than monks. The number of vows they take varies slightly between the different schools, but at around 360 is substantially higher than the 250 required of monks. At the same time, there is no tradition of fully ordained nuns in Tibet, and full ordination has only been possible since 1982. Living for the most part in separate monasteries from monks, nuns are nevertheless placed under the authority of a male spiritual teacher. There are also some women – usually the wives of spiritual teachers – who share the religious vocation but are not nuns.

Lines of reincarnation, the *tulku*

Religious life in Tibet is characterized by a great deal of flexibility between its different categories, and nothing prevents people from moving from one category to another, according to their aspirations. However, there is one religious class into which it is impossible to progress,

Incarnate lamas, or *tulku*, are unique to Tibetan Buddhism. At an early age they are recognized as reincarnations of their predecessors, then installed, and given the best possible education. Their aura reflects the prestige of their lineage, but they are always highly respected. In 1992, at the age of seven, the 17th Karmapa, Urgyen Trinley Dorje, arrived amid great ceremony at Tsurphu Monastery in central Tibet (above) from his home in Kham. Despite a show of Chinese 'benevolence', he fled to India in January 2000.

which is that of the incarnate lamas, who are known as the *tulku*, or 'emanated bodies', and who are addressed as *rinpoche*, or 'Precious One' – an honorary title also given to great religious figures who are not *tulku*. The state of reincarnation is one of the distinctive features of Tibetan Buddhism – a condition that Western society would equate with genetics; it is an integral and inalienable part of a child from birth. The child inherits the spiritual heritage which belonged to his predecessor in the line. He is therefore both himself and his predecessors at the same time, and so he bears the same name as them. A lineage of reincarnations begins when a guru declares that he will be born again in this world for the good of others.

Theologically justified by the theory of the Three Bodies of the Buddha, who can take on the form of an 'emanated body' (*tulku*) in our world, there is not in fact any historical mention of these incarnate lineages until the 13th century, when the Karmapa school was the first to introduce them. This form of succession for the hierarchs at the head of religious orders or monasteries gradually supplanted that of family succession, except among the

Once a *tulku* has been found by the entourage of his predecessor, he has to pass various selection tests, and finally must be recognized by a great lama. Nowadays it is usually the Dalai Lama who authenticates the child. Below, the Dalai Lama is placing a sash of benediction on the young Kalu Rinpoche, of the Kagyupa school. His predecessor, Kalu Rinpoche (1905–89), was a gifted teacher who helped to spread Tibetan Buddhism to the West.

Drukpa Kagyupa until the beginning of the 17th century, and the leaders of the Sakyapa school right up until the present day. Sometimes it even happened that the two methods coincided, and the reincarnated child proved also to be related to his predecessor.

When an incarnate lama dies, he is not regarded as dead but as 'absent'. When the child in whom he is reincarnated has been recognized, he is said to have returned. Recognition takes place after a complex process of prophecies, natural and supernatural signs, divinations, and a study of objects that had belonged to the previous incarnation. Sometimes there are several candidates, which can lead to religious and political problems. The child must ultimately be recognized formally by another great incarnate lama – often the Dalai Lama himself, now in exile – whereas in Chinese Tibet, it is the Chinese government that has now allocated this task to itself. Once the child has been recognized as the incarnation of his predecessor in the line, he is enthroned and takes the name of the lineage. Some of these *tulku* are also great spiritual teachers, or lamas, but except in the Gelugpa school, they are not obliged to take the vow of celibacy.

The pantheon

Whatever the religious school, Bönpo as well as Buddhist, the Tibetan pantheon contains an extraordinary and sometimes surprising profusion of deities of all kinds. These deities are personifications of philosophical symbols, and have no reality of

their own. The organization of this pantheon is complicated, and the deities take on different forms according to what aspects they are meant to symbolize. For ordinary Tibetans, however, they exist and can be approached by means of various rituals. Those deities that do not belong to the Buddhist religion but have been 'converted' into protectors of Buddhism are at the foot of the divine hierarchy, but they are still very important in daily life, because a family's prosperity may depend on them, in the form of good health, the harvest, and the cattle. The names and representations of these deities vary somewhat according to the different schools. They may be divided schematically into those of the

The bodhisattva of compassion, Avalokiteshvara, has several forms, one with eleven heads (opposite, 7th century). At the top of the hierarchy of deities are those that represent esoteric teachings. Above, the *Kalachakra*, the Wheel of Time, situated at the centre of a mandala. This diagram allows the initiated to become one with the divine.

The deities of esoteric cycles are complex and are often shown in sexual union with their consorts, symbolizing the union between compassion and wisdom which will eventually lead to Enlightenment. Opposite, Hevajra, deity of the tantra of the same name, and his consort, Nairatma, trampling the four illusions (Mara) underfoot (15th–16th century). The many hands carry attributes symbolizing their power. The necklaces of heads and the beings trampled underfoot are spirits or harmful desires that have been vanquished.

Iconographically and symbolically, the exact opposite of these tutelary deities is Tara (left, 16th century). Born from the tears shed by Avalokiteshvara out of pity for human beings, Tara is the female counterpart of this bodhisattva of compassion, and like him, she carries the attribute of the lotus, which stands for purity. She is an extremely popular deity, particularly among women. There are twenty-one forms of Tara, of which the best known are White Tara and Green Tara.

great tantric cycles, primordial Buddhas that may be peaceful or savage, Enlightened beings who are in the process of 'becoming Buddhas' (bodhisattvas), and also local deities.

Rituals and practices

Rituals (Tibetan: *choga, rimgro, to*; Sanskrit: *puja*) are a dominant feature of religious practice, and the Tibetans divide these into four categories: appeasement, development, submission, and destruction. Within this scheme, aims may range from pacifying or even exorcizing angry spirits to achieving long life, a safe journey, the prosperity of a region or country, a good harvest. There are also funeral rites and ceremonies commemorating important religious events.

The form that the ceremony takes will therefore depend on its type, its aim, the deity to which it is dedicated, and the religious school performing it. These rituals are often complex, and require elaborate preparations, such as ritual cakes (*torma*) and special offerings, a liturgy of song and recitation, different

The most popular daily practice is *sang*, or incense burning, a ritual of pre-Buddhist origin which pleases local deities and has a purifying effect. Prostration is also important as a mark of faith and of respect. The square in front of Jokhang Temple in Lhasa is the most sacred site for these activities (above). In the morning, bathed in fragrant smoke, hundreds of worshippers prostrate themselves full length, accumulating merits for their future life. At this altitude, physical exertion is a form of asceticism, especially when it is repeated dozens of times.

musical instruments and sometimes different music for the various parts of the same ceremony. They may be addressed to the Buddha, to Padmasambhava, to the deities of the pantheon, or to local gods. Those who perform the rituals will usually be members of the clergy, though not necessarily monks, or may simply be the head of a family if it is a matter of daily worship. Ceremonies may take place in a temple, a private chapel, or even a holy site in the open air if the deities addressed are not Buddhist.

The religious practices and fervour of the Tibetans are intense, and they are manifested daily in simple acts such as offerings of incense, butter lamps and bowls of water (symbolizing the senses), prayers, and circumambulation of holy sites. They are also manifested in local events: putting up prayer flags, pilgrimages, worship of relics, giving religious objects to the temples, participation in collective instruction, and building chortens. The aim of these practices, as far as lay people are concerned, is not so much to attain Enlightenment

Whether a ritual has been requested by a particular family, or

takes place as a celebration inside a temple, every one requires physical and spiritual preparation. In addition to the recitation or singing of particular texts, each ceremony has its own liturgy and music. The singing master conducts the songs and holds the cymbals, while other musicians play instruments, including the oboe (left). Among the ritual objects used are the *dorje* (Tibetan) or *vajra* (Sanskrit), meaning 'thunderbolt' (above), and the bell, symbolizing compassion and wisdom. Also important are sacrificial cakes made from grain.

as to accumulate merit, with a view to gaining a better incarnation in the next life that might take them closer to Enlightenment. It is generally believed that only holy men can hope for Enlightenment in this life, and even then, only those who have been given intensive tantric instruction.

'When you gallop on horseback across the plateau… do you not feel your heart swell with courage? According to the annals of the Tang, our ancestors… wore hats decorated with feathers and horns, and when they galloped away, they cried "Kihaha!" just as we do today,' exclaimed the poet Gedun Chöphel in 1950. While this enthusiasm enabled the Tibetans to build an empire, their conversion to Buddhism led to a symbiosis between state and religion that was to dominate the political scene until 1959.

CHAPTER 3

KINGS AND LAMAS: FROM EMPIRE TO THEOCRACY

The monuments of Lhasa, the Potala, the Jokhang and its monasteries are all illustrated in this 19th-century painting which is a condensed version of Tibetan history (left). It also features Samye Monastery, built by King Trisong Detsen (755–97?) (right, 15th-century statue in Gyantse).

An empire emerges from the high plateaux

Tibet arrived on the historical scene in the 7th century AD, and within a hundred years it ruled over a vast territory extending from north of the borders of Central Asia as far as China. Traces of settlements, in the form of stone tools, actually go back to the Paleolithic era, and remains of Neolithic settlements – cave paintings and carvings, pottery, burial sites – have been found all over the region. The 'Metal Age' covers a long period (from the 2nd millennium to the 6th century AD), and has left behind megaliths, tombs, and metal objects featuring animal motifs akin to the art of the steppes, though a lack of archaeological information makes them difficult to pinpoint. As for the social and political organization of the inhabitants during this early history, it is still unknown.

The chronology of the pre-monarchic period is equally vague. It might have been in the 6th century, or between the 2nd and 6th centuries, for Tibetan tradition speaks of a series of kings beginning in the 2nd or 3rd century, which would have been the Pugyal dynasty.

Society was probably divided into clans, ruled by

King Songtsen Gampo (above, portrait in the Potala) built the Tibetan empire in the 7th century through a series of rapid conquests. The story of this king, who was considered to be an incarnation of Avalokiteshvara, was retrospectively given a marked Buddhist slant by a text-treasure 'discovered' in the 12th century. 'Treasures' (*terma*) are texts or sacred objects said to have been concealed by Padmasambhava or his disciples so that they might be discovered at the right moment by a predestined master, the 'treasure finder' (*terton*).

independent lords and linked together by marriage. From that time onwards, Chinese annals recorded all information about Tibet as *Tufan*, and today they refer to the pre-monarchic and monarchic periods as *Tubo* or *Tufan*.

At the end of the 6th century, Namri Songtsen, one of the chiefs of the fertile valley of the Yarlung – a tributary of the Tsangpo (Brahmaputra) south-east of present-day Lhasa – began a campaign to unify the principalities of Central Tibet. His son Songtsen Gampo (*c.* 620–49) consolidated his father's achievements, set up his main residence in Lhasa, and from 640 made a series of bold, if not lasting, conquests: the valley of Kathmandu, west of Tibet, the annexation of Zhang Zhung which also encompassed western Nepal, south-eastern Tibet, and even the regions surrounding Lake Kokonor, which were inhabited by several different groups of Turco-Mongols. The king was required to take several wives, including a Nepalese princess and a Chinese princess, as a sign of these mighty political alliances.

Arising from the heart of Asia, the Tibetan empire spread and even took over the far western regions of Sichuan in Tang China. In 703 the Tibetan armies invaded Jan (part of what was to become Nanzhao) to the north-west of Yunnan, the land of horses and salt.

Advancing on China and Central Asia

For more than a century Tibet spread terror with its travelling armies, and carved out a place for itself on the map of Asia. This expansion brought Tibetans and Chinese head to head in a struggle for dominance over China's frontier lands, which included the oases of Central Asia and the turbulent region of Yunnan. Every year there was an exchange of tributes between these great neighbours – the

In order to consolidate his political alliances, King Songtsen Gampo married women from different countries. The most famous were Bhrikuti, a Nepalese princess (opposite below) and Wencheng, a Chinese princess (below; statues in the Potala). The founding of the temples of Jokhang and Ramoche are attributed respectively to these two princesses, and they are considered to have been emanations of Green Tara and White Tara.

kings of Kathmandu, the Palas of Bengal, and the Tang Dynasty.

The most significant expansion of the Tibetan empire took place in the 8th century, under a descendant of Songtsen Gampo, King Trisong Detsen (c. 755–97). He took advantage of a Tang empire weakened by the revolt of the Turco-Sogdian governor An Lushan and also by attacks from Arab-Turkish forces. The latter began their expansion into the Tarim oases after their victory over the Chinese in the Battle of Talas (now Kyrgyzstan) in 751. During the same period the Tibetans became allies of the kingdom of Nanzhao in Yunnan, and in 763, backed up by Uighur forces, they penetrated as far as the Chinese capital Chang'an (Xian), which they sacked before abandoning it. Peace was finally signed with China in 783, by which time the Tibetans controlled the oases of Central Asia, including Dunhuang. In 790 they reached the Amudarya river and the horse-rich region of Ferghana, which marked the furthest point of their

This modern map shows cultural and ethnic Tibet in the 7th and 8th centuries. The source material from this period includes the Dunhuang manuscripts which, despite their fragmentary state, are of incalculable historical and religious interest. The oasis of Dunhuang (opposite, a 9th-century drawing of the site) was strategically situated on the Silk Road, and was occupied during the 8th and 9th centuries by the Tibetans, who therefore came into contact with other Central Asian peoples.

expansion to the west, since they were held back by the forces of Harun al-Rashid, caliph of Baghdad.

A colossus with feet of clay…

The death of Trisong Detsen at the end of the 8th century sowed the seeds of the empire's disintegration. The Arabs formed an alliance with the Chinese, while the Uighurs – who were now at the height of their expansionist powers – continually harassed the oasis garrisons of the Tibetans in Central Asia. There were further futile skirmishes with China in the north-west until a new peace treaty was signed in 822–23. The text, which fixed the borders of the two empires, was written

W ritten in Chinese, Tibetan, Sanskrit and Uighur, the Dunhuang manuscripts were discovered *c.* 1900 – hidden in the walls of a cave in the oasis – by Wang, a Chinese Taoist monk. The scholars Aurel Stein in 1907, and Paul Pelliot in 1908, on archaeological expeditions to Central Asia, heard of this discovery, visited the cave, and both bought

in Chinese and Tibetan on three stone pillars: one in Chang'an, the second on the Tibetan-Chinese border, and the third in Lhasa. In 842 the Tibetan dynasty collapsed with the murder of King Lang Darma, which later Buddhist histories interpret as anti-Buddhist, though recently discovered documents suggest that this point of view may require some revision.

The fall of the Tibetan dynasty and the annihilation of the Uighur state by its old enemies from Kyrgyzstan,

a large number of the manuscripts from Wang. These have since been kept in the British Museum in London and the Bibliothèque Nationale in Paris, and are slowly being published. Microfilm copies have also been given to China.

resulted in further destabilization of this area of Central Asia. The Chinese renewed old alliances, and the Tibetans were driven out of the oases, including Dunhuang, Khotan and Hami. Tang China was, for the moment, the winner of the ultimate prize – control of the trade routes between China and Persia, and domination of the 'Barbarians from the West'.

By the sheer scale of its conquests, which brought with them a variety of peoples who could not be controlled, the Tibetan empire had proved to be a colossus with feet of clay. In fact ever since the time of King Songtsen Gampo, the various political marriages and changing regional alliances had been linked to a chain of brilliant conquests and swift losses, with the decline of the dynasty being exacerbated by religious conflict between Buddhism and the religion that had preceded it. It was a period of palace intrigues which involved a succession of plots and assassinations.

…but a cultural boom

Despite all of this, the dynastic era was also marked by a remarkable cultural and intellectual development. The Tibetans were influenced not only by the Chinese and Indian civilizations, but also by those of Zhang Zhung in western Tibet and the Greeks and Iranians. By merging these with their own indigenous traditions, they created the foundations of Tibetan culture as it is known today. They established a written language still in use, they translated canonical texts from Sanskrit into Tibetan, and Buddhism became the official state religion in the 8th century.

In the Tibetan view, 'three kings according to Buddhist law' (chögyel sum) played a major role: Songtsen Gampo, who is credited with the introduction of Buddhism, but who in fact maintained strong links with the pre-Buddhist religion; Trisong Detsen (755–97?), who built Samye, the first monastery, in 775 with the help of the Indian mystic Padmasambhava, and made Buddhism the state religion in 779; and Relpachen (815–38), along with his father, Senaleg (804?–15). The two latter kings

During the building of Samye Monastery, local deities were impeding the work. Trisong Detsen asked Padmasambhava to subjugate them, but when the two met, the king refused to bow to the guru who, with a gesture of authority, produced a jet of flame from his fingers… and the king prostrated himself (19th-century painting, Samye).

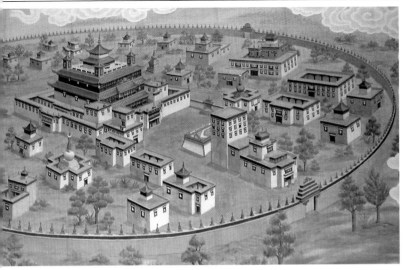

invited several spiritual teachers from India and Nepal – one result being a Buddhist Sanskrit-Tibetan dictionary still in use today, the *Mahavyutpatti* – and gave certain privileges to the clergy and the monasteries. This promotion of Buddhism annoyed the followers of the pre-Buddhist religion, who were present in large numbers in the court itself, and may have been at the root of Relpachen's assassination in 838 at the hands of his brother, Lang Darma, who was later depicted as a persecutor of the Buddhists. Lang Darma was in turn assassinated by a Buddhist monk in 842, and in little more than a hundred years, Tibet disappeared from the world stage.

After a century of obscurity, a Buddhist revival

Between 852 and 970 it is difficult to know what happened in Tibet, since no contemporary documents survive – not

Samye Monastery (modern painting, Tsetang) was built on the plan of the Odantapuri temple in India. It is a three-dimensional cosmic mandala, with the central tower representing the axis of the world – Mount Sumeru (or Meru) – the outbuildings being the continents, and the perimeter of chortens the wall of iron. The monastery was badly damaged during the Cultural Revolution, but has recently been restored; this stone pillar, dating from the 8th century (left), miraculously survived.

The inscribed edict established Buddhism as the state religion.

Tibetan monasteries were laid out in two different ways. The older ones, such as Samye (left, 19th-century painting) and Tholing (see overleaf) were built on flat terrain and often followed the mandala plan of Indian monasteries. From the 11th century onwards, however, they were constructed like fortified towns, with the buildings huddling below sheltered places on mountainsides, or even standing like true fortresses on rocky slopes. Whatever their layout, the buildings always served the same purposes: temples of different sizes, some with courtyards, a shrine to protective deities, cells or little houses for the monks, a kitchen, different storerooms, and toilets. Books were kept in the temples where teaching also took place, although some students went to the masters' homes. The monasteries were built of natural stone and wood which was sometimes transported over hundreds of miles. All the woodwork was first assembled on the ground (left).

even in Chinese. Buddhism was uprooted by the loss of its monastic communities and its royal patronage, but did survive in isolated pockets. The Buddhist revival sprang both from Amdo, in the east of Tibet, where some monks had taken refuge, and from the west, due to descendants of the scattered royal family who had established their own kingdom of Guge. It covered what was once Zhang Zhung, and was made up of the regions of Guge, Purang, Ladakh, Spiti and Kinnaur.

At the end of the 10th century, in order to re-establish Buddhism, the kings of western Tibet sent some young people to Kashmir and India, where they became translators. The most famous of these was Rinchen Zangpo (958–1055), who translated canonical texts, and revised the ancient tantras; he is credited with founding temples throughout the whole of western Tibet. Yeshe Ö, a Buddhist king of Guge, sponsored the building of monasteries – Tholing and Tabo – in 996. In 1042 his descendant Changchup Ö invited Atisha, a Bengali pandit and great Buddhist scholar, to take part in the Tibetan Buddhist renaissance. Atisha inspired a real revival both of the doctrines and of monastic life in Tibet, until his death in 1056. His disciples called themselves Kadampa – 'those who follow oral teachings'.

In the 10th and 11th centuries, western Tibet was a centre for the renaissance of Buddhism, and its proximity to India allowed the Tibetans to receive teachings from Indian masters. These included Rinchen Zangpo (above, painting from Alchi, Ladakh, *c.* 1200), who played a vital role in translating and disseminating Buddhist texts as well as the cult of the supreme Buddha; also Vairochana (below, painting from Tsaparang, 16th century), who is the principal figure in the tantra of that name. This text was immensely popular, in Japan too, as it brought together several other tantras.

The second diffusion of Buddhism: when faith met politics

During this time, monks who had taken monastic vows returned from eastern to Central Tibet, and set about establishing small communities. The whole land was a hive of spiritual and intellectual fervour. Many Tibetans went off to India, Nepal and Kashmir to seek out instruction, and this movement only ended with the Muslim invasions at the beginning of the 13th century.

This second wave of Buddhism is significant from both a spiritual and a political point of view. Given the importance of both teachers and oral teachings in tantric Buddhism, several charismatic figures emerged who gathered many disciples around them. These communities were supported by lay 'patron-donors', who helped them to build monasteries. Little by little, these monasteries grew to be centres of theology and literature, but also of economic power, thanks to gifts of land and cattle. Every school built monasteries affiliated to their main centre, and all tried to extend their religious influence as far as possible. Because of their prestige and the veneration in which they were held, monks began to play a larger role in negotiations between local lords.

In prehistoric times, western Tibet (Ngari) was the cradle of Zhang Zhung culture – of which hardly any trace now remains – and of the Bön religion; in the 10th century it was at the heart of the Buddhist renaissance, and until the 17th century it was the centre of the Guge kingdom, one of whose capitals was Tholing (below), situated in the magnificent Sutlej Canyon. Tholing was one of the first Tibetan monasteries (996) and like Samye, was built on a mandala plan. Despite the fact that it was a long way away from any centres of power, it was very badly damaged during the Cultural Revolution.

Unobtrusively, then, the Buddhist schools – already powerful forces in matters of religion and economics – became increasingly active politically, filling the power vacuum that had been left by the fall of the monarchy.

The Sakyapa and the Mongols

From the 13th to the beginning of the 17th century, the religious schools vied for political power, sometimes not directly in their own name, but through their alliances with powerful patron-donors, some of whom were not even Tibetan. The first school actually to assume political power, between 1260 and 1354, was that of the Sakyapa, who entered into a relationship of patronage with the Mongols. The armies of the latter launched many destructive raids against Central Tibet, but they received religious instruction from the lamas, spared Tibet, and actually became its protectors. Kublai Khan gave religious and political jurisdiction over the whole of Tibet to Phagpa, a Sakyapa lama, and when he became Emperor of China in 1260, the prestige of the Sakyapa grew still further. Succession from uncle to nephew within these religious schools ensured that the Sakya family held on to the reins of power. The influence of the Mongols was also a key factor in the complete reorganization of the Tibetan administrative system, titles, ranks, and costumes.

In the second half of the 14th century, the Sakyapa lost power to the Phagmodrupa, a branch of the Kagyupa whose most famous representative was Changchup Gyaltsen (1302–73), who severed all contact with the Mongol Yuan dynasty, and then with that of the Chinese Ming dynasty which succeeded it. He gained independence for Tibet, and established the administrative system of the *dzong* – or 'fortress-districts'.

The lama Sakya Pandita(1182–1251; 15th-century statue below), regarded as Tibet's greatest sage, was head of the Sakyapa school. In 1244 he was summoned to the region of Kokonor, where the Mongol prince Goden had set up camp and wished to receive instruction. Sakya Pandita remained at the prince's court until he died, and contributed greatly to the status of the Sakyapa from both a religious and a political point of view, because this was the beginning of their ascendancy in Central Tibet.

The Karmapa and the Gelugpa – rivals in the 15th and 16th centuries

Meanwhile, a new factor had emerged in Central Tibet, which was to transform the political and religious landscape. Tsongkhapa (1357–1419), a master from Amdo who had come to Central Tibet, attracted a number of disciples and lay patrons with his teachings. He preached a strict, reformed version of Buddhism, and his school took the name of Gelugpa, 'the Virtuous'. It revived the traditional teachings of the Kadampa, and was so successful that several large Gelugpa monasteries were founded in the Lhasa region, at Drepung, Sera and Ganden.

From the 12th century, first the Karmapa and then the Gelugpa broke with the system of hereditary power, and

Phagpa (1235–80), nephew of Sakya Pandita, accompanied his uncle to Kokonor. He was the first to enter into a formal relationship of patronage with a foreign leader, in this case the king of the Mongols, Kublai Khan (1215–94). The two men are shown in the painting above (Gyantse, 15th century), seated on a level with one another, to represent the equality of their relationship.

organized succession to the leadership of their school through lines of descent by reincarnation, the *tulku*. This system, which was later adopted by the other schools, brought about a profound political and religious change

The Kagyupa school split into several branches, of which today only the Drungpa, the Drukpa and the

in Tibet. In 1407, the 4th head of the Karmapa school and, some years later, the nephew of Tsongkhapa went to Beijing at the invitation of the Ming dynasty, but links between Tibetan Buddhism and China were not as close as they were during the Yuan period.

In 1434 the Phagmodrupa, who still had a degree of political control over Tibet, were challenged by the chiefs of Rinpung, an area north of Shigatse. There followed two centuries of sometimes insidious and sometimes open hostility between the two most important religious schools in Central Tibet at that time – the Karmapa and the Gelugpa – often brought about by the lay protectors to whom their fate was bound. The Karmapa were supported by the lords of Rinpung, while the Gelugpa were under the protection of the Phagmodrupa chiefs of the Lhasa region. The overthrow of the lords of Rinpung by one of their own feudal lords made no difference, as he installed himself at Shigatse, assuming the title 'King

Karmapa have survived. In the 15th and 16th centuries the Karmapa became rivals of the Gelugpa, who had established their main monasteries – including Drepung (above) – near Lhasa. Central Tibet was a battleground between these two schools until the Gelugpa emerged victorious in the early 17th century.

of Tsang', and his descendants continued to support the Karmapa. The Gelugpa found themselves in a difficult situation, because the Phagmodrupa were getting weaker and weaker.

The Mongols support the Gelugpa

In 1577 Sonam Gyatso, the 3rd Abbot of Drepung, was invited to Mongolia by Altan Khan, chief of the Mongol tribe of Tumed. He arrived there in 1578, and that is a highly significant date in the history of Tibet, for it marks the conversion of Altan Khan and his people to the Gelugpa school of Buddhism, as well as the conferment upon Sonam Gyatso of the Mongol title Dalai Lama. The Mongols became fervent and ferocious supporters of the Gelugpa, and the title of Dalai Lama was conferred

retrospectively on Sonam Gyatso's two predecessors on the throne of Drepung. After Sonam Gyatso's death in 1588, on his way back to Tibet, the 4th Dalai Lama (1589–1617) was chosen from among Altan Khan's close relations.

Although they now had the support of the Mongols, the Gelugpa were hardly in a position of any power in Central Tibet. It only needed the flimsiest of pretexts for hostilities to be resumed: an exchange of insults, failure

Scholarly debate (below) demanded knowledge of the texts, advanced logic, and great presence of mind. Noisily conducted by groups of monks, it took place in a monastery courtyard, sheltered from the wind. The questioner stood upright, facing his interlocutor, who was seated. Mime and gesture were important factors because he had to unsettle his adversary, and questions were not the only permitted means of doing so. The sound of prayer beads, hand claps, the thud of boots on the ground – these could all be used to break an opponent's concentration. This verbal jousting did not exist in the Kagyupa or Nyingmapa schools.

to show respect, destruction of property. In 1605 the King of Tsang and the Karmapa drove the Mongols out of the region of Lhasa, and for years tensions remained high, culminating in attacks on Gelugpa monasteries by Tsang troops in 1618.

Amid this political and religious turmoil, the recognition of the 5th Dalai Lama remained a closely guarded secret, because the Gelugpa feared for his life. Finally, after the Mongols attacked Tsang forces not far from Lhasa, the situation eased a little, and in 1622 the 5th Dalai Lama was publicly revealed and the child was enthroned at Drepung Monastery.

The rise of the Dalai Lamas, and 'The Great Fifth' (1617–82)

The 5th Dalai Lama is known by the Tibetans as 'The Great Fifth', because he gave Tibet a greatness and influence unequalled since the days of the empire. The incarnation of the bodhisattva Avalokiteshvara and of King Songtsen Gampo, it was he who consolidated the temporal supremacy of the line of Dalai Lamas and the Gelugpa school in Tibet. Linking back across the centuries to the imperial tradition, he moved his residence to the Potala in Lhasa, and made the city into a renowned capital. A scholar and a mystic, a remarkable politician, and a fine writer, he became one of the leading figures in Tibetan history.

In order to establish his power and to get rid of his enemies, the young Dalai Lama turned to the Mongol allies of the Gelugpa, and in particular to Gushri Khan, of the

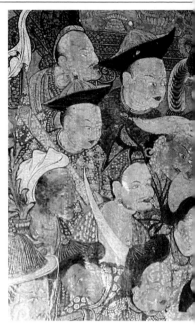

In Samye Monastery is a large 19th-century panel depicting donors from the different regions to which the influence of Tibetan Buddhism had spread (above). The Mongols and the Manchus are recognizable by their hats, while the people of the southern Himalayas wear turbans and elephant tusks; they are all keen to present their offerings to the 5th Dalai Lama and to receive his blessing (opposite). Two monks, at the foot of his throne, are trying to get them in line and re-establish ceremonial order.

Qoshot tribe. The latter launched his army first against eastern Tibet, and then against central Tibet, where he defeated the King of Tsang and the Karmapa. In 1642 a great ceremony was held in Shigatse, capital of Tsang, where the 5th Dalai Lama was invested by Gushri Khan with temporal power over the whole of Tibet, thus re-establishing the relationship of patronage that had begun in the 13th century with the Sakyapa lama Phagpa and Kublai Khan. The Manchu Qing dynasty thought that the 5th Dalai Lama would be able to control the wild Mongols, and invited him to Beijing in 1652–53.

The period from 1670 to 1685 was one of conquest: the Chumbi valley in the south of Tibet, some regions of Kham, and the western area of Tibet that had been under the control of Ladakh; only Bhutan succeeded in resisting this advance. These territorial conquests, which reunited Tibet for the first time since the empire, were naturally accompanied by the building of great Gelugpa monasteries. After the death in 1662 of his tutor, the

The greatest protector of the 5th Dalai Lama was the Mongol chief Gushri Khan (1582–1655; opposite below), who in 1642 masterminded the military and political victory of the 5th Dalai Lama's Gelugpa supporters over the King of Tsang, who supported the Karmapa. The 'Great Fifth', born into a noble family near Samye, was learned, pious and humorous. His political instinct made him leave Drepung Monastery and establish Lhasa as the political centre of Tibet, with the Potala Palace as his symbol.

Panchen Lama, the Dalai Lama introduced descent by reincarnation for the Panchen Lamas, who resided in Tashilunpo, near Shigatse. These two lines, however, were later to come into frequent political conflict.

This temporal power, gained with the support of the Mongol Qoshot tribe, was to have political consequences following the death in 1682 of the great statesman, whose life began and ended with a secret. Just as his accession had been kept hidden, his death was concealed by his regent, the *desi* (regent) Sangye Gyatso (1653–1705), a scholar of medicine and a statesman who, in order not to destabilize the political situation, preferred

not to announce the news. It was not made public until 1696, to the fury of the Qing dynasty, whose emissaries had been fobbed off in 1690, and the Mongols, who accused the regent of trying to keep power for himself.

Tashilunpo, the monastery of the Panchen Lamas, near Shigatse (drawing by Sven Hedin, 1907).

The latter was assassinated by Lhazang Khan, chief of the Qoshot, in 1705.

The 6th Dalai Lama ascended the throne at the age of 13. For a Gelugpa master, he was an eccentric character, and although his refusal to take all the monastic vows and his love of poetry and women endeared him to the people, it infuriated the Mongols and the Qing, who had already begun to lose confidence in the Tibetan regime.

The influence of the Qing dynasty – an 18th-century power struggle

The power vacuum, the absence of a strong and respected leader, and the turbulence of the Mongols all contributed to thirty years of trouble for Tibet, increasingly from the Qing. The 6th Dalai Lama was deposed, and died on his way into exile. Two Mongol groups took it in turn to occupy Central Tibet: the Qoshot, supported by the Qing Emperor Kangxi, and then the Dzungar in 1717; at first these were welcomed as liberators, but then they plundered and destroyed the monasteries that were not Gelugpa. The 7th Dalai Lama (1708–57), Kelsang Gyatso, who was born in Kham, was hidden from the Dzungar by his father and took refuge at Kumbum Monastery in Amdo, in north-eastern Tibet, where he was 'protected' by the Qing dynasty. The child was a political pawn, and in 1720 he was taken to Lhasa by a Manchu army which joined forces with the Tibetan troops under two generals and drove away the Dzungar. The Tibetans were therefore indebted to the Qing but did not realize the extent to which the country had now been placed under Qing influence.

The pro and anti-Qing struggle at the heart of collegial power intensified in Lhasa. The 7th Dalai Lama and his family were anti-Qing. The violent seizure of power by General Phola marked the beginnings of direct Chinese influence on the conduct of Tibetan affairs. The 7th Dalai Lama was banished to the extreme west of the country, parts of eastern Kham and Amdo passed into

Out of veneration for his master Lobsang Chögyen (1569–1662; opposite above, 18th-century painting) the 5th Dalai Lama established a lineage for the Panchen Lamas, who were considered to be the incarnation of the Buddha Amitabha (above, late 15th-century painting). Amithaba was the tutelary Buddha to Avalokiteshvara, of whom the Dalai Lamas are emanations. Lobsang Chögyen, who lived at Tashilunpo Monastery, was the first Panchen Lama, but the title was given retrospectively to his predecessors, and it was decreed that Kedrup Je (1385–1438) one of Tsongkhapa's disciples, was the first of the line. Tashilunpo Monastery, built in 1447, became the seat of this lineage during the 17th century.

the hands of the Qing, and small Chinese garrisons were set up in several regions, while two imperial Manchu commissioners, the *amban*, were posted to Lhasa and Shigatse. Titles and honours were granted to Tibetan nobles, and there was a huge increase in trade. The 'reign' of Phola (1728–47) was important because this was the first lay government that Tibet had had since the days of its empire. Phola, a statesman and diplomat, was able to stabilize the country, as the Manchus trusted him, and he succeeded in confining their interference in Tibetan affairs to a purely formal level.

When he died, power passed between the hands of the regents, Gelugpa followers, and for more than a century Tibetan politics took the form of intrigues among powerful ministers and the great families. Dalai Lamas succeeded one another without really assuming power, especially since the 8th had little interest in temporal affairs, and the 9th to the 12th all died young. The Panchen Lamas turned to the Qing. Because of quarrels over the minting of coins, the Tibetans were frequently attacked by Gurkha forces from Nepal, and needed the help of Manchu troops to repel them. As for the Manchus themselves, they were anxious to prevent the Tibetans from falling into the hands of the British or Russians, and so they supported the decision at the beginning of the 19th century to close Tibet to the West.

If Tibet was very much under the influence of the Manchus during the 18th century, this became weaker throughout the 19th century, the Qing dynasty having other more pressing priorities. Their garrisons were reduced to merely providing escorts, the *amban* regarded their posts as an exile, and relations between the Tibetans and the Manchus dwindled to an exchange of gifts and courtesies.

From the end of the 18th century relations between Tibet and Nepal deteriorated, giving rise to several armed expeditions. The Himalayas were not an impassable barrier, and the trade route through Kyirong also became an invasion route for the Gurkha army of Nepal, as happened in 1855 (below). On the pretext of trade violations by the Tibetans, the Gurkhas – led by the powerful minister Jung Bahadur Rana – occupied the frontier districts of southern Tibet; this invasion brought them into conflict with the Tibetan troops. A complex treaty of 1856 redefined relations between the two countries.

The 13th Dalai Lama, independence and the end of a world

The 13th Dalai Lama, Thubten Gyatso (1876–1933), having survived one assassination attempt, proved to be an outstanding politician at a time when the struggle between the great powers of Russia, Britain and China for supremacy in Central Asia was at its height. The British, who wanted to move into Tibet for commercial reasons, were met with a flat refusal by the Tibetan government. At the same time, rumours persisted of Russian influence over the 13th Dalai Lama – not to mention the possibility of an agreement between Russia and China on the subject of Tibet.

In 1904 the British launched a military expedition against Tibet and signed a trade agreement. The Dalai Lama fled to Mongolia. With the *amban* once more gaining authority in Lhasa, and the Tibetan government

The British East India Company saw it as a priority to establish trading relations with Tibet. In 1774 the emissary George Bogle (far left, in white) went to Shigatse and met Palden Yeshe, the 6th Panchen Lama. The meeting is immortalized in this painting (Tilly Kettle, Calcutta, 1775), which mixes the romantic style of the period with realistic details. Bogle got on well with the Tibetans, and even returned from his mission with a Tibetan wife.

incapable of action in the absence of the Dalai Lama, the latter then went to Beijing in 1908, where he met several diplomats, including the French, and reaffirmed Tibet's stance in relation to the Empress Cixi – the Chinese were once again patrons of Tibet, but nothing more.

From 1905 onwards, in the western regions of Tibet already under the Qing, there was a constant series of rebellions. An *amban* and some French missionaries deemed too close to the Chinese were killed. This revolt brought bloody retribution from the Manchu general Zhao Er Feng, 'the Butcher of Kham'. He imposed reforms based on the Chinese model, and created the province of Xikang in eastern Tibet, becoming its governor in 1908.

In 1909 the Dalai Lama returned to Lhasa after five years of exile, and immediately came into open conflict with the amban, Lian Yu, who called in reinforcements of 2,000 men from Sichuan. Parts of Lhasa were ransacked. The Dalai Lama sent emissaries to the great powers, but these were no longer interested in Tibet. He then went back into exile, this time to British India,

Having failed to achieve their commercial ends, and in the spy mania of the 'Great Game' that was poisoning the whole atmosphere of Central Asia, the British sent an expeditionary force to Tibet in 1904 (below, illustration from *Le Petit Journal*, February 1904). Under the command of Colonel Younghusband, it set out to force the Tibetans to establish relations with British India, and so counterbalance any possible Russian influence. After the massacre at Kuru, the British advanced as far as Lhasa, where they were met by some Tibetan officials.

where he was given a friendly welcome. Great Britain launched an official protest to the Qing court concerning its interference in the internal affairs of Tibet. The period between 1907 and 1911 is in fact the only one prior to modern times in which the Chinese used force to try and impose themselves on Central Tibet, and this attempt caused bitter resentment.

After the fall of the Qing dynasty in 1911, the 13th Dalai Lama officially broke off relations with China and announced that its protection was neither necessary nor desirable. The last Chinese soldiers were driven out of Tibet, and in 1912 the Dalai Lama returned to Lhasa. He was the first Dalai Lama after The Great Fifth to assume political power. In 1914 the British signed an agreement with the Tibetans, recognizing them as equals.

The Dalai Lama had to reach compromises with a powerful bureaucracy, the 20,000 monks from the great monasteries around Lhasa – some of whom hankered after the kind of sumptuous gifts they had received from the Manchu emperors – and the Panchen Lama, whose lineage had become a kind of state within a state. Misunderstandings led to the 9th Panchen Lama fleeing to China in 1923. Although there were a few Tibetans, like General Tsarong or the intellectual Gedun Chöphel,

The 13th Dalai Lama, Thubten Gyatso (1876–1933) was a skilled politician (above, in exile at Kalimpong, c. 1910), who devoted himself to the cause of Tibet, declaring its independence in 1912 after the fall of the Qing dynasty in China.

who recognized the need for modernization within Tibetan society, the forces of conservatism were too powerful and were too frightened of the potential damaging changes that might arise from contact with foreigners. Reforms of the army and police were suspended, and the British school, which had been opened in Gyantse in 1924, was closed after two years. The Dalai Lama gave way to the critics of modernization – even on a limited scale – and the chance of opening the country up was lost for ever.

The 13th Dalai Lama died in 1933. The Chinese sent a delegation to convey their condolences, and then reopened their mission. In 1936 a small British mission was opened in Lhasa, with the agreement of the Tibetan government, who were happy to welcome another power as a counterbalance to the Chinese – something which the Nepalese and Bhutanese representatives had never been during their two hundred years in Lhasa.

Furthermore, high society in Tibet was very interested in trading with British India, especially in products such as glass, arms and cotton fabrics. Some noblemen's children were sent to fashionable boarding schools in Darjeeling and Kalimpong, and in 1944 a school was

In 1922 – under the influence of the 13th Dalai Lama, some Tibetan officials and the British – Tibet experienced a very tentative form of modernization. The image above strikingly encapsulates the period. Seated are officials wearing brocaded costumes or Western uniforms, and General Tsarong Dazang Dadul (centre) wears a uniform with lanyards and polished boots, although his hairstyle is Tibetan. An ambitious man, who pursued a policy of openness and also modernized the army, he was dismissed from his posts as commander-in-chief and minister in 1925.

The Tsarongs were a powerful family in Central Tibet and along with the Pandatshangs, who came from eastern Tibet, they controlled part of the great caravan trade (below). This trade between India, Tibet and China required substantial capital, and also involved some risk because of bandits and bad weather. The caravans of yaks and mules were accompanied by armed guards. Cotton goods, tools, rifles and fancy goods came from India, and tea and silk from China, while Tibet exported wool, gold, and musk. The route ran from Central Tibet to Kalimpong in East

opened in Lhasa, but was rapidly forced to close owing to monastic opposition.

The 14th Dalai Lama, Tenzin Gyatso, was born in Amdo in 1935 and ceremonially enthroned in Lhasa in 1940. He was much too young to prevent internal politics from once more degenerating into quarrels between the regents. The country went through the Second World War in a state of blissful ignorance, and both the upper classes and the monks continued to live as if the world had not changed in the slightest, and as if the signs of impending disaster had nothing at all to do with the East. In 1947 the British left India, and in 1949 the Communists took power in China. This was to have dramatic consequences for the fate of Tibet.

India, near Bhutan, and was dominated by Mount Jomolhari (7320 m).

'What then is the formidable charm of this strange country, to which those who have once glimpsed it always return? To rediscover its mountains and its people, one must cross the ocean, traverse entire kingdoms, the whole of China… And one arrives in frozen deserts so high that they no longer seem to belong to the Earth… One sees houses like huge castles, all humming with prayers and smelling of rancid butter and incense. This land is Tibet… forbidden to foreigners, isolated from the world, and so close to the sky….'

Jacques Bacot, 1912

CHAPTER 4

THE QUEST OF THE WEST

In the 18th century, explorers painted watercolours (left, Samuel Davis, 1783). At the beginning of the 20th century, photography became the favoured medium. Opposite: Alexandra David-Néel with Khampa warriors (Kanze, 1924).

• For it is in this part of India that the sandy desert lies. Here, in this desert, there live amid the sand great ants, in size somewhat less than dogs, but bigger than foxes.... Those ants make their dwellings under ground, and like the Greek ants, which they very much resemble in shape, throw up sand–heaps as they burrow. Now the sand which they throw up is full of gold. The Indians... go into the desert to collect this sand.... When the Indians reach the place where the gold is, they fill their bags with the sand, and ride away at their best speed: the ants, however, scenting them, as the Persians say, rush forth in pursuit. •

Herodotus, *Histories*

Left, a 15th-century woodcut showing ants digging for gold.

At the beginning of the 20th century, this mythical land of which all Westerners dream was nothing but a large blank patch on the map of Asia. Furthermore, influenced by the rivalry between the three great powers of Russia, China and Britain, it was more than ever a forbidden and jealously guarded country. However, this was not always so, and over the centuries there have been many intrepid travellers who have experienced its mysteries. Missionaries, explorers, representatives from British India, spies and adventurers – all in their different ways told tales of a land and a city that was virtually 'inaccessible', where the grandeur of nature gave rise to such mystical exaltation that dream and reality became confused. There is probably no country in the world that has so excited the human imagination, which has spent hundreds of years trying to penetrate its mystery.

Herodotus was the first writer to allude to Tibet when he wrote of an area in the upper regions of the Indus where there were ants that dug for gold. Subsequently all accounts of Tibet mention the prospectors and gold

mines, thus nourishing the myth of a mysterious land full of hidden treasure.

The name 'Tibet' first appeared in Western literature in an account written by the Spanish explorer Benjamin de Tudela. He travelled to Central Asia in the 12th century, and reported 'that a few days' walk away from Samarkand extends the province of Tibet, whose forests provide shelter for the beast which produces musk.' His source is probably Arabic literature which, from the 7th century onwards, mentions Tibet (*Tubbat*) in association with musk – the substance produced by a gland in the male musk deer (*Moschus moschiferus*) and used by the Arabs since antiquity for making perfume. In around the 10th century, Arabic literature also includes the earliest references to a city named Lhasa.

The earliest travellers

The first wave of travel to Central Asia took place in the middle of the 13th century. In 1241 Europe was barely recovering from the terrors of the Mongol invasion, which had ended when the Mongols suddenly withdrew on the death of their khan Ogodei. The Pope and King Louis IX of France (later St Louis) decided to send emissaries to the great Khan of Mongolia in order to find out about

The first detailed, though not entirely accurate map of the Orient, commissioned in around 1290 by the Polo brothers while they were still in China. In 1380 the *Catalan Atlas* shows Asia from the Black Sea to the Pacific Ocean in four sections, and pinpoints the major cities of China. But it is on Fra Mauro's map of 1459 that there is the first clear mention of 'Tebet'. Fra Mauro, a Venetian, was influenced by the maps and accounts of the Polo brothers. The map depicts China in illustrations that are typical of the Middle Ages. North China with the Yellow River is situated at the bottom, while South China with the Yangtse is at the top. Tibet can be seen on the left of the map (left, detail from Fra Mauro's map, 1459). In the 17th century, Johann Grueber's map showed Tibet as the water tower of Asia, a geographical fact confirmed by explorers two hundred years later.

his future intentions. Jean du Plan Carpin, a Franciscan monk, arrived at the court of Khan Kuyuk in 1246. He returned from this mission and wrote *The History of the Mongols*, in which is to be found the first information on Tibet. He tells how 'the Mongol army reached the country of Burithabet, which it conquered by force; they are pagans who have an incredible and rather deplorable custom that if someone's father has paid his natural tribute to death, all the relations gather round to eat him: we were assured that this was so.' The origin of this rumour was the ritual of the sky burial, and for over two centuries travellers would continue to refer to this in their accounts.

In 1253 another emissary from King Louis, Guillaume de Rubrouk, arrived at the court of Khan Mangu. In his account of this journey, he gave a first impression of Tibetan Buddhism, quoting the famous mantra *om mani battam* (in fact: *Om mani padme hum*), and said that he even took part in a religious debate. He spoke of idolatrous monks who believe in the transmigration of the soul and in spirits, and also reported that there were cannibal men, the 'tebet', who drank from the skulls of their relatives.

Marco Polo was also interested in Tibetan customs. He arrived at the court of Kublai Khan in 1275, where he noted the presence of 'sorcerers' and Tibetan priests.

During his journey, he crossed the border regions of Tibet, which he said were inhabited by bands of ferocious bandits, filthy and idolatrous, but with some surprising customs.

For a long time the Franciscan missionary Odoric of Pordenone was considered to have been the first Westerner to reach Lhasa. He left Europe in 1318 and travelled to the kingdom of Riboth. 'In its white city, named Gota, no one dares to spill human blood, and yet

The compliance attributed to Tibetan women fired Marco Polo's imagination, even though he had never visited the country. 'The old women come with these virgins, their daughters or relatives, and present them to passing strangers....' The illustration (below, *The Travels of Marco Polo*, c. 1400) shows horsemen offering a ring to some young girls, and probably echoes the reference to the traveller who in the morning hands over 'a ring or a little trinket'. The many popular accounts of Marco Polo's travels had a major influence on the way in which Westerners imagined the East from the 15th century onwards.

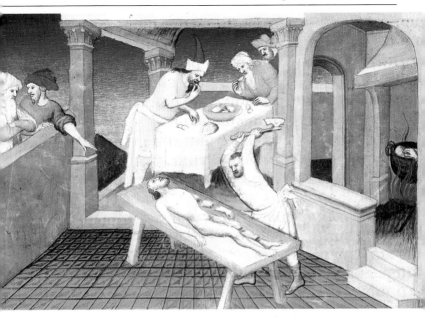

they practise sky burials and other abominable customs.' In fact, Odoric must have gone not to Lhasa but to Khotan, in Central Asia, and was simply repeating information he had been given by the local people.

During the 14th century, the Mongol empire lost its power. It no longer struck fear into the hearts of Europeans, who then stopped sending emissaries. At the same time, new and easier trade routes were opened, and so missionaries and traders ceased to venture forth into the countries of Central Asia. But through the accounts of those who had visited them, these lands remained cloaked in mystery and peopled by phantoms of the medieval imagination.

Missionaries on the roof of the world

At the end of the 16th century, the Society of Jesus, founded in 1534, established missions in India and China which very quickly began to look for lands to convert. Sure enough, they turned their attention to Tibet. Antonio de Andrade, a Portuguese Jesuit, is

The concept of the dismemberment of the dead shocked people from the West. It was described *c.* 1330 by Odoric of Pordenone, who could only have known about it through hearsay; '...they carry the dead body out into the fields, and right there on a table... the priests cut the body into pieces, and then the eagles and vultures come and they throw each one a piece....' (Above, from *The Travels of Marco Polo, c.* 1400; a similar illustration can be found in *The Travels of Sir John Mandeville*, from 1365.)

considered to be the first European to have truly reached
the heart of Tibet. He crossed the Himalayas from the
west and, although this was an extremely arduous route,
he entered the royal city of Tsaparang in 1624, where he
was received by the King of Guge. At the time, this
independent kingdom was just as important as Central
Tibet. In his account, Andrade says how moved he was
by the particularly warm welcome he was given by the
king, who expressed interest in his religion, and allowed
him to set up a mission and build a church. He also
found that there were a lot of similarities between the
two religions, but deplored the evident hostility of the
Buddhist clergy towards him. During his stay, he heard
tell of another region called Greater Tibet, or the
'Kingdom of Utsang', situated a month and a half's walk
away to the east. His advice was to try and approach it
from the southern side of the Himalayas, from the
direction of Bengal.

The country had become a theocracy in 1642, with
the 5th Dalai Lama at its head, and in 1661 the first two
Europeans to officially enter Lhasa were Father Johann

Grueber and Father Albert d'Orville. The former was
Austrian, the latter Belgian, and they were based in

Missionaries such as
Grueber, Desideri
and Andrade (above,
aged 54, portrait
painted in India, 1634)
provided the first
accounts of the country
and also of its 'king', in
fact the 5th Dalai Lama,
who had built the
Potala. Grueber took
back a sketch of it
(below left). His
descriptions of Lhasa,
which had recently
become the capital of
Tibet, were the first
eyewitness account,
and their publication
by Kirchner in 1677
created a great deal of
interest in this strange
country. Among the
illustrations is that of
'Two idols in the town
of Barantola' (opposite),
representing the
historical Buddha and
the eleven-headed
Avalokiteshvara, before
whom two Tibetans are
bowing in reverence.

China but had found it impossible to get back to Europe by ship. They therefore decided to go to India by crossing China. They reached Lhasa on 8 October 1661, and stayed there for over two months. Their notes and sketches were published in Latin in 1677 by Athanasius Kircher, and are especially notable for including the earliest references to the Dalai Lama and the Potala.

At the beginning of the 18th century both Jesuits and Capuchins, simultaneously and without prior knowledge of each other's intentions, set out to establish missions in Tibet: this subsequently led to a dispute over rights of anteriority. The Capuchins chose the more accessible and in fact the shorter route from the south of the Himalayas, whereas the Jesuits followed Antonio de Andrade's arduous route from the west, across the high Tibetan plateaux of Ladakh. Their journey to the 'third and great

Despite the efforts of these pioneering missionaries, the West still knew little about Tibet. In effect, the Christian church proved incapable of imposing itself on this part of the world, and so tried not to lose face: firstly, it sought to discredit Buddhist beliefs and practices, which it suddenly condemned as barbarous and primitive, although previously it had presented them as being similar to Christianity; secondly, it divulged only a tiny part of the accounts written by its missionaries. It must be said that the reports of these audacious travellers

Tibet' was gruelling and took them more than seven months. In 1716 the Capuchin father Orazio Della Penna and the Jesuit fathers Emmanuel Freyre and Ippolito Desideri all found themselves together in Lhasa. Even if they were not exactly enthusiastic over this forced cohabitation in the same city, Desideri and Della Penna soon came to have a great deal of respect for each other, and set about studying Tibetan together. Their aim was

were unanimous in their praise of the spirit of tolerance mixed with curiosity shown by the Tibetan clergy, who allowed them to live in their country and even establish missions there.

to convert people, not by ridiculing the Buddhist theories of the great lamas, but by refuting them. They were both admitted to Sera Monastery, near Lhasa.

Desideri left Tibet in 1721, and on his return to Rome he wrote an account of his travels which was not published until 1904, perhaps because the Church did not want to reveal too openly the tensions that existed between the Capuchins and the Jesuits. His book was ultimately to gain wide – though long delayed – recognition as a remarkable work by a scholar, geographer and explorer, and it made a major contribution to a better understanding of Tibet and of Lhasa. He described the workings of the government, and also the intense trading activity in Lhasa – a crossroads where all the arts and cultures of Asia came together. He was present during the Dzungar Mongol invasion of 1720, and witnessed the political changes that took place before and after the death of the 6th Dalai Lama. As for Della Penna, he spent sixteen years in Tibet. During this time the Manchus undermined the

Exaggerated images became popular in the West ('Burning of a lama's body', above, late 18th century), but some drawings were of genuine ethnographic interest (below, left and opposite).

monks' trust in all things Western, and the last missions soon closed.

Emissaries and adventurers

During the second half of the 18th century, missionaries were replaced by travellers whose main aim was to find new avenues for trade. The East India Company, particularly well situated in Bengal, was keen to open up new markets, but in order to do this, political intervention was sometimes necessary. In 1774 the Governor-General of India, Warren Hastings, decided to send a mission to Tibet in order to negotiate future Anglo-Tibetan relations. George Bogle, a young Scotsman, was ordered to go to Shigatse, rather than to Lhasa, because the young Dalai Lama was only fifteen, and so the real spiritual and political

In 1759, the *Alphabetum Tibetanum* was published in Rome by the Congregation of the Propagation of the Faith, which in 1703 had sent the Capuchins to evangelize Tibet. Largely based on letters written by the Capuchin Della Penna, this book contained remarkably accurate illustrations. The Tibetan liturgical objects were well reproduced, in particular the prayer wheels and flags that so intrigued the missionaries. In 1740

power lay with the 6th Panchen Lama – one of the most important in the lineage, who lived in Tashilunpo Monastery near Shigatse. At first Bogle was disappointed by the monotony of the landscape, but he gradually grew interested in the people. He became a personal friend of the Panchen Lama, studied the language and customs of the country, and married a Tibetan woman, but he was to die prematurely in 1781. Although his mission was not a commercial success, his own account of it– which was not published until a century later, in 1876 – contains valuable information about this period of Tibetan history.

In 1783, in recognition of the 4th Panchen Lama, Hastings sent a second mission led by Captain Samuel Turner. His account, published in 1800, was used as a reference work for more than a century, since it provided

Della Penna returned to Tibet, accompanied by Fra Cassiano da Macerata, who produced a journal with sketches of great historical and ethnographical interest (above, a procession of monks, Gyantse). The Capuchin mission to Tibet ended in 1741 through lack of financial support and because of the hostility of the Buddhist clergy towards the missionaries – in marked contrast to their attitudes of the previous century.

clear explanations of relations between Tashilunpo, Lhasa and the Manchu dynasty of the Qing.

A forbidden land

It was just as the colonial powers were building their empires that the Tibetan government decided in 1810 to close Tibet and Lhasa to all foreigners. The Tibetans were encouraged in this policy by the Manchus, who ruled China and who saw this as a means of protecting their own relations with Tibet against all foreign influence. Later the British took the same line, because among other things they wanted to establish trade relations with Tibet while also warding off any Russian interference. Thus it was that at the beginning of the 19th century Tibet became a forbidden land or, in the imagination of the West, a forbidden fruit that became more and more of a temptation.

In the course of this century, however, three travellers succeeded without too much difficulty in crossing Tibet and staying in the 'Forbidden City'. It may have been because he was a doctor that Thomas Manning was allowed to accompany a Chinese general whom he met in 1811 at the frontier. His true destination seems to have been China itself, for which he had a true passion, and his descriptions of Tibet and of Lhasa are rather negative: the climate was harsh, the country very dirty and completely under the control of the Chinese, who were extremely civilized compared to the Tibetans. Apart from the Potala palace, which was more impressive than he

Although eastern Tibet (Kham and Amdo) were relatively accessible – a lot of Westerners explored and stayed in the region during the 19th and early 20th centuries – Central Tibet became out of bounds. Nevertheless Fathers Huc and Gabet (opposite below, in Chinese dress, 1852)

reached Lhasa in 1846. Huc wrote of Lhasa, its monks and its mendicant pilgrims (above, painting by H. A. Oldfield, 1852).

had imagined, he was disappointed by the city itself: 'There is nothing striking, nothing pleasing in its appearance. The habitations are begrimed with smut and dirt. The avenues are full of dogs....' The journal of Manning, the first Englishman to reach Lhasa, was published in 1876.

In 1846, two French Lazarists, Father Evariste Huc and Father Joseph Gabet, reached Lhasa after a gruelling journey of nearly two years across China, the Gobi Desert, Mongolia and north-eastern Tibet. Their primary purpose was to convert the Mongols, but in the course of their work and through various chance meetings they began to grow attracted to the holy city. They took advantage of an unexpected meeting with the caravan of some emissaries from the Dalai Lama who were returning from the court at Beijing, and joined up with them. On 29 January 1846 they entered Lhasa. Although Huc and Gabet were both missionaries, they were also good observers. Their account of Tibetan culture is precise and invaluable. In particular, they lay emphasis on the bustle in the centre of Lhasa, and on the ethnic diversity to be found there. As the report continues, the two priests

In 1791 the Nepalese Gurkhas once more invaded Tibet and ransacked Tashilunpo Monastery in Shigatse (above, mausoleum at Tashilunpo, Samuel Davis, 1783). The Qing dynasty reacted sharply, and on the pretext of protecting Lhasa against the 'English expansionists' – whom they accused of being behind the invasion – they pushed for a total ban on Westerners in eastern Tibet.

Westerners found many different reasons for crossing the Tibetan borders. At the beginning of the 19th century, a Hungarian, Csoma de Körös, the first Tibetologist, spent some years studying Tibetan at Zanskar and Kinnaur in the Himalayas. In 1890 Henri d'Orléans and his companion Gabriel Bonvalot set out to contradict the rumours and prove that Huc and Gabet had truly reached Tibet; the two explorers ended their journey not far from Lhasa. Henri d'Orléans took back an extensive photographic record of Tibet. (Above, women with braided hair, Amdo, 1890).

make less and less effort to hide their aversion to the Chinese and their liking for the Mongols and the Tibetans who had made them very welcome. They never tried to conceal their own foreignness, and were finally expelled from Lhasa, taking more than three months to go back across eastern Tibet. As soon as it was published, their report was an outstanding success, and when, in 1890, French duke Henri d'Orléans set out for Asia, having decided to go to Tibet, he paid tribute to Father Huc: 'Always and everywhere we have been surprised by the accuracy of the French missionary's descriptions…'. It was, however, after these unwanted visits that the Manchus and Tibetans decided to completely exclude all foreigners.

'The Great Game'

The second half of the 19th century was an era of intense rivalry between Britain and Russia for control of Central Asia and Tibet. Of the Russians, the most resolute was Colonel Nikolai Prejevalsky of the Imperial Army, who led an expedition to northern Tibet in 1872. In 1879 he organized another expedition across Mongolia and northern Tibet in order to enter Lhasa, but he was stopped 250 km north of the capital. He died in 1883 on the shore of Lake Issyk Kul in the Tien Shan Mountains, once more on his way to Lhasa.

The British for their part mounted a campaign of 'clandestine cartography'. They employed some Indian agents, who set off for Tibet disguised as pilgrims, having first been taught to note down the topography. From 1865 to the end of the 1880s, these pandits – the most famous of whom were Nain Singh, Kishen Singh and the heroic Kintup – risked their lives to provide the British with a vast quantity of scientific information. The pandit Sarat Chandra Das, immortalized in Rudyard Kipling's *Kim* under the name of Mookerjee, was in Central Tibet from 1879 to 1881 and wrote a Tibetan-English dictionary which is still used as a reference book today.

Everyone with a spirit of adventure began to launch the craziest schemes in order to get themselves to Central Tibet and the Forbidden City. Most of them never got anywhere near, often being stopped at Nagchu, the gateway to Central Tibet 300 km north of Lhasa, either at the guard posts in eastern Tibet or by the British guards on the foothills of the Himalayas. Virtually all these expeditions ended in failure. This was certainly the case for the English missionary Annie Taylor, and for the Englishman Henry Savage

Born in Chittagong, India, Sarat Chandra Das (left, mounted on a yak, 1881) was both a scholar and a British spy in Tibet. The British were increasingly concerned about the supposed influence of the Russian empire on Tibet, especially when they heard in 1901 about the mission of Dordjieff (above), a Buddhist monk of Buryat origin, who acted as a go-between for Tsar Nicholas II and Lhasa, where he had been studying since 1880. Accused of being an *éminence grise* paid by the Russians to influence the 13th Dalai Lama, he was one of the reasons for the British expedition of 1904.

Landor, who was imprisoned in 1897 in southern Tibet. Two expeditions came to a tragic end in eastern Tibet: that of French explorer Dutreuil de Rhins in 1893, and that of the Dutch missionary Petrus Rijnhart, who was accompanied by his Canadian wife Susie and their baby son Charlie in 1898. Only his wife survived the adventure.

Worried by what they considered to be the empire-building ambitions of the Russians, the British launched an expedition to Tibet in 1904 under the leadership of Colonel Francis Younghusband. This led to the death of

An official from Lhasa (on the left) accompanied the Abbot of Tashilunpo to southern Tibet in order to negotiate with the Younghusband expedition, which was threatening Shigatse and Lhasa. A servant is standing behind the lama, next to a little altar on which there are ewers and sacrificial

a thousand Tibetans, and by the time the British army reached Lhasa, the 13th Dalai Lama had fled to Mongolia. Perceval Landon, the *Times* correspondent who accompanied the mission, observed Tibetan society and took home sketches and photographs. He wrote: 'I have said much in these volumes to the discredit of Lamaism, and I have said it with deliberation and conviction; but this panorama of Lhasa batters down

cakes. There are cups of tea on the low tables. Salted butter tea is a staple drink, and is ritually served and drunk; it is even given to enemies (photo Jean-Claude White, 1903).

helplessly the prejudices of a quieter hour. Lamaism may be an engine of oppression, but its victims do not protest.... To Lamaism alone we owe it that when at last the sight of the farthest goal of all travel burst upon our eyes, it was worthy, full worthy, of all the rumour and glamour and romance with which in the imaginings of man it has been invested for so many years.'

All these men who set out to conquer Tibet gradually found themselves being conquered by it, starting with Colonels Waddell and Younghusband, whose initial scepticism gave way to the same lyrical enthusiasm. L.A. Waddell, the expedition's head doctor and a devout Scottish Presbyterian, wrote; 'Wreathed in the romance of centuries, Lhasa, the secret citadel of the "undying" Grand Lama, has stood shrouded in impenetrable mystery on the Roof-of-the-World, alluring yet defying our most adventurous travellers to enter her closed gates.' Younghusband left Lhasa with thoughts that were to change his whole way of life: 'I was insensibly suffused with an almost intoxicating sense of elation and good-will.... Never again could I think evil, or ever again be at enmity with any man.'

In 1907, and then again in 1909–10, the French explorer Jacques Bacot crossed eastern Tibet, which at the time was ruled by the Manchus. He took an ethnological viewpoint, and his account bears witness to the disasters caused by the war between the Chinese and the Tibetans. The poet Victor Segalen, who was in China at the same time as his friend Bacot, experienced the fascination of Tibet in a mystical manner. He never succeeded in reaching Tibet itself, but wrote a whole collection of poems in its praise: 'Lha-sa, your roofs of

Camps punctuated the life of travellers in Tibet. Settlements were rare, and pack animals had to be fed. Water and, if possible, wood were necessities, as seen here in Kham (photo Jacques Bacot, Yarlung valley, 1909). On arrival at the camp, the mules and yaks were unsaddled, and a fire lit in order to prepare tea and food, provide warmth, and frighten away wild animals. All Westerners took their own food and personal effects with them. Some of them even travelled in style. At Christmas 1903 the members of the Younghusband expedition complained that their champagne was undrinkable at -40 degrees C.

'I rejoiced at the thought that I was the first European to wander in the solitude of those mountains, where the only tracks were those trodden by yaks, wild donkeys and antelopes….'
Those were the words of Sven Hedin (1865–1952), the famous Swedish explorer who crossed the whole of western Tibet between 1906 and 1909, and accomplished extraordinary feats of cartography and orography: he discovered and named the Transhimalayan range, the sources of the Indus, the Brahmaputra and the Sutlej, not far from the sacred Mount Kailash. An artist and a painter, he depicted in the brightest of colours the landscapes, villages, temples and people – such as the women from western Tibet with their festive headdresses (left), a monk pushing the door of a mausoleum in Tashilunpo (opposite, below), and the little monasteries near the Tsangpo river (opposite, above). Towards the end of his life, Hedin shocked his colleagues and compatriots with his Nazi sympathies, but nevertheless left behind some remarkable maps and books.

gold, o Lha-sa, and yet it is over, finished, it is ended, sung and played, too distant...too late, Lha-sa, I shall not go to Lha-sa!'

In 1924, at the age of 56, Alexandra David-Néel (opposite) reached

First White Woman to Enter For

Rare visits by Westerners

After the fall of the Manchu empire in 1911, the 13th Dalai Lama proclaimed the independence of Tibet in 1912 – a declaration that was not recognized by the government of republican China. The only Westerners who were legally allowed to travel to Central Tibet at the beginning of the century were British representatives posted at Sikkim. Of these, David MacDonald and Sir Charles Bell – the only foreigners allowed into Lhasa in 1921 – became acute observers of Tibetan culture, and it was their writings that at last rendered this culture

Lhasa after an exhausting journey over thousands of miles. Disguised as a beggar, she was the first European woman to enter Lhasa. She too succumbed to the charms of Tibet: 'I remain enchanted… I was on the edge of a mystery…Yes, I shall dream about it for a long time, all my life, and a bond will remain between me and this land of clouds and snows.'

accessible to Europeans. In 1927 it was a Frenchwoman, Alexandra David-Néel, who achieved a resounding success in Europe and the US with the publication of her book *My Journey to Lhasa*. She helped greatly to popularize an image of Tibet in the West that reached beyond the rather restricted circle of Orientalists and diplomats.

Other British representatives made brief visits to Tibet, but one of them, Hugh Richardson, stayed in Lhasa for eight years, from 1936 to 1940, and from 1946 to 1950. He was a fine photographer and an expert on Tibetan society and history, and on his retirement from diplomatic service he became an eminent Tibetologist and a fervent supporter of Tibetan independence. There were two other Britons who were employed as radio operators: Reg Fox, who arrived in Lhasa in 1937 and married a Tibetan girl, and Robert Ford. In 1950 the latter watched in despair as the Chinese army took Chamdo, a town in eastern Tibet that commands the route from eastern Tibet to Lhasa. He was taken prisoner and spent five years in Chinese gaols for espionage.

den City of Tibet

There were also some non-British Westerners who succeeded in climbing the bureaucratic fence and spent weeks or even months in Tibet. At the beginning of the 1930s the American naturalist Brooke Dolan went twice to eastern Tibet, accompanied by a young German zoologist, Ernst Schäffer. In 1938–39, Schäffer went to Central Tibet, this time with a team of scientists who were all members of the SS and were financed by Himmler. The latter was fascinated by Tibet, and wanted to prove that the land of Shambhala truly existed, and that Tibet was one of the cradles of mankind. The expedition returned with a film, photographs of 2,000

•The town is not very interesting. I've had my fill of visits to monasteries; I've seen so many! ...The palace of the Dalai Lama... has nothing very special about it [opposite, photo by Hugh Richardson]. In town, instead of exotic objects, the shopkeepers lay out piles of aluminium saucepans.•

Alexandra David-Néel, letter to her husband.

The Second World War brought the first official American mission to Tibet (left, the Tolstoy mission between the Upper Yangtse and the Upper Mekong, 1942). The Cuttings, rich financiers from New York, had links with the 13th and 14th Dalai Lamas, and had already visited Lhasa in 1935 and 1937. Since the beginning of the century, a handful of American missionaries had also been living in Amdo and Kham, in eastern Tibet, and had set up small schools and health centres.

Tibetans, the anthropometric measurements of 376 people, and some casts of Tibetan heads.

Brooke Dolan himself returned to Central Tibet from Sikkim in 1942, during the war. He was then a lieutenant in the OSS (precursor of the CIA), and was accompanied by a young OSS captain, Ilya Tolstoy, grandson of the great Russian novelist. This was the first American mission to Tibet. Their official task was to negotiate with the Tibetan government for permission to fly planes carrying war equipment through Tibetan airspace. In fact, however, they really wanted to know if they could construct a road across Tibet. The two officers spent several months in Lhasa, and finally left for China at the end of the winter of 1942–43, travelling via north-eastern Tibet.

The great Italian Tibetologist Giuseppe Tucci, accompanied by the photographer Petro Mele and the young Fosco Maraini, managed to make eight scientific expeditions to Tibet between 1933 and 1948, the year when he finally got to Lhasa with authorization from the Tibetan government. The Italians moved on to Tsaparang and Tholing in western Tibet, where they met the lama Anagarika Govinda – a Buddhist originally from Germany – and his wife Li Gotami, who had gone there in 1947–48. They all returned with invaluable photographic records of temples, paintings and statues that have since been destroyed.

The general public got a taste of everyday life in Lhasa in the middle of the 20th century through the adventures of two Austrian mountaineers, Heinrich Harrer and Peter Aufschnaiter. Having escaped from

a prison camp in India, they crossed the Himalayan barrier, and after wandering for months across the high plateaux, they reached Lhasa in 1946. The 14th and present Dalai Lama was then an adolescent who was extremely curious to know about the outside world, and the two men won his confidence. Harrer's book *Seven Years in Tibet* became an international bestseller during the 1950s, and was made into a successful film in 1994.

Tourists, students, the 'tolerant years'

After 1951 and the Chinese invasion, or 'peaceful liberation', the bamboo curtain fell over Tibet, which became more inaccessible than ever except for a few envoys from 'brother countries' whose tenets followed the Communist Party line. The Cultural Revolution increased this isolation, and the Red Guards caused destruction with impunity.

In 1981 the Tibet Autonomous Region (*Xizang* in Chinese) – founded in 1965 and incorporating

In summer 1939, at Kumbum Monastery in Amdo, a caravan (below) prepares to accompany the young 14th Dalai Lama to Lhasa. He recalls in his memoirs: 'The party was large. Not only did it consist of my parents and my brother...[but] a number of pilgrims came too. There were also several government officials in attendance, together with a great number of muleteers and scouts.... The journey to Lhasa took three months. I remember very little detail apart from a great sense of wonder at everything I saw.'

central and western Tibet – was opened up again under the iron rule of the Chinese, who realized that Tibet was a potential tourist attraction and as such, a potentially considerable source of income. Groups of tourists were encouraged to come, and countless individuals undertook the extremely arduous journey. A cautious form of liberalism began to emerge, through the efforts of Hu Yaobang (who was swiftly deposed by the Party) and the 10th Panchen Lama, who died in 1989. These were the so-called 'tolerant years'.

In the second half of the 19th century, Europe developed a passion for mysticism which crystallized around the name 'Tibet'. Theosophists, inspired by Helena Blavatsky and Georgei Gurdjieff, were convinced that the land was a source of mystical

Demonstrations for Tibetan independence took place in Lhasa in 1987, 1988, and 1989, and led to riots that were bloodily suppressed. Hu Jintao, then head of the Communist Party in Tibet, brought in martial law in 1989. Once again it became increasingly difficult to travel to Tibet except in supervised groups and at an exorbitant cost. Nevertheless, despite these hostile political conditions, Western tourists still flocked to Tibet, which then swiftly set up the infrastructures to accommodate them – including air links. In 2000, there were 132,000 foreign visitors to the country.

In the name of evangelism

Among these crowds of foreigners were new waves of missionaries, mainly evangelical. These groups, based in USA or Hong Kong, saw Tibet and Bhutan as the 'last

knowledge, and Walter Evans-Wentz, the first translator of the *Tibetan Book of the Dead* (1925), was a theosophist. James Hilton's novel *Lost Horizon* (1933), which Frank Capra filmed in 1937 (film poster above), was influenced by these ideas, and describes a paradisal land called Shangri-La, hidden in the heart of the Himalayas. In modern times, the Chinese have given the name Shangri-La to a valley in eastern Tibet.

frontier', the last bastion against Christianity. Even though at the end of the 19th and beginning of the 20th centuries there had been Catholic and Protestant missionaries in eastern Tibet, as well as priests from foreign missions on the borders of Tibet and Yunnan, the number of Tibetan converts was negligible. In 1986 the Chinese government began to recruit English teachers, which presented the missionaries with a golden opportunity, and a large number of so-called 'teachers' duly arrived with Bibles in their bags. Similarly, during the mid-1990s the University of Tibet offered courses in Tibetan to foreigners, and some of the American and Korean students were also missionaries. China turned a blind eye to their activities, because the government tended to take a positive view of anything that might remove the Tibetans from Buddhist influence, but the Tibetan people themselves seemed to have little desire to be converted.

Conversely, the West developed a passion for Tibetan Buddhism – as propagated by the spiritual teachers who went into exile during the 1950s – and interest in Tibetan culture increased, especially through the charismatic figure of the 14th Dalai Lama, who won the Nobel Peace Prize in 1989. The 'fashion' for Tibet was spread by the media, film stars and publicity, and the New Age movement adopted some of the values of Tibetan Buddhism. But historical and political realities were eclipsed by these religious trends and by international commerce. Once more, as at the time of Herodotus, the West only saw that part of Tibet which nourished its fantasies of the moment; Tibet remained a prisoner of the image of Shangri-La, the paradisal valley invented in 1933 by James Hilton in his novel *Lost Horizon*.

Countless artists have been fascinated by Tibet and its myths. The films *Seven Years in Tibet* (1994) and *Kundun* (1997) were seen by huge audiences. The comic book *Tintin in Tibet* (1960) is one of the most popular in the Tintin series, and is fairly well researched, although it does reuse some of the old clichés like the levitating monk shown here. Its Chinese edition, under the title *Tintin in Chinese Tibet* (2001), was at first withdrawn from sale, but has recently been

reissued under its original title.

'We must be ready to defend ourselves. Otherwise our spiritual and cultural traditions will be completely eradicated. Even the names of the Dalai and Panchen Lamas will be erased.... The monasteries will be looted and destroyed, and the monks and nuns killed or chased away.... The birthrights and property of the people will be stolen. We will become like slaves to our conquerors, and will be made to wander helplessly like beggars. Everyone will be forced to live in misery, and the days and nights will pass slowly, and with great suffering and terror.'

Testament of the 13th Dalai Lama, 1931

CHAPTER 5

INVASION AND COLONIZATION: TIBET TODAY

Soldiers and the Chinese flag in front of the Potala Palace (opposite); statues destroyed by the Chinese (right): the words of the 13th Dalai Lama ring out like a prophecy.

In 1947 the Tibetan government sent a trade mission to the West. The Americans and the British stamped the Tibetan passports with visas, and thereby recognized the independence of Tibet. In July 1949, with a Communist seizure of power imminent in China, the Tibetan government expelled all Chinese, including traders. But the new Chinese government saw Tibet as an integral part of their country, and Chinese radio announced that Tibet must be 'liberated from the British imperialist yoke'. Isolated by its own foreign policy during the last two hundred years, Tibet received no support from the West – not even from Great Britain. Furthermore, the USSR took China's side, and India recognized China's suzerainty over Tibet.

The 'liberation' of Tibet

This sad period forces us to believe that the Dalai Lama and the Panchen Lama – two adolescents who knew nothing of the modern world and its politics – were manipulated by their respective entourages, whose primary concerns were to protect their own status. Indeed, the very young Panchen Lama (born in Qinghai

In October 1951, thousands of soldiers of the People's Liberation Army marched into Lhasa from Sichuan and Qinghai. They had come 3000 km through this inhospitable land, galvanized by Mao, with orders to 'peacefully' liberate the country from the 'imperialist yoke' and its people from slavery, so that they could be reunited with the 'mother country'. The problem of the Chinese in Lhasa was not the resistance of the Tibetans, but logistics: how were thousands of soldiers to be fed and housed? But the soldiers themselves were disciplined and earned the admiration of the local people.

in 1938), or rather his advisers, did believe at the time that the Dalai Lama and his court at Lhasa could benefit from the situation, and it was they who sent a message to China asking them to send in the People's Liberation Army (PLA).

On 1 January 1950, Radio Beijing announced that Tibet was about to be liberated. Finally in Lhasa fear began to mount, but even then the danger had been underestimated. The troops were reinforced on the eastern frontiers of Tibet, and the Chinese invaded the whole of Kham, reaching the Yangtse river. The Tibetan government was incapable of responding, due to a lack of trained soldiers and a pro- and anti-Chinese split within the monastic and aristocratic hierarchy. On 7 October 1950, 40,000 Chinese soldiers, on orders from Deng Xiaoping, political commissioner for the army at Sichuan, crossed the river. Under the command of Ngapo Ngawang Jigme they took Chamdo, the great city of the east, on 17 October after three weeks of fighting. Eight thousand Tibetan soldiers were killed. The route to Central Tibet was now open. Of course India protested, but the West abandoned Tibet to its fate, being more concerned about the situation in Korea. El Salvador took Tibet's case to the UN in November 1950, but without success. Tibet was regarded as an internal affair of China – a refrain that has been repeated many times over the last fifty years.

Propaganda photos from 1950–51 show Tibetans giving an enthusiastic welcome to the Chinese army. Here in Kangting (Dartsendo/ Tachienlu) in Kham, a delegation of women carrying flowers and banners greet the Liberation Army. In order to win the people over, the soldiers were given strict orders: not to occupy houses without permission from the inhabitants; not to kill birds or fish; to respect customs and all sacred objects; not to allow any female staff to enter the monasteries. This public relations exercise also extended to the nobles and the clergy. Mao's orders were to 'make every possible effort by all appropriate means to win over the Dalai Lama and the majority of the upper classes, and to isolate the minority of bad elements in order to achieve the long-term objective of transforming the economy and politics of Tibet gradually and without bloodshed.'

During this time the Dalai Lama, at the age of fifteen, was enthroned in Lhasa as head of state. Ngapo, now vice-President of the Committee of Liberation, called on the Tibetan government to negotiate with China. This was a parody of compromise. It was impossible for the Tibetans to oppose the Liberation Army, and the Chinese only wanted to negotiate in order to justify themselves to the Tibetans and to the international community. A high-level Tibetan delegation, led by Ngapo, was sent to Beijing in April 1951. The text of the agreement was already fixed; no negotiation was possible. After some equivocation, the Tibetan delegation unwillingly signed the '17-Point Agreement' on 23 May 1951, handing Tibet over to the Chinese. The 1st article stated that the Tibetan people would return to the family of the mother country, the People's Republic of China. It was a clear but contradictory statement: clear because it announced that Tibet was now a province of China; contradictory because it implied that Tibet was not in fact part of China.

Chinese policy in action

In autumn 1951 the Liberation Army reached Central Tibet, approaching simultaneously from the east and the

Mao invited the 10th Panchen Lama (on his right) and the 14th Dalai Lama (on his left) to make an official visit to China, and he received them in Beijing in 1954 (above). The young Dalai Lama was at first charmed by Mao's conciliatory words and apparent interest in Tibet. He remarked how kind Mao had been, and formed a genuine respect for him. On the occasion of their final meeting, however, Mao dropped his mask and said that although he understood the Dalai Lama's point of view, he regarded religion as a poison. It has, he said, two faults: it destroys a race, and it slows down a country's progress.

north-west: 'On 26 October the People's Army of Liberation marched into the interior of Tibet, and the Tibetan people were liberated from imperialist aggression and returned to the great family of the People's Republic of China' (Xinhua, the Chinese news agency). When the Liberation Army reached Lhasa, it marched in orderly fashion, with red flags and portraits of Mao, parading before an anxious and bewildered people that had little knowledge of what was going on. Within a few months, 20,000 Chinese soldiers were stationed in Lhasa – half the city's population at the time.

For some years the Chinese behaved themselves, and gave gifts to the nobles, many of whom came over onto their side. Schools and hospitals were provided. At the same time army garrisons were set up all over Tibet, virtually locking it in. Roads linking Tibet to China, finished in 1954, facilitated the transport of troops.

Also in 1954, the Dalai Lama and Panchen Lama were invited to Beijing, where they were received with great ceremony by Zhou Enlai and Mao Zedong. The teenage Dalai Lama was quite charmed by Mao, who made soothing comments about religion, right up until their last meeting, when Mao told him that in fact religion was a poison. On his return journey in 1955, the Dalai Lama could see only too well the hold that the Chinese had on his native province, Amdo. Away from Lhasa, the Communist reforms were well and truly underway. The monasteries had gradually been stripped, and the Tibetans slowly realized that they had no say in their own affairs.

In 1956 the 'Preparatory Commission for the Autonomous Region of Tibet' was created, with General Ngapo as its

Mao's cult of personality reached Tibet and was adapted to local customs. Below, an East Tibetan monk places Mao between two great lamas of the Gelugpa school in a model of the Forbidden City's temple, with Chinese flags flying from the top.

secretary, and this culminated in the creation of the Tibet Autonomous Region in September 1965. The Dalai Lama was its president, but he was only a puppet. Power now lay exclusively with the Committee of the Communist Party.

Rebellion and the flight of the Dalai Lama

Infuriated by the Chinese reforms, attacks on their religion, and the fact that they were even forced to feed the occupying armies, the Tibetans of Amdo and Kham rebelled in 1955. These people, often divided in the past, now united against the invader. Even monks took up arms. There was now a bloody guerrilla war with the Chinese. At

this point the US, furious with the Chinese for their role in Korea, began to take a new interest in Tibet. The CIA ran secret training courses in the US and delivered arms and radio equipment to the guerrillas in the east. This operation did not officially end until 1971, when Henry Kissinger went to Beijing to try and normalize relations between China and the US.

In 1956 Beijing sent 150,000 men to Kham, supported by air raids. Tibetan resistance was shattered by these 'balls of fire' falling from the sky, and the

The Tibetan flag became a symbol of resistance and of a free Tibet (top). The monks were also involved in resistance. They were forced to surrender their weapons after the 1959 rebellion in Lhasa. (The photo above is probably a reconstruction.)

Chinese army regained control of Kham in a bloodbath. Reprisals, particularly against the clergy, were horrific, and whole villages were razed.

No Tibetan in Lhasa would or could grasp the situation. Neither did news travel abroad. Chinese propaganda claimed that the Dalai Lama had been authorized to go to India to celebrate the 2,500th anniversary of the birth of the Buddha. Nehru met him but could give him no hope or support other than to advise him to cooperate with the Chinese. The Dalai Lama returned to Lhasa when rumours of a general uprising in Central Tibet began to grow. In 1958 tensions became even greater when thousands of East Tibetans arrived in Lhasa with news of more disasters.

No photos of the Lhasa rebellion are available. For one thing, no foreign journalists were present; the Chinese did not want to show the Tibetan people in revolt at a time when they were supposed to be grateful for their 'liberation'. However, there are some rare photos of the surrender, for these prove that the 'dangerous element of the feudal society' were defeated. Against the

On 10 March 1959 the crisis was heightened when the Chinese authorities issued an unusual invitation to the Dalai Lama: he was to come alone to the Chinese camp to attend a theatrical performance. When he refused to accept the invitation, the Chinese decided to 'liberate' him from reactionary forces. Having got wind of this, the Dalai Lama fled with his entourage and an escort of Khampa guerrillas during the night of 16–17 March 1959. On 30 March 1959 he arrived in India, where Nehru gave him political asylum. The Chinese did not

background of the Potala, a line of men walk single file, their hands in the air. Their clothes suggest that they are nobles, but ordinary people – including women – also took part in the fighting. This photo may be a reconstruction for propaganda purposes.

learn of his escape straight away, and were taken aback by the scale of the insurrection.

From 20 to 22 March 1959, Lhasa was ablaze, and the fighting became all the more bloody and all the more one-sided as the Chinese brought their tanks into action. Estimates of the Tibetan death toll varied from 2,000 to 10,000, while some 4,000 were taken prisoner. Between 1959 and 1960, faced with such violent repression, at least 80,000 Tibetans fled either to India, following the Dalai Lama, or to Nepal. Poverty-stricken, weak, and unused to the Indian climate, many died of tuberculosis or diarrhoea in the camps that were set up by the High Commission for Refugees (HCR) and the Indian government.

In lay clothing (below) the Dalai Lama escaped from Lhasa on horseback with a hundred friends and relatives and four hundred resistance fighters. The Chinese did not learn of his escape until 48 hours later, and attacked Norbulingka, where they thought he would still be. The fugitives took fifteen days to cross the mountains and reach Tawang in India.

A nation in exile

Tibet suddenly hit the headlines in the West. The Dalai Lama immediately gave a press conference denouncing the 17-Point Agreement, and the UN passed a resolution condemning Chinese policy in Tibet. The Indian government gave assistance to the Tibetans, and put the ancient colonial town of McLeod Ganj, above Dharamsala, at the disposal of the Dalai Lama. In 1960 a

'There was nothing dramatic about the crossing of the frontier. The country was equally wild on the other side and uninhabited. I saw it in a daze of sickness and weariness and unhappiness deeper than I can express.'

14th Dalai Lama

government-in-exile was established, and the Tibetans began to get organized, with Indian and international aid. In the course of the years and with a good deal of financial support, there gradually came into being a Tibet in exile, with administrative centres, children's villages, monasteries, libraries and records offices. But after 45 years of iron rule by China, Tibetans must still risk their lives to cross the Himalayas.

Democratic reforms and the working classes

Since 1959 Tibetan culture has suffered numerous attempts to destroy it. The years that followed the flight of the Dalai Lama were appalling. There were bloody reprisals against the people, compulsory Communist

OVER 65,000 TIBETANS EXTERMINATED
Dalai Lama appeals to civilised world

indoctrination, redistribution of land to the 'working classes', public sessions of 'criticism' which often degenerated into torture, annihilation of monastic life, and the removal of works of art to China. The aim was to 'exterminate the reactionary forces of Tibet', to 'emancipate the slaves'. 'Democratic reform', with the aid of these Tibetan slaves, was completed in 1961. Famine was everywhere, as in China itself. Family and religious structures collapsed, and 'counter-revolutionaries' and 'reactionaries' were systematically rounded up and sent for re-education at labour camps – the *laogai* – where many of them died. The exact number of these prisoners is not known, but some estimates put it at 70,000.

The Panchen Lama, who had remained in Tibet, appeared to sanction this situation, and

Nehru, the Indian Prime Minister (below, with the Dalai Lama), granted asylum to the Dalai Lama and the Tibetan refugees, but this gesture put him in a difficult position with China, who accused him of 'imperialism and expansionism'. Nehru could not defend Tibet against China, and so the Dalai Lama placed his hopes in the UN, which in October 1959 passed a resolution upholding the rights of the Tibetans, but this had no effect.

The first refugees reached the Indian plains after travelling across the Himalayas in appalling conditions. They were placed in camps, and had to endure the humid heat of India, in stark contrast to the dry cold that they were used to. Still dressed in their heavy Tibetan garments, here they seem bewildered by the climate, fatigue, grief, fear of the future – their faces locked in an expression of uncertainty as they wait. All they know is that the Dalai Lama is also in this country, which for them is the land of the Buddha. Many died of dysentery or tuberculosis. Once in India, the Tibetans fashioned a way of life which they thought would only be temporary. Other Tibetans dispersed to Nepal, Australia, Europe, Canada and the United States. The nation set up a government-in-exile, and since 2001 has had a Prime Minister elected by universal suffrage, Samdhong Rinpoche. Tibetan Buddhism is enjoying great popularity today, not only in the West. The Chinese in Taiwan and the diaspora all flock to the lamas. But refugees continue to arrive from Tibet, and the 'temporary' way of life has now gone on for fifty years.

held the post of Vice-President of the People's Consultative Assembly. In fact, however, in 1962 at the age of 24 he sent a petition to Mao, vehemently denouncing Chinese policy in Tibet. Early in 1964, having made a public speech in Lhasa calling for the Dalai Lama to return to the throne, he was submitted to a terrible session of 'criticism', sent to prison in China, and not released until 1978.

Tibetans indoctrinated by the Chinese duly took up executive positions in the Party and became cogs in the new administrative machinery. In 1965 the Tibet Autonomous Region became a reality, but it represented no more than a third of cultural and ethnic Tibet.

The Cultural Revolution

The Cultural Revolution which hit China in 1966 only worsened the situation in Tibet. The Red Guards, Tibetan as well as Chinese, destroyed every vestige of the old regime. Monasteries, castles, books, statues, paintings, chortens, and all traces of 'superstition' were savagely smashed to pieces. As in China, denunciations, torture and executions followed one another down through the years, and isolated rebellions were drowned in blood. The Cultural Revolution affected every region of Tibet, even the distant, desolate west; the artistic treasures of the ancient kingdom of Guge were destroyed.

In 1964 the Panchen Lama was accused of being an enemy of the people, of the Party, and of Socialism. For fifteen days he endured a session of public 'criticism', the violence of which heralded the Cultural Revolution (left). This began in 1966, transformed Tibet into a mass of ruins, (above, Ganden Monastery), and shattered the majority of pious Tibetans, who were forced against their will to help in the destruction of the monasteries and their contents.

The monasteries, 'nests of reactionaries and superstitions' which had survived the invasion, were systematically wiped out – often dynamited – and their contents smashed. The most valuable were sent to Beijing, where they were melted down, although in 1983, 26 tonnes of relics were discovered hidden in the Forbidden City. Of the 6,000 temples and monasteries that had existed in Tibet before 1959, practically nothing remained by 1976. A culture had been physically defiled and destroyed. Just a few Tibetans, defying all the risks, managed to hide some statues and books by burying them and transforming the temples into barns.

From 1969 onwards, people's communes were set up, and collectivization finished in 1975. Privacy disappeared. Instead of the traditional crop of barley, wheat had to be grown and harvested annually. Since the army were given priority use of all cereal crops, there was more famine amongst the civilian population.

In 1969, the bloody Nyemo rebellion was led by a woman, Trinley Chödron. She was captured and publicly executed in Lhasa, along with other partisans.

Finally, in 1975 the Chinese government introduced a policy for Han Chinese to immigrate to Central Tibet. Amdo and part of Kham – integrated with the Chinese provinces of Gansu, Qinghai, Sichuan and Yunnan – were already mixed, but the Tibet Autonomous Region was not. Now thousands of Chinese began to arrive. Statistics are incomplete, non-existent or doctored, and so it is difficult to give precise figures, but one official estimate suggests that 96,000 Han Chinese – not including military personnel – entered Central Tibet after 1982. The city of Lhasa was no longer recognizable. At the same time it is estimated that more than a million Tibetans, including those in Amdo and Kham, died between 1951 and 1976. The 13th Dalai Lama's prediction had come true.

During this period, guerrilla warfare was still being waged from the Mustang region, a Tibetan enclave in Nepal. It only ended in 1974, when the American and Nepalese governments withdrew their aid to these, the last freedom-fighters, some of whom killed themselves in despair.

A taste of liberty, 1979–87

In 1978 Deng Xiaoping received the Central Committee's backing to begin reforms. This was a new chapter in the post-Mao era. The Tibetans began to notice changes, particularly when the General Secretary of the Communist Party, Hu Yaobang, toured Tibet in 1980 and had the courage to criticize the colonialist policy of the past and the mistakes that the Chinese had made in Tibet. On seeing the poverty of the Tibetans, he could have wept for shame, and he set in motion a series of targeted economic measures, advocated autonomous decision-

The Chinese opened schools in Tibet, but all the teaching was done in Chinese, and of course the propaganda shows young girls immersed in Chairman Mao's *Little Red Book* (below). During the 1960s, many young Tibetans were sent to China to study and be indoctrinated. When they returned, they expected to be given positions of responsibility, but in fact they were sent to remote areas in order to gain 'revolutionary experience', where they remained until the end of the 1970s. These young people had hoped for a Tibet in which they could play an active role, and so were disappointed to see that China was only interested in ideological education and the class struggle, rather than the economic development of Tibet. With the creation of the Tibet Autonomous Region in 1965, 'former peasants' were promoted to administrative positions, but since they were illiterate in both Chinese and Tibetan, they were assisted by 'Party work teams' that were made up of Chinese officials.

making for the Tibetans, and decided that 85 per cent of the Chinese officials should leave the country. Prisoners were released, and the Tibetan language was once more taught in schools. In 1982, article 35 of the Chinese Constitution guaranteed freedom of worship, provided it did not endanger order and the State. Monasteries were rebuilt, and monks began to study

In effect it was not until 1980 that there was any improvement in the situation. Emphasis was then laid on economic development and on giving increased responsibility to Tibetan officials. Many projects

again. Tibet was opened to foreigners, and the University of Lhasa was created in 1985.

But in Tibet and Beijing, the Party faithful were vehemently opposed to this open policy, and Hu was deposed in January 1987. The deposing of Hu Yaobang and the mysterious death of the 10th Panchen Lama signalled the end of the one period of relative liberalization that Tibet had experienced since 1959.

were launched to improve the infrastructure, using mainly female Tibetan workers (above). Tibet was opened up both to investment and to the first influx of Chinese traders. Tourism was seen as a source of revenue for the region, but proved a double-edged sword for the Chinese, because it helped to publicize the Tibetan cause internationally.

Internationalization and riots

The Chinese realized that not only had they failed to crush the Tibetans, but also that Tibetan nationalism was a reality. The paradox was that they had succeeded in creating a unified opposition to themselves among Tibetan peoples who, from a political point of view, had

During the 1980s, the economy was liberalized and the Tibetans, who consumed 90 per cent of what they produced, were encouraged to develop a market economy. The first Chinese Muslim market-gardeners (the Hui) arrived and took over most of the trade in fresh products. In towns like Lhasa (left), nomads and Tibetan peasants sold their wares: bread, butter, vegetables. Religious practices were revived, and people gathered round the principal temple in Lhasa, the Jokhang, selling foodstuffs and holding their prayer wheels. The 10th Panchen Lama, who was compelled to renounce his monk's vows and to take a Chinese wife, returned to Tibet in 1982, where he was greeted with respect and affection (above).

not always been on the best of terms. The nuns and monks were the spearhead of this nationalism, and Buddhism was one form of its expression.

In 1987 the Dalai Lama addressed the US Congress, and the following year he delivered his Strasbourg appeal, in which he outlined his plan for Tibet. He had abandoned the idea of independence, but asked for an association between a greater, genuinely autonomous Tibet and China, for the basic rights of Tibetans to be respected, for an end to Chinese immigration, for Tibet no longer to be used as a nuclear dumping ground, and for the creation of a peace zone. A lot of Tibetans were shocked by his abandonment of the principle of independence, and the Chinese rejected his proposals because they did not contain the one clause they deemed essential: that Tibet had always been part of China.

Nevertheless, the Dalai Lama's influence grew still further when he was awarded the Nobel Peace Prize in 1989. The Tibetan cause was taken up by a number of Westerners who were interested in Buddhism, and these included famous actors and singers. This sympathy

The 1987 riots sounded the death knell of liberalization, and brought home to the Chinese that the Tibetan people had not given in. The police manhandled the monks who were proclaiming that Tibet was a free and independent nation. The police station in front of the Jokhang was set on fire by the Tibetan crowd, and the riot was bloodily put down in full view of dozens of Western tourists. Six policemen were killed according to Chinese reports; according to Western observers six Chinese policemen and seven Tibetans were killed, and dozens were injured.

filtered through into Tibet itself. Radio programmes in Tibetan were broadcast from the West, and tourists often demonstrated their support. The Tibetan cause became international, and the Dalai Lama made his voice heard in many foreign parliaments, to the fury of the Chinese, who protested vehemently. For the world outside China, Tibetan politics and religion were once more symbolized by the Dalai Lama. The time had long passed since the British Prime Minister Neville Chamberlain was able to call this 'a quarrel in a far-away country between people of whom we know nothing.'

At the end of September 1987, a week after the Dalai Lama's speech in Washington, a series of pro-independence rallies took place in Lhasa, led initially by monks and nuns. It is clear that the welcome accorded to the Dalai Lama by such a powerful nation had sparked new hope, but this was rapidly and bloodily extinguished by the police. Nevertheless, small-scale demonstrations continued until 1989, causing increasing embarrassment to the Chinese government. After the death of the Panchen Lama, Tibetan resentment exploded and, at the beginning of March 1989, there was the biggest ever anti-Chinese demonstration in Lhasa. Conscious of the symbolism underlying this, the 30th anniversary of the rebellion in Lhasa, the Chinese took no risks. The demonstration was savagely crushed, with dozens of Tibetans killed. On 8 March 1989 martial law was imposed on the whole Autonomous Region by the new Party Secretary for Tibet, the brilliant but shrewd Hu Jintao, who today is on the verge of becoming the most powerful man in China. To the Tibetans, the massacre of March 1989 was on a par with the events that took place in Beijing's Tiananmen Square

In the course of time, the Dalai Lama became a great deal more than the 'simple monk' he once aspired to be. As political head of Tibet, he had to act directly on behalf of his people, and extend international contacts. His Nobel Peace Prize in 1989 was a slap in the face to the Chinese at a time when there were more and more demonstrations in Tibet.

In Dharamsala, the Dalai Lama took part in protests against Chinese repression (above). His charisma and his speeches calling for tolerance won over many Westerners – including non-Buddhists – to the Tibetan cause. China, however, launched vehement personal attacks against him, which alienated still further the Tibetans in Tibet.

four months later. Martial law was finally lifted at the end of April 1990

'Cutting off the serpent's head'

Since then, particularly since the 3rd Work Forum in Tibet in 1994 and the crisis concerning the 11th Panchen Lama in 1995, Chinese policy in Tibet has been characterized by religious repression, political indoctrination, increased capital investment to build the economy and the infrastructure, and the promotion of massive Chinese immigration. All these policies are interdependent, because the Chinese government see economic development as an antidote to the poison of religion, and in the middle term the Tibetans have to be demographically absorbed in the Autonomous Region just as they have been in other provinces. The Tibetan exception must be eliminated, along with separatism and the demands for restoration of annexed Tibetan lands.

A propaganda document circulated after the 3rd Forum, in typical Communist jargon, clearly articulates the policy of repression: 'As the saying goes, to kill a serpent, we must first chop off its head. If we do not do that, we cannot succeed in the struggle against separatism.... It is not a matter of religious belief nor a matter of the question of autonomy, it is a matter of securing the unity of our country and opposing separatism.... Any separatist activities and convictions must be continuously crushed, according to the law. We must heighten our vigilance, and watch out for those few who are holding to a reactionary standpoint, and who are launching vengeful counterattacks and harming our cadres at the grassroots level. They must be struck down and punished severely....' (3rd Work Forum report, 1 October 1994).

A colonial policy

In addition to its strategic geographical position, Tibet is also Asia's 'water tower'. All the great rivers of Asia have their sources here, and their upper regions cross the country: the Yangtse, the Yellow River, the Mekong, the Salween, the Irrawaddy, the Indus, the Sutlej, the Brahmaputra. Reckless deforestation in the south-eastern

The image above symbolizes Chinese Tibet, on two levels. The Chinese would see it as showing the harmony between the army and the people, as they watch a religious ceremony together. But what is striking is the presence of the Tibetan and Chinese soldiers in the foreground, relaxing in their chairs, while the ordinary people stand or sit on the ground.

regions of Tibet (Kongpo and Kham) has massively eroded the soil and increased the risk of violent floods throughout South and South-East Asia, as well as on the Chinese plains. Even though a partial ban was placed on deforestation in December 1998, the exploitation continues with the active participation of the army. In forty years, forested areas throughout Tibet are estimated to have declined from 25.2 million hectares to 13.57 million, and 18 million m³ of timber have been transported from south-eastern Tibet to China. In the same period, the Chinese have given a figure of 54 billion US dollars earned through timber taken from the Autonomous Region alone.

Furthermore, the postures of the soldiers – legs stretched out or crossed, one of them reading – shows no respect for the masked dancer, who represents a fearsome deity. The irony of the spectacle is that his task is to castigate the enemies of religion with his sword. Religion has been reduced to folklore – a mere show devoid of its ritual meaning.

Tibet is also rich in minerals: gold, uranium, coal, copper, chromium, mica, borax, iron, zinc and lithium, of which it has the second largest reserves in the world. But for the moment it is too difficult and too costly for these resources to be exploited, with the exception of gold. Potential hydroelectric resources are enormous: 250,000 MW, or 57 per cent of China's potential, and power stations have been built in order to export electricity, primarily to China's paddy fields.

In this fragile ecology, with poor soil and a harsh climate everywhere except in the south-east, the soil of Tibet cannot at present sustain high yields or intensive farming. Even though the country is sparsely populated, any demographic influx would pose great dangers to an ecosystem already undermined by deforestation, soil erosion, the disappearance of some species of animals, hunted for their commercial value, and in the north of Tibet, nuclear waste.

This is a colonial economy, exploiting the riches of the country not for the benefit of the Tibetans but for that of the Chinese, and this is confirmed by the number of

Ancient buildings were demolished, and new blocks were put up with no regard for traditional architecture. Broad streets open the way for wind and dust; inelegant buildings of concrete and glass are totally unsuited to the weather conditions; the modern plumbing should have been beneficial, but the water supply is irregular; rubbish is only collected occasionally; at 7 a.m. Beijing time, which is still nighttime in Tibet, loudspeakers greet the new day in military fashion. This is modern Tibet, Chinese style (below).

Tibetan officials in positions of responsibility within the TAR: only 34 per cent of jobs at prefectorial level and above are occupied by Tibetans, and only 16 per cent in the armed forces. Furthermore, not one Communist Party Secretary in the Autonomous Region has ever been Tibetan.

The current situation

The Dalai Lama's doctrine of non-violence has been opposed since 1988 by some Tibetans who believe that middle-of-the-road pacifism simply doesn't work, especially since all attempts at negotiating with the Chinese have proved futile and have so far brought not the slightest relief to the Tibetan people. The Chinese media and officialdom now more than ever condemn the Dalai Lama as a 'separatist', and any allusion to the situation in Tibet by a foreign power is dismissed as interference in the internal affairs of China. The Chinese know that after 45 years, they still have not won the hearts of the Tibetans. Any untoward event is perceived as a violation of Party policy and is attributed to the Dalai Lama's 'clique': in 1995 the chosen reincarnation of the 10th Panchen Lama, who had died in 1989; in 1997 the publication of the secret 1962 report by the Panchen Lama; in December 1999, the flight to India of

In Chinese, Tibet is called *Xizang*, or 'Western Treasure House'. These 'treasures' include minerals, hydraulic power and forestry. The deforestation of eastern Tibet has been an environmental disaster (above, Serthar, eastern Tibet), as it has increased flooding in the Chinese plains. Tibet also contains huge uninhabited spaces, which China lacks, and these offer much scope for nuclear research. The '9th Academy' was established in the 1960s for this purpose in Qinghai, near Lake Kokonor; it has since been closed, but the untreated radioactive waste has polluted the region. However, no nuclear tests have ever been carried out in Tibet.

the young Karmapa, head of the Karma Kagyu school, who until then had been a political puppet of the Chinese.

Sometimes the Chinese government is so desperate to maintain total control over everything that the situation becomes absurd. The current situation includes a Communist state giving itself the right to recognize reincarnated lamas. The 11th Panchen Lama, Gedun Choekyi Nyima, recognized by the Dalai Lama in Tibet, disappeared in 1995, and was replaced by a Panchen Lama chosen by the Chinese. The disappearance of the Tibetan child, six years old at the time, makes him the youngest political prisoner in the world. He has not been seen for seven years, but the Chinese government assures everyone that he is well.

On 24 October 2001, addressing the European Parliament in Strasbourg, the Dalai Lama renewed his appeal for negotiations in the interests of both Tibet and China: 'I have led the Tibetan freedom struggle on a path of non-violence and have consistently sought a mutually agreeable solution of the Tibetan issue through negotiations in a spirit of reconciliation and compromise with China.... My proposal... envisages that Tibet enjoy genuine autonomy within the framework of the People's

The disappearance of the 11th Panchen Lama, recognized in Tibet by the Dalai Lama in 1995, and the fact that no foreign delegation or UN representative has ever been able to meet him – in spite of repeated demands to do so – have provoked much anger among human rights campaigners. The Chinese government merely says that the child and his parents are in good health, but it will not provide details or photographs. The boy is now aged fourteen, but the only photograph of him was taken in the year of his recognition, when he was six (above).

Republic of China. However, not the autonomy on paper imposed on us fifty years ago in the 17-Point Agreement, but a true self-governing, genuinely autonomous Tibet, with Tibetans fully responsible for their own domestic affairs, including the education of their children, religious matters, cultural affairs, the care of their delicate and precious environment, and the local economy. Beijing would continue to be responsible for the conduct of foreign and defence affairs. This solution would greatly enhance the international image of China and contribute to her stability and unity – the two topmost priorities of Beijing – while at the same time the Tibetans would be ensured of the basic rights and freedoms to preserve their own civilization and to protect the delicate environment of the Tibetan plateau.'

Even if Tibet prior to 1950 was a society in need of profound reform, was there really no other means than the destruction of a culture and the subjugation of a nation by a foreign armed force and ideology? The drawing below, by a child who lived in Tibet, is a poignant illustration of parents being separated from their children so that the latter may receive a Tibetan education in exile.

Violated rights and economic integration

Religious repression and the campaign of reeducation are once more in full swing. The recently built Serthar Monastery in Amdo (Sichuan), under the leadership of the charismatic Khenpo Jigme Phuntsok, and containing 5,000 monks and nuns including some Chinese, was destroyed in July 2001.

NAME= Phur bu Tsering
class = V.e
Tittle = About 1959 in Tibet

On 7 March 2002, Paula Dobriansky, the US State Department's Special Coordinator for Tibetan Issues, informed Congress: 'The situation on the ground in Tibet remains grave. The State Department's annual Human Rights Report for 2001, in the section on China, clearly states that tight controls on religion and other fundamental freedoms remain serious problems. The report describes in detail widespread human rights and religious freedom abuses, including instances of arbitrary arrests, detention without public trial, torture

As for the 'second generation' Tibetans born in the West or in India, even though they are of course influenced by the way of life in their host countries, they remain deeply attached to their culture and their faith, of which they consider themselves the guardians.

in prison, and official controls over Tibetan monasteries and institutions on monks and nuns. Tibet remains China's poorest region even though China has devoted substantial economic resources to Tibet over the last twenty years. Language problems severely limit educational opportunities for Tibetan students, illiteracy rates are said to be rising, and non-urban children in some regions are chronically undernourished. Some reports suggest that privatization of health care, increased emphasis on Chinese language curriculum, and continuing Han migration into Tibet are all weakening the social and economic position of Tibet's indigenous population…'

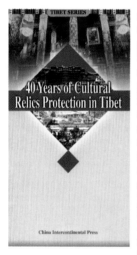

Because terror, ideology and collaboration have all failed, the Chinese government is now proceeding by means of demographic assimilation; Tibet is being populated by Chinese coming in from the 'mother country' – small traders, drivers, construction workers, and road and railway workers, not to mention the military, whose numbers are kept secret but are estimated at around 500,000, while prostitutes believed to number around 10,000. All are flocking to this inhospitable, sparsely populated country where wages are three times as high as they are in China. The government has even coined a slogan: 'Go west'. Today a railway is being constructed between Golmud, in Qinghai, and Lhasa, built by thousands of Chinese workers. It will be 1,084 km long, will cross mountain passes 5,000 m high, and will cost 2.34 billion US dollars (official figures, 1995). It is a gigantic undertaking carried out in the most testing climatic conditions, and it is due to be finished in 2007. It is 'of extreme importance to the consolidation of the south-

Mao, Deng and Jiang smile against the background of the Potala and invite Tibetans to follow them into a new era (above) – and the destruction counts for nothing in *40 Years of Cultural Relics Protection in Tibet* (left). The propaganda continues, and Chinese tourists come flocking: 404,000 in 2001 (official statistic). Foreigners require a Chinese visa and also a special permit to visit the TAR.

拉萨市政府 宣

|ལམ་སྟོན་པ་ཡིས། ང་ཚོ་དུས་རབས་གསར་པའི་ཕྱོགས་སུ་འཁྲིད།

领路人，带领我们走进新时代。

west frontier of the mother country, for the exploitation of the natural resources along the route, and for the establishment of direct economic and political links between Tibet and other parts of the country' (5th Development Plan of the Tibet Autonomous Region).

In 2002 a 35-metre high monument was constructed in front of the Potala, to the glory of the People's Liberation Army; the town itself is dominated by the new public security building. Thus the ancestral fear of the 'Barbarians from the West', shared by all Chinese governments since the Eastern Zhou dynasty (8th–3rd centuries BC), would seem for the moment to have been allayed.

A half-smile: in late June 2002, the Dalai Lama visited Prague, and received a portrait of himself from Vaclav Havel.

DOCUMENTS

Travellers in Tibet

'In the whole history of exploration, there is no more curious map than that which shows the tangled lines of traveller's routes towards this city (Lhasa), coming in from all sides, north, south, east and west, crossing, interlocking, retracing, all with one goal, and all baffled, some soon after the journey had begun, some when the travellers might almost believe that the next hill would give them a distant glimpse of the golden roofs of the Potala.'

Perceval Landon, 1904

Great piety

The Jesuit Antonio de Andrade (1562–1607) travelled across the whole of Central Asia and in 1626 established the first church in Tibet at Tsaparang, in the kingdom of Guge.

It is because of this piety and this inclination towards the things of God that they continually ask for crosses and reliquaries which they like to hang around their necks. The mother of the king lives in a different country which is two days' journey away from here; even before speaking to me, she sent someone to ask me for some holy object of this order. I sent her a cross and a reliquary, which gave her great pleasure. In addition to a golden cross, the king himself wears round his neck our rosary which also bears the sacred cross, and a gold reliquary with two of our relics inside. I took theirs away from them and burned them.

…It is out of pure piety as well as their good nature that they also worship our images with such devotion. We have several in this church, which is very well furnished. All the nobles and many ordinary people come flocking to it; they prostrate themselves upon the ground three times, as is their custom, and they worship the sacred images and ask for the Holy Bible to be placed on their heads; in this way we have plenty of opportunities to explain the mysteries of the faith to them.

…The opportunity arose for the king to watch us offering Holy Communion at mass. He returned to the house a few days later, and asked to see the Host again. I showed him one, broke it, and put it in his hand, saying: 'At the moment, Sire, it is only bread. But when one offers it to God, by the force of the words that He Himself taught us, it changes into his own body.' – 'Well,' he replied, 'since at the moment it is only bread, give me permission to eat it.' He took a tiny piece, and divided the rest among his servants who were present, just like someone handling a relic, a very sacred thing.

Antonio de Andrade, 1626
taken from Les Portugais au Tibet, les premières relations jésuites (1624–1635),
ed. Hugues Didier, Paris, 1996

On the Buddhist Trinity

Francisco de Azevedo (1578–1660) was also a member of the Tsaparang mission, which he joined in 1631. His interpretation of the Buddhist trinity – the Buddha, Buddhist law and the community of monks – is very interesting.

These people are clothed in coarse woollen tunics and breeches of the same material, with boots, the men as well as the women. They wear nothing on their heads, and wear their hair in little tresses that fall down their backs and are carefully coated with butter; for jewelry they wear amber or coral chains around the neck or on the chest. They are all as dirty as one another. From the forehead to the middle of the head falls a cord in which are threaded some rough green stones called turquoises. But some of them are beautiful. They eat meat which is either raw or barely cooked, flour made from roasted barley, and cooked vegetables. They have fresh ones all year, because during the summer they dry them at home in the shade. When they want to eat them fresh and green, all they have to do is soak bunches of them in water for half a day. Thus they are as fresh as if they had just been picked. If these are served to you, the menu is not bad.

…They believe that God is threefold. They call Him Conja Sumbo [*C'os dkon gsum pa*]. They call the Father Lama Conjo [*bLa ma dkon mc'og*], the Son Cho Conjo [*C'os dkon mc'og*], the Holy Spirit Giundu Conjo [*dGe dun dkon mc'og*]. They believe that the Father begat the Son in accordance with His word, and that the Holy Spirit was born of them both. They call Our Lady Gelobo Lunze [*Ses rab p'a rol tu p'yn pa*]. They believe that the Son is incarnated in her. God had wanted to send her an angel as His envoy, but the latter had caused much resentment among the men because they considered that in this manner he had touched her. And so God, in order to prevent disputes, had sent an elephant as his envoy. At least that is what is written in their book.

Francisco de Azevedo, 1631
taken from Les Portugais au Tibet, les premières relations jésuites (see above)

At Tashilunpo monastery

George Bogle (1746–81), a keen young man with great respect for local customs, wrote an excellent description of life in Tashilunpo Monastery, and the mutual curiosity with which Tibetans and Westerners regarded each other.

'From the day of our arrival at Teshu Lumbo till the 18th of January, 1775, the [Panchen] Lama was engaged in receiving visits and presents. Among the rest of his votaries were a large caravan of Kalmuks, who offered up to his shrine talents of silver, furs, pieces of silk, and dromedaries. They remained about a month at Teshu Lumbo, and then proceeded to Lhasa....

I was not present on any of these occasions, but remained at home, where I had enough visitors of my own; for crowds of *gylongs* [monks] used to come into my room to see me at all hours, or get upon the leads and look down upon

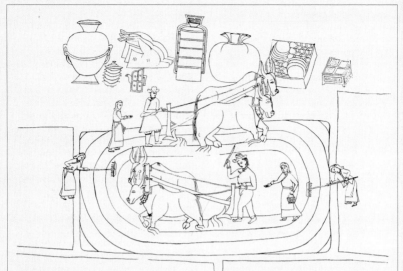

me. Among these last came the Shigatzé Killadars, dressed in their feminine attire. I never forbade anybody; and after giving them a pinch of snuff and indulging them with a look at the chairs, &c., which always produced an exclamation of "Pah-pah-pah, tze-tze-tze!" they used to retire and make way for others. This continued, more or less, all the time I was at Teshu Lumbo....

The priest, who every morning came to me with boiled rice and tea from the Lama, was called Debo Dinji Sampu. He was about fifty, marked with the smallpox, his eye mild and candid, and himself of great singleness of mind and simplicity. He came to understand my imperfect attempts to speak the Tibetan language tolerably well, and we used to have long chats together. I grew very fond of him, and he, which showed his sagacity, took a great liking to me. He always kept a box of excellent snuff, and was not niggardly in offering a pinch of it. But with all Debo Dinji's good

qualities, he was as averse to washing his hands and face as the rest of his countrymen. He happened one morning to come in while I was shaving, and I prevailed upon him for once to scrub himself with the help of soap and water. I gave him a new complexion, and he seemed to view himself in my shaving glass with some satisfaction. But he was exposed to so much ridicule from his acquaintances, that I never could get him to repeat the experiment.'

George Bogle, 1775
taken from *Narrative of the Mission of George Bogle to Tibet and of the journey of Thomas Manning to Lhasa*, ed. Clements R. Markham, London, 1879

The battle of Kuru

Perceval Landon (1869–1927), a reporter for The Times*, accompanied the British expedition to Tibet led by Colonel Francis Younghusband in 1904. His poignant description of the battle of Kuru and his* *dispatches from Lhasa stunned and thrilled his readers.*

By this time the storm had broken in full intensity, and from three sides at once a withering volley of magazine fire crashed into the crowded mass of Tibetans. It was like a man fighting with a child. The issue was not in doubt, even from the first moment; and under the appalling punishment of lead, they staggered, failed and ran. Straight down the line of fire lay their only path of escape. Moved by a common impulse, the whole mass of them jostling one against another with a curious slow thrust, they set out with strange deliberation to get away from this awful plot of death. Two hundred yards away stood a sharply squared rock behind which they thought to find refuge. But the Gurkhas from above enfiladed this position and the only hope they had lay in reaching the next spur half a mile away. Had we been armed with their weapons, another hundred yards would have brought them into safety, even in the open. It was an awful sight. One watched it with the curious sense of fascination which the display of unchecked power over life and death always exerts when exercised. Men dropped at every yard. Here and there an ugly heap of dead and wounded was concentrated, but not a space of twenty yards was without its stricken and shapeless burden. At last, the slowly moving wretches – and the slowness of their escape was horrible and loathsome to us – reached the corner, where at any rate we knew them to be safe from the horrible lightning storm which they had themselves challenged.

All this was necessary, but none the less it sicked those who took part in it, however well they realised the fact.

This was no fighting in the usual sense of the word. As soon as their first assault had failed there was nothing for the Mission escort to fear except, perhaps, the bullets of their own companions....

As I have said, Lhasa would remain Lhasa were it but a cluster of hovels on the sand. But the sheer magnificence of the unexpected sight which met our unprepared eyes was to us almost a thing incredible. There is nothing missing from this splendid spectacle – architecture, forest trees, wide green places, rivers, streams and mountains, all lie before one as one looks down from the height upon Lhasa stretching out at our feet.... The beauty of Lhasa is doubled by its utter unexpectedness... there was nothing – less perhaps in such maps and descriptions of Lhasa as we had than anywhere else – to promise us this city of gigantic palace and golden roof, these wild stretches of woodland, these acres of close-cropped grazing land and marshy grass, ringed and delimited by high trees or lazy streamlets of brown transparent water over which the branches almost met....

Lamaism may be an engine of repression, but its victims do not protest; and there before one's eyes at last is Lhasa. It may be a barrier to all human improvement; it may be a living type of all that we in the West have fought against and at last overcome, of bigotry, cruelty and slavery; but under the fierce sun of that day and the white gauze of the almost unclouded sky of Lhasa, it was not easy to find fault with the creed, however narrow and merciless, which built the Potala palace and laid out the green spaces at its foot. In this paradise of cool water and green leaves, hidden away among the encircling snows of the highest mountain ranges in the world,

Lamaism has upraised the stones and gold of Lhasa, and nothing but Lamaism could have done this thing. To Lamaism alone we owe it that when at last the sight of the farthest goal of all travel burst upon our eyes, it was worthy, full worthy, of all the rumour and glamour and romance with which in the imaginings of man it has been invested for so many years.'

Perceval Landon, 1904
taken from *Lhasa: an Account of the Country and People of Central Tibet and of the Progress of the Mission Sent There by the English Government in the Year 1903-4*, London, 1905

Dances at Patong

The French explorer Jacques Bacot (1877–1965) never succeeded in reaching Central Tibet, but his travels in the border regions of Tibet gave him an intimate knowledge of the customs, which he described in colourful style.

Yesterday evening, at the twilight hour, after we had had a good laugh at the crude or naive clowning, the festivities ended with the song of *Om mani padme*. While the three oldest men of Panong threw fistfuls of grain to the spirits of the four cardinal points, the entire crowd – men and women – started singing. Mystic syllables, whose meaning scholars search for in vain; but a magnificent sound with its fullness and its aching melody, with the voices rising very high, as high as hope can rise, and then falling again in disappointment and a profound lamentation. No one knows who composed this song, but it is without the artifice of composition. It is the work of centuries and of a whole nation, a synthesis, the very cry of human distress and hope, despairingly and eternally uttered from the depths of the abyss. It sums up all of the Tibetan religion, and all religions.

Jacques Bacot
taken from *Le Tibet révolté*, Paris, 1912.

My adventures in the land of France

Ardjroup Gumbo (died 1910) gives a Tibetan traveller's view. He went to France with Jacques Bacot, and observed and compared French and Tibetan societies with directness and gentle humour. In his book Le Tibet révolté *(1912) Bacot, whom Gumbo called* Ta-jen *(master), pays homage to him: 'I owe to him feelings that people of our time no longer know and perhaps will no longer understand.'*

…I went out to visit Marseilles. On a mountain nine storeys high there is a large church; to climb this mountain there are several sorts of path. As for me, in order to climb it I entered a little house at the foot of the mountain [the lift that goes up to Notre-Dame de la Garde], and saw some men sitting down. In the time it takes to utter a cry, the house was transported to the top of the mountain and the doorway to the church. In this church there were statues of saints and virgins. At the sight of them I rejoiced and knelt down to pray. Having come up in a vehicle, we went down again to the foot of the mountain.

When we arrived at an arm of the sea, a lot of men were standing in a house suspended above the water [the transporter bridge]. And this house crossed the space above the water. We came back into town in a vehicle, and a lot of men were looking at me.

…In the inn there were more than eight storeys and a hundred rooms.… In these rooms were beds that had been made, covered with silken fabrics, and also tables loaded with ornaments. Silken fabrics without any grime covered these tables. In the evening, so that we could sleep some servants stretched the beds out, and in the morning they folded them up.

I ate with the masters of the inn at a round table. The custom in the morning is to eat a small meal of milk, coffee, butter and sugar. At midday and in the evening, there are two big meals of meat, fish, fruit and sweet things.

Before having these meals, one must wash one's body and hands, and shake the dust from one's clothes. And when I go home to my country, when I say, contemptible dog, that I am following this custom, all the men will be incredulous and will stop their ears.

Before entering the house, one must wipe one's feet on woven carpets. Not everyone is allowed in. At the main door there is a guard. First you must approach the guard, and he lets some in and not others. If he says yes, he accompanies you into the house... On every floor there are little wheels, and if you turn them a quarter turn, they give light, water, heat, everything you want; and you do not need oil or fire. I did not know how it was done, but when I looked closely I saw that underneath the house, in the earth, there was a great fire and an abundance of water.

...There is a large room where people only go to eat meals. The men eat with the women, all mixed together at a round table. In order to enter the room, the men link arms with the women and bow to them. The French like women very much, bow to them deeply, and when they talk to them, they have smiling faces and their voices are full of sweetness.

...The Ta-jen has a large country house in addition to his house in Paris... This house is as big as a fortress and is built on a little mountain. But the Ta-jen is not the chief of the country, because in France those who live in palaces have become the subjects of their farmers. The poor have become powerful, having been elected by the people, and have left their goods to the rich. But now they are beginning to want them back.

Everywhere in this house there are paintings, depicting trees, the water of lakes and rivers, gardens and fields such as one sees in the country. In these paintings there is not one god or saint to be seen, because they have not been done by priests but by clever men. And French people like looking at these paintings inside their houses.

...For three months I suffered a lot, because the cook disliked me. This female cook had a moustache; she was dirty, nasty, and did not fear God. She gave me my food as if I was a dog. After three months the Ta-jen drove her out of the house....

I've seen other bad women, but their husbands were good. In France, when a married woman has committed adultery, her husband does not kill her, as a virtuous husband must do in Tibet and China, but he goes peacefully about his affairs while everybody laughs at him and mocks him....

Ardroup Gumbo
taken from 'Impressions d'un Tibétain en France', in Jacques Bacot, *Le Tibet révolté* (see above)

A Tibetan perspective

Trade was dependent on great caravans transporting goods between the regions. These were major expeditions which lasted for months and had to protect themselves against wild animals and bandits.

Every morning, with great precision, the enormous machine got itself ready to depart: everyone got up very early, two or three hours before daybreak, at the moment when the night was at its coldest, when it was freezing enough to split stones. While the cook did what he could to heat the water for tea, the teamsters harnessed the horses. Only then did they set about loading the yaks and dismantling the camp. Every move was calculated: they needed two men per animal; it took them half an hour to load forty. They began with the animals that would be leaving first – those which had spent the night closest to the track. It was the head teamster who would decide the day before which of the yaks would go at the head of the caravan – whichever was the best; it would be constantly under surveillance, and he would guard it with his life against accidents and bandits, if necessary. The honour of the head teamster depended on it and so, by extension, the fate of all the other men.

When the caravan moved off in the morning, everything had to be done at speed in order to keep up with the front of the column, but also not to keep the rear of the column waiting. Faster! Faster! This was the constant cry that reverberated the length of the caravan and had the men complaining. Having had enough of being told that he must go faster, one of the men would sometimes do the opposite of what the master had ordered. It only needed one man to disobey, and the effect would be felt by the whole caravan. As soon as twenty yaks had been loaded, they would set off without waiting, accompanied by a teamster on horseback; then there would be another teamster accompanying twenty more yaks, then another, until finally the head teamster would set off with the last twenty yaks. Each group that followed

would wait until its predecessor had departed. There was never a gap in the long line. It took an hour for the circle finally to unwind and for the whole caravan to be on the move. The last group could always sleep an hour longer than the first, and so each group took it in turns to take the lead.

That was the caravan: always in a hurry, always needing to go faster, always exciting; and yet the caravan was slow; it set off in the morning at about 5 a.m., and stopped around midday after seven hours on the move. How far did it travel each day? Fifteen to twenty kilometres.

...On its journey the caravan crossed land that belonged to different tribes of nomads; the caravan had long since made agreements with them, and every year the traders exchanged tea for skins and wool. If the caravan was simply crossing the land without trading, it would pay a toll. Most of the time there was nothing to fear – not even from the Gologs, who also needed tea. It was always the head of the caravan who negotiated with the nomad chiefs.

...In the desert, which looks completely empty, the smallest clod of earth has its own peculiarities, and the head of the caravan is first and foremost a man who knows the country; this place is good for camping because it's sheltered from the wind; the water is bad here because it comes from peat bogs; over there you'll find fuel; careful, this is a valley where you're likely to be attacked by bandits; there's the rock you have to climb to spot an ambush in the distance; this is the hollow where you can defend yourself against an attack.

The camp leader had a troop of horsemen at his disposal, changing each day; they would take it in turns to leave their duties with their respective groups, and would be designated as 'guards'. The leader would then have them under his command as a separate unit, and he would know each one by reputation. The risks would vary according to the day's itinerary. There were some stages of the journey where the countryside was open and one could see everything coming from afar. On those days the camp leader knew that he did not need the best of the guards. But there were other days when the area to be crossed was dangerous: it might be a broad, peaceful valley, but the leader knew that

often stopping to examine prints in the ground; 'So many riders passed this way yesterday; judging by their number, their direction, the weight of their mounts, they were hunters.' These advance riders were able to decide where to pitch camp. Some time before reaching the stopping place, they would be joined by the troop of men sent on by each group to set up the camp and tighten the ropes before the yaks arrived.

Other horsemen escorted the caravan en route. They protected its flank by

the only route the caravan could take was a narrow track, squeezed between the foot of the mountain and the marshes. It was from the neighbouring valley four years previously that the Gologs had mounted their attack. On such days, the camp leader appointed his best men to be guards; he knew them all, even if they did not belong to his own people.

Every morning, well before the departure of the great caravan, a small group of six to eight horsemen would leave early; they too had to be top men. Their task was to clear the road about two hours in advance of the caravan. Always in twos, they advanced along the crests from one side of the valley to the other. They reconnoitred all the valleys,

staying on higher ground. They were very independent, always galloping ahead, behind, to the sides, climbing to the tops of the hills, disappearing into the distance, always in pairs, patrolling the neighbouring valleys. Last thing in the evening, the camp leader would station the nightwatchmen on the ridges, overlooking the great circle in which the caravan spent the night.

From Samten Karmay and Philippe Sagant, *Les neuf forces de l'homme*, Nanterre, 1998.

Poetic songs

'The Tibetan language is extremely well adapted to poetic creation... because it allows the insertion of syllables without any real meaning into the body of the text, and permits some grammatical connections to be omitted in order to change the rhythm... Moreover, the Tibetans have always loved to sing, dance and shout at and to one another, and compete in verbal jousts. People of words, they have always valued language: from infancy they are still lulled to sleep by the mantras their mothers recite, or by the fabulous tales of King Gesar that are sung by the bards. Poetry is the offspring of this ambiance of song.'

Françoise Robin, *Action Poétique 157, Tibet aujourd'hui*, 1999.

The anonymous Saga of Gesar is a long sequence of thousands of verses, and has been put together over several centuries. Sung by bards who specialize in particular chapters, it is extraordinarily popular.

Instructions from Ma-ne-ne to Jo-ru

The song is *a-la tha-la tha-la tha-la*, that is the way that a speech is fashioned. *A-la* is the beginning of the speech. *Tha-la* is the way of expressing a word. And now, Jo-ru, divine son, listen to the song which I, your aunt, sing to you. In the furrows of the field in a sheltered valley, the blue-green shoots have sprouted; If the field is not adorned with fruits of good quality, in case of misfortune, how will the 'black heads' live? The blue leaves which feed the animals, even if they grow in quantities, are of no use. In the azure tent of the lofty sky, when the myriad stars are sparkling, if the full moon does not come to adorn them, who will lead them along the path of darkness? These constellations, like a guide through the darkness, even though they are great in number, are of no use. On the earth of the many-coloured Glin, Jo-ru has brought forth emanations of all kinds; if Jo-ru does not understand the sovereignty of the white Glin, will Jo-ru ever do good for all beings? When he is taken in by the deception of his emanations, it is like a sign of the dominance of Uncle Khro-thun.

The Saga of Gesar

Milarepa (1052–1135) was one of the greatest mystics and ascetics of Tibetan

Buddhism, and one of the founders of the Kagyupa order.

There are four great rivers
Birth, old age, disease and death.
They exist for all beings in this world,
    and none are spared.
Ah! Solitary site of the fortress of the
    Enlightenment!
High up near the glaciers live gods and
    spirits, the tower at the foot of the
    terraces is filled with benefactors.
Behind, a mountain holds out its curtain
    of white silk.
The paradisal groves thicken before.
I watch the water birds swing down
    from the mountain pass on to the
    bank of the pool.
Slaves tied to their worldly desires fill
    the earth, striving for material
    possessions.
The yogi who observes them clearly
    from the height of the precious rock,
    takes them as an example of the
    impermanence of all things.
They think of their own desires, like the
    trembling water, like the vision of a
    diseased eye.
The yogi looks on this life as the illusion
    of a dream.

*

I am a strange man, a hermit dressed
    in cotton, meditating in the months
    of summer in the snow-covered
    mountains: the Breath of new life
    cleanses all the mists of the body.
In the month of autumn, I beg for alms;
    nothing more than some barley to
    keep me in health.
In winter I meditate in the deep forests
    which protect me from the biting
    attacks of the wind.
In spring I dwell in the fields and hills
And so I free myself from phlegm and
    bile.

                      Milarepa

Drukpa Kunley, 'the divine madman' (1455–1529) belonged to the Buddhist school of Drukpa, and was one of the great family of the Gyas from whom the leaders of the Drukpa school traditionally came. However, his refusal to take established holy orders, his wanderings, his eccentric and shocking behaviour, and the songs that he used to teach the essence of faith all give him a unique place in Tantric Buddhism.

I take refuge in the quietened penis of
    the old man, dried up to the root,
    broken like a dead tree;
I take refuge in the flaccid vagina of the
    old woman, collapsed, impenetrable,
    like a sponge;
I take refuge in the warlike manhood of
    the young tiger, indifferent to death;
I take refuge in the lotus of girls, making
    them feel waves of bliss, freeing them
    from shame and inhibitions.

*

The lama without a disciple, the student
    without perseverance,
The pandit without an audience, the
    woman without a lover,
The farmer without a farm, the nomad
    without cattle,
The monk without discipline, the
    Gomchen without instruction,
The nun obsessed with sex, the man
    incapable of erection,
The whores running after money and
    the girls sighing for sex,
How ridiculous they are, how laughable
    they are!

                  Drukpa Kunley

The 6th Dalai Lama Tsangyang Gyatso (1683–1706) did not take monastic vows, and until his tragic death was torn between his religious duties and his love of pleasure. His simple poems are among the most beautiful in Tibetan literature.

White crane, lovely bird,
Lend me your wings!
I am not going far:
One day I shall return, through the land
    of Litang.

                    *

When the arrow is fired,
Its point sinks into the earth.
As soon as I saw my childhood
    companion again,
My heart was set upon her.

                    *

For so long I meditated
on the face of my lama,
yet nothing took form in my mind
except the features of my beloved!

                    *

If my mind which wanders and wanders
    again,
Thought only of the Dharma when she
    is absent,
then in just one lifetime, in just one
    body
I would become Buddha!

                    The 6th Dalai Lama

*Born in Litang, in eastern Tibet, the 7th
Dalai Lama, Kelsang Gyatso (1708–57),
was confronted by a difficult political
situation. He took refuge in spirituality
and religious practice, and devoted much
of his time to writing.*

What is the essence
Of all secret teachings?
That which benefits the mind
And frees it from illusion
The Sky of immaculate space
I thought to melt my mind in it;
The centre of the fresh, floating clouds
I thought to touch their softness.

                    The 7th Dalai Lama

*Nyoshul Khenpo Rinpoche (1932–99), an
ascetic with no affiliations, was one of the
masters of the spiritual tradition of the*

*Great Perfection (Dzogchen). Born in
Kham, he studied under the greatest lamas
of his time, and then went into exile.*

Actions and passions torment the mind
    unsparingly
Like violent waves, battering again and
    again
In this ocean, so unlike the Cycle
    without shores.
May it find the great peace that is its
    nature!

                    Nyoshul Khenpo Rinpoche

*Orgyän Dorje (born 1961) was born
in southern Tibet to a peasant family,
and worked on a literary magazine in
Tibet; he is one of the most typical of
contemporary poets.*

Untitled
Deprived of the sunlight
My body has become a block of ice
Deprived of the moonlight
What I can see is obscured in the half-
    light
What will nature grant me?
A violent rain to darken the hills and
    valleys?
A pure sky to dispel the half-light?
I wait, I wait for the response of the
    clouded mind.

An endless evening
The willows wave in all directions
The cold wind wounds my face
The troop of my companions
Disappears into the edge of the sky.
Before my eyes
Nothing remains but a broad empty
    plain
The song of yesterday mingles with the
    refuse
The radiance of smiles merges with the
    snow
At first I thought that all of this

Was nothing but one long sigh,
Now – it is one long evening, endless.

Orgyän Dorje

*Palden Gyal (1968–) was born in
Repkong in Amdo (Qinghai), and gained
a diploma at the Qinghai Institute of
Nationalities. In 1989 he went into exile
in India, then in England, and finally the
USA, where he is still pursuing his literary
career while working for Radio Free Asia.*

The Offering

Last night I passed from sleep
Into a terrifying world
Today I lost my being
I stuck a sharp dagger into my heart,
sliced off my head
And offered it, ornament of Mount
Kailash
I plunged my right hand into the head
of Magyäl Pomra
And stretched out my left hand towards
the summit of Khangka' Riwo
I offered my right foot to Lake Konokor
And dipped my left foot in Lake
Manasarovar
This whole body, so hard to obtain
Everywhere I make it my offering, seed
of my limbs.

Palden Gyal

*Born in Amdo, Gedun Chöghel
(1904–51), former monk, eclectic and
iconoclastic spirit, loved women and travel,
and was one of the line of 'mad saints'. He
called himself the 'beggar of Amdo' and
was a philosopher, poet and artist. His
critical view of lay and monastic society
earned him the hostility of the Tibetan
government, and imprisonment in 1947.*

Wherever it may be, whomever it may
be,
In Calcutta, in Nepal, in Peking
Or in Lhasa, in the land of snows,

If I observe them, all men seem to me to
behave in the same way, when they
see tea, butter and clothes.
Even those who do not like noise and
chatter, whose manners are calm and
disciplined, have no thoughts other
than those of an old fisherman.
The proud and filthy nobles like praise
and flattery, the common people like
trickery and deceit.
The young like games and the pleasures
of love, and now almost everyone
likes beer and tobacco.
People are attached to their families, but
hate and reject those of a different
origin.
To me, every human being has a nature
as brutal as an ox!
They go on pilgrimages to Tsari to
improve their reputation, they
practise the difficult mastery of heat
and cold in order to feed themselves,
they recite the words of the
Conqueror to gain some reward.
When one reflects, it seems clear that
everything is done for the profit one
can draw from it.
Sacrificial cakes, offerings of food and
drink, all those rituals that we
perform are nothing but a sumptuous
display.
Although there is no happiness, neither
in the valley nor at the top of the
mountain, we have no choice other
than to live on this earth, as in the
cowshed or in the kennel, until this
illusory body of flesh and blood
disappears.
Adzi! Such frankness may not be to
everyone's taste!

Gedun Chöphel

Tibetan Medicine

Based on Buddhist principles, this originated at the time of the kings (7th–9th centuries), and came under various foreign influences, especially Indian and Chinese. In the 12th century, Yuthok 'the Young' adapted Indian concepts to a Tibetan context in the Four Medical Tantras. *Tibetan medicine came of age in the 17th century, when Sangye Gyatso, the regent of Tibet, revised the Four Tantras and wrote a commentary,* The Blue Beryl, *illustrated with 79 paintings. In 1695, he founded the Chakpori school of medicine in Lhasa, for monks only.*

The physiological and pathological theories propounded in the Four Tantras were borrowed mainly from Indian *ayurveda*. The basic elements are the three humours (bile, phlegm and wind) which act upon the structures formed by the seven types of body tissue: chyle, blood, flesh, fatty tissue, bone, bone marrow and reproductive fluids (sperm or menstrual blood). While the anatomy of the organs is rudimentary, the system of channels through which the humours and other fluids circulate is, by contrast, described by sophisticated concepts that reflect the spiritual content of the tantras, in particular those enumerated in the *Kalachakra* tantra. Illness is defined as an imbalance of humours that can be caused by various factors: food, lifestyle, time of year, evil spirits, etc. Nevertheless, the function of medicine would be problematical if it did not also embrace the theory of absolute determinism that shows how past actions affect the destiny of the

individual (karma). Tibetan medicine also includes a concept developed earlier in the *Astanghrdaya Samhita* of Vagbhata, which states that there are three types of disease: those which are due to 'pathogenical factors of present life', and which can be cured by medical remedies or by exorcisms (in cases where the cause is evil spirits); those which manifest themselves with no apparent immediate cause and are the 'maturation of the fruit of past bad actions' (if severe, these can only be curbed by the ten virtuous practices); finally, those which are serious although their direct causes are minimal, and which combine pathogenical factors of present life with the effects of past bad actions.

In practice, the basic method of diagnosis is the taking of the pulse, which is a method borrowed from the Chinese, in addition to questioning, examination and, more rarely, study of the urine. Of the many different therapeutic methods taught in the Four

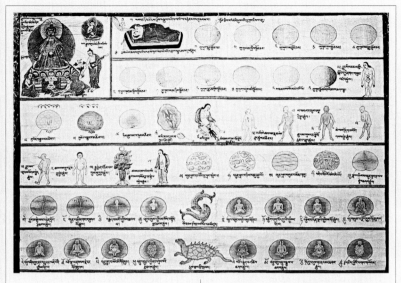

Tantras, after prescribed changes to food and lifestyle, the most commonly employed are infusions, powders and pills made up of a wide range of medicinal substances – animal, vegetable and mineral – as well as practices such as moxibustion from China.

The concepts of the Four Tantras create a 'rational' link between the biological theories inherited from Indian *ayurveda* and the foundations of Buddhist philosophy.... As the Four Tantras say, 'suffering is part of every being, even when he feels well, just as the shadow follows the bird, even though he is flying in the sky.' Tibetan medicine has not only taken up the classic comparison between the three moral poisons of Buddhism and the three humours of ayurvedic doctrine, but it has also formulated a causal link between the two.... By incorporating the three moral poisons and, ultimately, our non-cognizance of the origin of the humours and hence of life, Tibetan medicine extends the ancient concepts of *ayurveda* in order to link them with basic Buddhist philosophy, which holds that life in all its forms is affected by mental processes, and that the chain of rebirth can only be broken through access to knowledge.

...Tibetan medicine is also closely connected with the spiritual domain both in its transmission and in its institutions.... Medical practice strictly speaking has never been clearly separated from ritual or liturgical practices – the latter being dedicated essentially to the Master Buddha of Medicine – although these are not necessarily performed by the same specialist or for the same beneficiary.

Fernand Meyer,
taken from 'Médecine et bouddhisme au Tibet', *Grand Atlas des Religions*, Paris, 1988

Tibet and China: the 17-Point Agreement

The Chinese government forced the Tibetan leaders to sign this document in April 1951, when the Chinese army was already in eastern Tibet. The Chinese never respected the agreement in any case, and it became a cause of disillusionment to those Tibetans who had believed in Communism. 'The Chinese authorities seem to have a short memory,' wrote a Tibetan official, 'they have forgotten what they said. Mao… announced at the time that the Chinese government would send a few soldiers and officials to help the Tibetan people and, once the situation had improved, the Chinese military and officials would immediately return to China.'

In the latter part of April, 1951, the delegates with full powers from the Local Government of Tibet arrived in Beijing. The Central People's Government appointed representatives with full powers to conduct talks on a friendly basis with the delegates of the Local Government of Tibet. The result of the talks is that both parties have agreed to establish this agreement and ensure that it be carried into effect.

1. The Tibetan people shall be united and drive out the imperialist aggressive forces from Tibet; that the Tibetan people shall return to the big family of the motherland of the People's Republic of China.

2. The Local Government of Tibet shall actively assist the People's Liberation Army to enter Tibet and consolidate the national defences.

3. In accordance with the policy towards nationalities laid down in the Common Programme of the Chinese People's Political Consultative Conference, the Tibetan people have the right of exercising national regional autonomy under the unified leadership of the Central People's Government.

4. The Central Authorities will not alter the existing political system in Tibet. The Central Authorities also will not alter the established status, functions and powers of the Dalai Lama. Officials of various ranks will hold office as usual.

5. The established status, functions and powers of the Panchen Erdeni shall be maintained.

6. By the established status, functions and powers of the Dalai Lama and the Panchen Erdeni is meant the status, functions and powers of the 13th Dalai Lama and of the 9th Panchen Erdeni when they were in friendly and amicable relations with each other.

7. The policy of freedom of religious belief laid down in the Common Programme of the Chinese People's Political Consultative Conference will be protected. The Central Authorities will not effect any change in the income of the monasteries.

8. The Tibetan troops will be reorganized step by step into the People's Liberation Army, and become part of the national defence forces of the People's Republic of China.

9. The spoken and written language and school education of the Tibetan nationality will be developed step by step in accordance with the actual conditions in Tibet.

10. Tibetan agriculture, livestock raising, industry and commerce will be developed step by step, and the people's livelihood will be improved step by step in accordance with the actual conditions in Tibet.

11. In matters relating to various reforms in Tibet, there will be no compulsion on the part of the Central Authorities. The Local Government of Tibet should carry out reforms of its own accord, and when the people raise demands for reform, they must be settled through consultation with the leading personnel of Tibet.

12. In so far as former pro-imperialist and pro-KMT* officials resolutely sever relations with imperialism and the KMT and do not engage in sabotage or resistance, they may continue to hold office irrespective of their past.

13. The People's Liberation Army entering Tibet will abide by all the above-mentioned policies and will also be fair in all buying and selling and will not arbitrarily take even a needle or a thread from the people.

14. The Central People's Government will handle the external affairs of the area of Tibet; and there will be peaceful co-existence with neighbouring countries and the establishment and development of fair commercial and trading relations with them on the basis of equality, mutual benefit and mutual respect for territory and sovereignty.

15. In order to ensure the implementation of this agreement, the Central People's Government will set up a military and administrative committee and a military area headquarters in Tibet, and apart from the personnel sent there by the Central People's Government it will absorb as many local Tibetan personnel as possible to take part in the work. Local Tibetan personnel taking part in the military and administrative committee may include patriotic elements from the Local Government of Tibet, various district and various principal monasteries; the name list is to be prepared after consultation between the representatives designated by the Central People's Government and various quarters concerned, and is to be submitted to the Central People's Government for approval.

16. Funds needed by the military and administrative committee, the military area headquarters and the People's Liberation Army entering Tibet will be provided by the Central People's Government. The Local Government of Tibet should assist the People's Liberation Army in the purchases and transportation of food, fodder and other daily necessities.

17. This agreement will come into force immediately after signatures and seals are affixed to it.

* KMT: the Kuomintang, the Chinese Communist Party

The Tibetans, the Party and the Lamas

The political problems between China and Tibet cannot simply be reduced to a conflict between the Dalai Lama and the Chinese government. Other lesser-known participants also play an important role, and religious history and the Communist Party must also be taken into account. This political issue rests on the shifting sands of historical forces, Party edicts, and the conclusions that can be drawn from these.

In 1950, true to the spirit of Mao, the Marxist view of religion as the 'opium of the people' was to be imposed, the temporal and spiritual influence of the Dalai Lama was at all costs to be undermined, and the feudal society overturned. This was the ultimate aim which nothing was to prevent, and many sectors of Chinese society, as well as some Tibetans, were totally sincere in their desire to build a new society in Tibet. The dominance of the Chinese army and party representatives, the thousands of prisoners thrown into labour camps, the famine caused by the 'great leap forward', the Cultural Revolution, the bloody repressions of the late 1980s, the death of the Panchen Lama in 1989, and the disappearance of his reincarnation in 1995, and finally the constant attacks on the Dalai Lama and the refusal by the Chinese to engage in any form of dialogue – all these destroyed the illusions of those Tibetans who had trusted the invaders.

It is true that the Tibet Autonomous Region is making some progress, at least from the point of view of economic statistics. The Chinese government and provinces are helping to improve infrastructures, telephones work, markets are well stocked and shops are bursting with goods, including the latest two-in-one shampoos. But behind the facade lie severe social problems: Tibetans who do not speak Chinese are marginalized; shops are mainly owned by the Chinese; Lhasa has the greatest number of prostitutes per head of the population of any town in Asia; alcohol and gambling are the only escape routes.

In order to endure and survive a situation in which political change is only possible by way of conflict within the Party, Tibetans have become a schizophrenic people. They profit from the economic progress, comply with political directives, and live side by side with the Chinese because they know that any open revolt will be futile given the military might of the army. They 'negotiate' their lives within the constraints of the Party line. At the same time, they laugh at themselves and their karma, despise the Chinese who are doing so well out of them (interracial marriages are rare), and no change escapes their mordant humour. They manage to keep practising their religion, with a faith that nothing can shake, and they venerate the lamas. Many are ready to make huge sacrifices to give their sons and daughters a good education, and are even prepared to be separated from their children forever in order to let them study in India. Fifty years of political instruction have simply passed them by. Their obvious resilience is matched only by their deep determination. The 10th Panchen Lama, who died in 1989, was a symbol for the Tibetan people, and the image of him as a collaborator, opposed to that of the Dalai Lama as a resistance fighter, is simplistic.

What is true, however, is that since his exile in 1959 and his Nobel Peace Prize in 1989, the Dalai Lama has become a major international figure. His charisma has united all the exiled Tibetans behind him, regardless of their religious affiliation; he also favours an ecumenical movement among the different Buddhist schools. Some of the great religious figures from his own school, the 5th and 8th Panchen Lamas, were members of Bönpo families, and today – as the 5th Dalai Lama did in the 17th century – the 14th Dalai Lama recognizes the Yundrung Bön as one of the spiritual schools of Tibet on a par with the four Buddhist schools. Although each school has its own leader – like the Karmapa, exiled in India since 2000 – the Dalai Lama is the political figure around whom they all revolve. For the vast majority of Tibetans in Tibet, after the death of the 10th Panchen Lama, he has become an object of worship – more or less covertly through fear of reprisals – as a symbol of resistance against Chinese oppression.

The matter of the 11th Panchen Lama, however, remains a burning issue. In 1642 the 5th Dalai Lama became political head of Tibet, and the religious school of Gelugpa grew in influence. In 1662, to pay homage to his master, who lived in the Tashilunpo Monastery in Shigatse, the 5th Dalai Lama established the incarnate lineage of the Panchen Lamas. But from the 6th Panchen Lama in the 18th century onwards, these became more and more independent in their relations with the Tibetan government and the Dalai Lama, and directed their sympathies towards the Qing dynasty, who played one hierarchy off against the other.

When the Chinese invaded in 1950, the young 10th Panchen Lama was in Amdo and was taken captive by the Communists. He was therefore brought up partly by the Chinese, but after 1959 remained in Tibet. His criticisms of Chinese policies in Tibet, however, cost him 18 years' imprisonment in Beijing. Having been 'rehabilitated', he returned to Tibet in 1978 and was appointed Vice-President of the Autonomous Region; as such he worked for the good of the Tibetan people despite the very strict limitations on his actions. Greatly respected, he opposed the construction of a hydroelectric dam on the sacred lake of Yamdrok Tso. He died under mysterious circumstances in 1989, at the age of 51, in Tashilunpo.

The 11th Panchen Lama was recognized by the Dalai Lama in Tibet in 1995, but the Chinese government rejected this decision, and the child disappeared, thus becoming the youngest political prisoner in the world. The Chinese government recognized a different 11th Panchen Lama, who had been brought up in Beijing and was 'in good health through the care of the Central Committee and the efforts of the different departments' (Xinhua). When he visited Tibet in June 2002, he declared that 'the changes in present-day Tibet have made me more confident in the wise governance of the Central Committee of the Party' (Xinhua).

Beyond the sad tale of a child who has disappeared, and the pronouncements made by another child of 12 who has no say in his own fate, there is a political problem in the making. Since the Dalai Lamas and the Panchen Lamas take it in turns to recognize each other's succeeding incarnations, the Chinese government will in future be in a position to allow their own Panchen Lama to recognize the reincarnation of the current Dalai Lama. The irony here is that the Communist Party, for whom religion is anathema, still discusses and decides the selection of reincarnations. The current Dalai Lama is therefore confronted now with questions of succession which, as is always the case in Tibet, are both political and religious. He has declared that the 15th Dalai Lama will be born 'in a free country'.

Françoise Pommaret

The hopes of the Dalai Lama

...Within the context of the present tense political atmosphere the Chinese authorities in Tibet have continued in the past year to subject Tibetans inside Tibet to gross violations of human rights, including religious persecution. This has led to an increasing number of Tibetans risking their lives to flee Tibet and to find refuge elsewhere. Last summer the expulsion of thousands of Tibetan and Chinese monks and nuns from a Tibetan Buddhist learning institute at Serthar in Eastern Tibet highlighted the intensity and scale of the repression in Tibet. These abuses of rights are a clear example of how Tibetans are deprived of their right to assert and preserve their own identity and culture.

I believe that many of the violations of human rights in Tibet are the result of suspicion, lack of trust and true understanding of Tibetan culture and religion. As I have said many times in the past, it is extremely important for the Chinese leadership to come to a better and deeper understanding and appreciation of the Tibetan Buddhist culture and civilization. I absolutely support Deng Xiaoping's wise statement that we must 'seek truth from facts'. Therefore, we Tibetans must accept the progress and improvements that China's rule of Tibet has brought to the Tibetan people and give recognition to it. At the same time the Chinese authorities must understand that the Tibetans have had to undergo tremendous suffering and destruction during the past five decades. The late Panchen Lama in his last public address in Shigatse on January 24, 1989 stated that Chinese rule in Tibet had brought more destruction than benefit to the Tibetan people.

The Buddhist culture of Tibet inspires the Tibetans with values and concepts of compassion, forgiveness, patience and a reverence for all forms of life that are of practical benefit and relevance in daily life and hence the wish to preserve it. Sadly, our Buddhist culture and way of life are under threat of total extinction. The majority of Chinese 'development' plans in Tibet are designed to assimilate Tibet completely into the Chinese society and culture and to overwhelm Tibetans demographically by transferring large numbers of Chinese into Tibet. This unfortunately reveals that Chinese policies in Tibet continue to be dominated by 'ultra-leftists' in the Chinese government, despite the profound changes carried out by the

Chinese government and the Party elsewhere in the People's Republic of China. This policy is unbefitting of a proud nation and culture such as China and against the spirit of the 21st century....

It is my sincere hope that the Chinese leadership will find the courage, wisdom and vision to solve the Tibetan issue through negotiations. Not only would it be helpful in creating a political atmosphere conducive to the smooth transition of China into a new era but also China's image throughout the world would be greatly enhanced. It would have a strong, positive impact on the people in Taiwan and will also do much to improve Sino-Indian relations by inspiring genuine trust and confidence. Times of change are also times of opportunities. I truly believe that one day, there will be the chance at dialogue and peace because there is no other choice for China or for us. The present state of affairs in Tibet does nothing to alleviate the grievances of the Tibetan people or to bring stability and unity to the People's Republic of China. Sooner or later, the leadership in Beijing will have to face this fact. On my part, I remain committed to the process of dialogue. As soon as there is a positive signal from Beijing, my designated representatives stand ready to meet with officials of the Chinese government anywhere, anytime. My position on the issue of Tibet is straightforward. I am not seeking independence. As I have said many times before, what I am seeking is for the Tibetan people to be given the opportunity to have genuine self-rule in order to preserve their civilization and for the unique Tibetan culture, religion, language and way of life to grow and thrive. For this, it is essential that the Tibetans be able to handle all their domestic affairs and to freely determine their social, economic and cultural development.

In exile we continue with the democratization of the Tibetan polity. Last March, I informed the elected representatives of the Assembly of Tibetan People's Deputies that the Tibetan exiles must directly elect the next Kalon Tripa (Chairman of the Tibetan Cabinet). Consequently, last August for the first time in Tibet's history, the Tibetan exiles directly elected Samdhong Rinpoche as the new Kalon Tripa by a margin of over 84 per cent of the total votes cast....

I take this opportunity to thank the numerous individuals, including members of governments, of parliaments and of non-governmental organizations who have been continuing to support our non-violent freedom struggle. It is most encouraging to note that universities, schools, religious and social groups, artistic and business communities as well as people from many other walks of life have also come to understand the problem of Tibet and are now expressing their solidarity with our cause. Similarly, we have been able to establish cordial and friendly relations with fellow Chinese Buddhists and ordinary Chinese people living abroad and in Taiwan....

Finally, I pay homage to the brave men and women of Tibet who have and who continue to sacrifice their lives for the cause of our freedom and pray for an early end to the suffering of our people.

Statement made by His Holiness The Dalai Lama on 10 March 2002 in Dharamsala, India, on the 43rd Anniversary of Tibetan National Uprising Day

THE DALAI LAMAS AND PANCHEN LAMAS

THE DALAI LAMAS

1st Dalai Lama (named retrospectively): Gendun Drub (1391–1475)

2nd Dalai Lama (named retrospectively): Gyalwa Gendun Gyatso (1475–1542/3)

3rd Dalai Lama: Gyalwa Sonam Gyatso (1543–88)

4th Dalai Lama: Yonten Gyatso (1589–1617)

5th Dalai Lama: Ngawang Lobsang Gyatso (1617–82)

6th Dalai Lama: Rigdzin Tsangyang Gyatso (1683–1706)

7th Dalai Lama: Kelsang Gyatso (1708–57)

8th Dalai Lama: Jampel Gyatso (1758–1804)

9th Dalai Lama: Lungtok Gyatso (1806–15)

10th Dalai Lama: Tsultrim Gyatso (1816–37)

11th Dalai Lama: Khedrup Gyatso (1838–56)

12th Dalai Lama: Trinley Gyatso (1856–75)

13th Dalai Lama: Thubten Gyatso (1875–1933)

14th Dalai Lama: Tenzin Gyatso (born 6 July 1935)

THE PANCHEN LAMAS

The dates differ slightly according to the source

1st Panchen Lama (named retrospectively): Kedrup Je (1385–1438)

2nd Panchen Lama (named retrospectively): Sonam Choklang (1439–1504)

3rd Panchen Lama (named retrospectively): Lobsang Dondrup (1505–66)

4th Panchen Lama (the first to be named in his lifetime): Lobsang Chögyen (1567–1662)

5th Panchen Lama: Lobsang Yeshe (1663–1737)

6th Panchen Lama: Palden Yeshe (1738–80)

7th Panchen Lama: Tenpe Nyima (1782–1853/4)

8th Panchen Lama: Tenpe Wangchuk (1854/5–82)

9th Panchen Lama: Choeki Nyima (1883–1937)

10th Panchen Lama: Choeki Gyaltsen (1938–89)

11th Panchen Lama (recognized by 14th Dalai Lama in 1995, but since imprisoned by Chinese government): Gedhun Choeki Nyima (1989–)

11th Panchen Lama (chosen by the Chinese government; dubbed 'the Chinese Panchen Lama'): Gyaltsen Norbu (1990–)

FURTHER READING

BOOKS

Adhe Taponstsang, *Ama Adhe, The Voice that Remembers: the Heroic Story of a Woman's Fight to Free Tibet*, Boston, 1997

Anagarika Brahmacari Govinda, *The Way of the White Clouds: a Buddhist Pilgrim in Tibet*, London, 1966

Ani Pachen & Donnelley, Adelaide, *Sorrow Mountain: the Journey of a Tibetan Warrior Nun*, London, 2000

Arpi, Claude, *The Fate of Tibet: When Big Insects Eat Small Insects*, New Delhi, 1999

Avedon, John F., *In Exile from the Land of Snows*, New York and London, 1985

Avedon, John F., *Tibet Today*, London, 1988.

Bacot, Jacques, *Milarepa*, Paris, 1971

Baker, Ian A. & Shrestha, Romio, *The Tibetan Art of Healing*, London and San Francisco, 1997

Bogle, George & Manning, Thomas, *Narratives of the Mission of George Bogle to Tibet, and of the Journey of Thomas Manning to Lhasa*, ed. Clements R. Markham, London, 1876

Buffetrille, Katia & Diemberger, Hildegard (eds), *Territory and Identity in Tibet and the Himalayas*, Leiden and Boston, 2002

Cornu, Philippe, *Padmasambhava*, Paris, 1997

Dalai Lama, *Freedom in Exile: the Autobiography of the Dalai Lama*, London and Berkeley, 1990

Dalai Lama and Rowell, Galen, *My Tibet*, New York and London, 1990

David-Néel, Alexandra, *My Journey to Lhasa*, London, 1983 (1st ed. 1927)

David-Néel, Alexandra & Lama Yongden, *The Superhuman Life of Gesar of Ling, the Legendary Tibetan Hero*, trans. Violet Sidney, London, 1933

Didier, Hugues, *Les Portugais au Tibet, premières relations jésuites*, Paris, 1996

Dodin, Thierry & Rather, Heinz (eds), *Imagining Tibet: Perceptions, Projections, and Fantasies*, London, 2001.

Donnet, Pierre-Antoine, *Tibet: Survival in Question*, trans. Tica Broch, London and Delhi, 1994

Fisher, Robert E., *Art of Tibet*, London and New York, 1997

Föllmi, Olivier, *Homage to Tibet*, London, 1996

Ford, Robert, *Captured in Tibet*, Hong Kong and Oxford, 1990

Goldstein, Melvyn, *A History of Modern Tibet, 1913-1951, The Demise of the Lamaist State*, Berkeley, 1989

Havnevik, Hanna, *Tibetan Buddhist Nuns: History, Cultural Norms and Social Reality*, Oslo, 1989

Heller, Amy, *Tibetan Art: Tracing the Development of Spiritual Ideals and Art in Tibet, 600–2000 AD*, Woodbridge, NY, 1999

Hergé, *Tintin in Tibet*, London and Boston, 1990

Jackson, David Paul, *A History of Tibetan Painting: the Great Tibetan Painters and Their Traditions*, Vienna, 1996

Jones Tung, Rosemary, *A Portrait of Lost Tibet*, photos by Ilya Tolstoy and Brooke Dolan, Berkeley, 1996

Landon, Perceval, *Lhasa: an Account of the Country and People of Central Tibet and of the Progress of the Mission Sent There by the English Government in the Year 1903-4*, London, 1905

Lehman, Steve, *The Tibetans: a Struggle to Survive*, London, 1999

Lobzang Jivaka, *The Life of Milarepa: Tibet's Great Yogi*, London, 1994

Lopez Jr, Donald S., *Prisoners of Shangri-La. Tibetan Buddhism and the West*, Chicago and London, 1998

Meyer, Fernand, *Gso ba rig pa. Le système médical tibétain*, Paris, 2002 (1st ed. 1988)

Nyoshul Khenpo Rinpoche & Surya Das, *Natural Great Perfection: Dzogchen Teachings and Vajra Songs*, Ithaca, NY, 1995

Palden Gyatso, *Fire under the Snow*, trans. Tsering Shakya, London, 1997

Pommaret, Françoise, *Les Revenants de l'au-delà dans le monde tibétain*, Paris, 1998 (1st ed. 1989)

Pommaret, Françoise (ed.), *Lhasa in the Seventeenth Century: the Capital of the Dalai Lamas*, trans. Howard Solverson, Leiden and Boston 2002

Rawson, Philip, *Sacred Tibet*, London and New York, 1991

Ribes, Jean-Paul, *Karmapa*, Paris, 2000

Ricard, Matthieu & Föllmi, Olivier & Danielle, *Buddhist Himalayas: People, Faith and Nature*, London and New York, 2002

Samten Gyaltsen Karmay, *The Treasury of Good Sayings: a Tibetan History of Bon*, London, 1972

Samten Gyaltsen Karmay, *Secret Visions of the Fifth Dalai Lama. the Gold Manuscript in the Fournier Collection*, Musée Guimet, Paris, London, 1998

Snelling, John *The Buddhist Handbook: a Complete Guide to Buddhist Teaching, Practice, History and Schools*, London, 1987

Stein, R. A., *Tibetan Civilization*, trans. J. E. Stapleton Driver, London, 1972

Tashi Khedrup, *Adventures of a Tibetan Fighting Monk*, Bangkok, 1986

TIN (Tibet Information Network), *Cutting off the Serpent's Head*, London, 1996

TIN (Tibet Information Network), *Leaders in Tibet*, London, 1997

Tsering Shakya, *The Dragon in the Land of Snows: a History of Modern Tibet since 1947*, London, 1999

Tucci, Giuseppe, *Tibet: Land of Snows*, trans. J. E. Stapleton Driver, London, 1967

Willis, Janice D. (ed.), *Feminine Ground: Essays on Women and Tibet*, Ithaca, NY, 1989

CD-ROM

Thurman, Robert A. F., *Illuminated Tibet*, Mystic Fire, 2000.

AUDIO CDS

Philip Glass, *Kundun*, Warner Music, 1997.

Lama Gyurme & Jean-Philippe Rykiel, *Rain of Blessings/Vajra Chants*, Real World, 2000.

Ngawang Khechog, *Quiet Mind*, Tibet Universal Music, 1991.

Tenzin Gönpo, *In Memory of Tibet*, Tshangpa, 1999.

Yangchen Lhamo, *Tibet, Tibet*, Real World, 2000.

SELECTED WEBSITES

Tibetan Government-in-Exile: www.tibet.net

Dalai Lama's official site: www.dalailama.com

Himalayan Art Project (S. & D. Rubin Foundation): www.tibetart.com

International Campaign for Tibet (USA): www.savetibet.org

Radio Free Asia: www.rfa.org

Tibet Information Network (TIN): www.tibetinfo.net

Tibetan Bulletin: tibetnews.com

China's Tibet: www.tibetinfor.com

LIST OF ILLUSTRATIONS

CHAPTER 5

DOCUMENTS

INDEX

PHOTO CREDITS

An anthropologist and historian, Françoise Pommaret has travelled widely in Tibet and has lived and worked in Bhutan since 1981. She has worked for the Bhutan Tourism Corporation (1981–86) and the Department of Education of the Royal Government of Bhutan, and now works as a researcher for CNRS, specializing in the history of the Tibetan region, and for INALCO, the French National Institute for Oriental Languages and Civilizations. She is the author of many books and articles of both scientific and general interest.

For S. K. and the people of Tibet

Translated from the French by Barbara Mellor and David H. Wilson

For Harry N. Abrams, Inc.
Project Manager: Susan Richmond
Cover designer: Brankica Kovrlija

Library of Congress Cataloging-in-Publication Data

Pommaret-Imaeda, Françoise.
   [Tibet : une civilisation blessée. English]
   Tibet: an enduring civilization / Françoise Pommaret.
     p. cm.
Includes bibliographical references and index.
   ISBN 0-8109-9112-8 (pbk.)
   1. Tibet (China)—History. I. Title.

DS786.P58513 2003
951'.5—dc21

                                              2003002557

Printed and bound in Italy by Editoriale Lloyd, Trieste

10 9 8 7 6 5 4 3 2 1